YALE HISTORICAL PUBLICATIONS

Lewis P. Curtis · Editor

MISCELLANY

LII

THE THIRTIETH VOLUME
PUBLISHED UNDER THE DIRECTION OF
THE DEPARTMENT OF HISTORY ON THE
KINGSLEY TRUST ASSOCIATION PUBLICATION FUND
ESTABLISHED BY
THE SCROLL AND KEY SOCIETY
OF YALE COLLEGE

British Policy
and the Independence of
Latin America,
1804-1828

BY

WILLIAM W. KAUFMANN

NEW HAVEN

YALE UNIVERSITY PRESS

LONDON · GEOFFREY CUMBERLEGE · OXFORD UNIVERSITY PRESS

1951

TO MY MOTHER

NETTIE CRAMER KAUFMANN

PREFACE

A NEW STUDY of British policy toward Latin America in the years between 1804 and 1828 requires a measure of justification. American and English historians have devoted time, energy, and ample space to a description of that policy, and the results of their investigations are generally known. The two volumes on Castlereagh by Charles K. Webster and the study of Canning by Harold Temperley are perhaps sufficient evidence of the quality of scholarship represented in the field. They may also provide a warning of the dangers which another author, perforce, must face. He is traveling along a well-worn path; he observes the surroundings through his predecessors' eyes; and, as likely as not, the conclusions he reaches regarding his journey will echo faithfully the inductions of those who went before. Comparisons are in order and may prove fatal.

What, in the face of such risks, are the compensations? At the present time an intimate knowledge of early British policy toward Latin America implies a similar acquaintance with a multitude of sources. Since the chief purpose of this study is to trace the evolution of that policy from its confused origins in 1804, through a great war, the difficulties raised by the Monroe Doctrine, and recognition, to a point where Great Britain attempted to bring the independent states of Latin America into a world balance of power, what follows may have some justification as a synthesis of both fact and interpretation. But there is another aim as well: to observe how one of the many dilemmas which statesmen face came to be resolved. The study of an episode, however remote, in terms of the problem posed, the alternatives available, and the diplomacy employed, may reflect some light upon the dilemmas of our own time.

If I have avoided any of the pitfalls, or attained any of the objectives, here set forth, it is because of the kindness and guidance of the following members of the Yale faculty: Samuel Flagg Bemis, Lewis P. Curtis, William T. R. Fox, Bernard Brodie, and Miss Betty Martin of Yale University Press. The resources of the Sterling Memorial Library at Yale University were, and are, a researcher's delight and a scholar's pride. A Sterling Fellowship and a Social Science Research Council Fellowship afforded me the freedom with which to make this study. The patience and assistance of my wife remain beyond computation. For so much aid I am deeply grateful. For the contents and imperfections of the pages that follow I acknowledge complete responsibility.

For permission to quote from works published by them I am indebted to *The American Historical Review*, G. Bell and Sons Ltd., the Carnegie Endowment for International Peace, E. P. Dutton and Company, Inc., Harvard University Press, the Controller of His Britannic Majesty's Stationery Office, Longmans, Green and Company, Inc., John Murray, Oxford University Press and the Ibero-American Institute of Great Britain, and the University of North Carolina Press.

W. W. K.

New Haven, Connecticut
September, 1950

CONTENTS

I

THE BASIC DILEMMA

THE first years of the nineteenth century witnessed a series of upheavals such as had not shaken Europe since the Thirty Years' War. The French nation, following upon a revolution of singular violence, embarked upon a career of expansion under the leadership of Napoleon Bonaparte. Fifteen years of almost continuous conflict ensued, and only after a succession of great coalitions, led by Great Britain, Russia, and Austria, had formed against the aggressor did a semblance of peace return to the distracted continent.

That a conflict of such proportions should have been felt in the Western Hemisphere is hardly surprising. But, in the light of the order imposed upon Europe at the Congress of Vienna, it is somewhat disconcerting to discover that the colonists of Latin America responded almost unmolested to the very revolutionary principles which elsewhere had been so zealously repressed. Why was it that all the trappings of Legitimacy were restored to Spain and Portugal while their transatlantic dominions went free? Were distance and an especially determined spirit responsible, or had some other equally influential forces been at work as well?

Certainly the inhabitants of Latin America must be credited in large measure for the change which took place in their fortunes. The example and assistance of the United States must also be remembered. But in order to understand fully the reasons for this transformation, the inquirer must turn to a consideration of British policy between 1804 and 1828.

Policies generally possess more casual origins than either statesmen or historians willingly admit, and British policy toward Latin America offers no exception to this rule. The function of logic proved relatively insignificant during the formative years of that policy. Even tradition played a less imposing role than might have been anticipated. England had established many contacts with Latin America between the sixteenth and nineteenth centuries, and these contacts were to influence the minds of responsible ministers.

Tradition, after all, is always more persuasive than logic. But stronger than tradition or logic was the pressure of events originating outside the orbit of British control. Under the impact of Bonaparte's agility, decisions tended to yield to the circumstances of war rather than to precedent or calculation.

If, in the beginning, the ordinary eighteenth-century mind reacted apprehensively to this disorderly state of affairs, the sensitive intelligence of England's first minister responded with a particular agitation. For nearly ten years the younger Pitt had attempted to combat the expansion of France with variations of the traditional strategies which had served his father so well. He met with an unbroken succession of failures. What should have sufficed, according to precedent, was the containment of France by means of continental alliances. Great Britain, for her part, would put limited forces into Europe, seize the last of her ancient rival's colonial possessions, and erase French commerce from the seas. But the course of this war had proved unlike that of 1759. The French showed a surprising indifference to the loss of their colonies and, supported by their new faith, fought on in Europe not only with tenacity but with extraordinary success. No Frederick the Great arose to thwart them. Prussia and Austria, instead of marching upon Paris, indulged in another partition of Poland. And Russia fell under the dominion of a Tsar who was both mad and pro-French. Two coalitions, organized to stamp out the revolutionary madness, quickly collapsed, and, instead of filching sugar islands, Pitt found himself slipping ever deeper into the bog of continental warfare.

There had been only one respite from this dreary business. Pitt, sulking, had retired from office in 1801, and his timid successor, Henry Addington, had negotiated with Bonaparte the Peace of Amiens—that celebrated treaty of which Madame de Staël remarked, next to the fault of signing it, that of not breaking it would have been the greatest. But the peace had provided a respite and no more. The conflict resumed on May 18, 1803, and early in 1804 Pitt returned to the familiar surroundings of Downing Street, bearing with him a set of revised strategic concepts.

During the gloomy years of retirement Pitt had apparently persuaded himself of the futility attached to the diffuse strategy of his first administration. Indeed, if previous experience had not forced this conclusion upon him, the presence of a French army of invasion at Boulogne, under the direct orders of Bonaparte himself, should have sufficed to drive it home. To end the wasting conflict surely this much must be done: France must be brought to bay in Europe. There was no further warrant for dispersals of effort, distracting side shows, or piecemeal offensives. As in the days of Marlborough, the main strength of England must be concentrated directly upon the enemy. The primary obligation of government would be a continental strategy.

As Pitt pursued further his analysis of the situation, he concluded with some logic that England alone could not deal the coup de grâce to France. Her seagoing commerce might wither away, a strict blockade could wound her seriously, and Nelson might even destroy her fleet. But, finally, England would require help to deal her a mortal blow. Once returned to office, therefore, Pitt applied himself to the task of winning allies to his cause. The moment proved propitious. Russia, under a new Tsar, had already indicated some interest in a third coalition; even Austria had expressed a timid and secret desire to cooperate; and so, as the summer months of 1804 slipped by and Napoleon waited feverishly upon the Channel, a new and more powerful alliance began to take form. Agreement with Russia, although difficult, approached a certainty, and the prospects of gaining the support of Austria, Prussia, and Naples improved.[1] Hopes in London rose higher despite the ever present menace of invasion. And then as the general confidence increased Pitt seemed to waver and weaken in his initial resolve. Just as his plans approached fruition the problem of Latin America arose to distract him. That this weakening should have occurred at so crucial a moment seems strange, and yet, in the light of Pitt's complex personality, it is not entirely incomprehensible.[2]

Pitt must remain something of an enigma to the present generation; his greatness is of that secret and personal sort which communicates itself only with difficulty through the passage of time. His oratory, so impressive in its day, leaves the modern reader unmoved. His record as a financial expert retains its interest principally as an economic curiosity. And the history of his war

1. J. Holland Rose, ed., *Select Despatches . . . Relating to the Formation of the Third Coalition against France, 1804–1805* (London, Royal Historical Society, 1904), pp. i–xii.

2. While the sketch of Pitt that follows is based in good part upon the work of J. Holland Rose, *William Pitt and National Revival* (London, G. Bell, 1911), and *William Pitt and the Great War* (London, G. Bell, 1911), the conclusions are my own.

ministries, extending over a period of fourteen years, would suggest the maddest kind of optimism, were it not for the list of naval victories which culminated in the destruction of the French fleet at Trafalgar. The sum total of his career is hardly impressive if one forgets that, almost singlehanded, he persuaded England to contest the expansion of France. The rolling speeches with their elaborate metaphors somehow elevated the spirits of his followers, his financial manipulations evoked universal if misplaced confidence, and his perseverance as the first minister of a half-mad sovereign inspired his countrymen to even greater feats of endurance of their own. George Canning, as was his wont, captured the general sentiment when in 1802 he exclaimed, "Whether Pitt *will* save us, I do not know, but surely he is the only man that *can*." [3]

The magnetism of Pitt's personality matched the extremity of his perseverance. He possessed the enviable ability of attracting the ambitious young men of the day to his side, not so much by reason of his patronage as by the speculative grandeur of his ideas. Castlereagh, Canning, Liverpool, and all the Wellesleys professed to be his most devoted adherents. At the age of forty-five he had reached in his compatriots' minds a singular pinnacle of sagacity, his vaulting imagination an endless source of inspiration upon such diverse subjects as the sinking fund and the balance of Europe, Catholic Emancipation and territorial guarantees, the reorganization of Parliament and the defeat of France.

But there was another side to Pitt, a more mundane side which left him a prey to vacillation. As a politician he showed a marked reluctance to give practical application to his ideas. He had been "so bred in a riding-house," William Windham remarked, "so completely put upon his haunches, that he [could] never fairly lay himself out *ventre-à-terre* so as to win the prize in the race of renown and glory." [4] How, indeed, could he have been otherwise? As a mere boy he had labored over the intricacies of parliamentary procedure; he had spent over twenty of his forty-five years in the singular atmosphere of the House of Commons. Political associates surrounded him, and his working hours were occupied with the manipulation of votes. Is it any wonder, then, that of a particular measure he was inclined to think not how effective will it be but how many interests will it appease?

3. J. W. Fortescue, *British Statesmen of the Great War, 1793–1814* (Oxford, Clarendon Press, 1911), p. 167.
4. *Ibid.*, pp. 39–40.

This deference to political expediency had proved a useful characteristic in the domestic arena; but if expediency contributed to governmental longevity, it also tended to impede the fruition of Pitt's more statesmanlike ideas. Nowhere was this hesitation more obvious than in the formation of the Third Coalition. Having brought his creation to the brink of reality, Pitt commenced to wonder if he had not been too single-minded in his purpose. At one moment he congratulated himself upon the achievement of his chief objective; at the next he speculated on the consequences of disaster. Alternating between hope and uncertainty, besieged with doubts, fascinated yet fearful, he turned for an instant to the articulate and mellifluous voices which advocated vigorous British action in Latin America.[5]

The voices which sounded in 1804 were new and persuasive, but their refrain bore the accents of a well-worn litany. Counterparts could be found ringing through English history almost from that day on May 4, 1493, when Pope Alexander VI granted to Spain and Portugal an exclusive title to Latin America. Drake and Hawkins had advocated raids in the Caribbean as a means of thwarting the aspirations of Spain in Europe, and at the end of the sixteenth century a brief interlude of looting and rapine had split the quiet of the West Indies. But the vigor of the Elizabethans had faded into the senescence of the Stuarts. British energies were diverted to North America where New England received its embittered saints and Virginia its unrepentant sinners.

Successive generations saw a revival of the interest. Cromwell, planning to carve out an empire in Latin America, had conceived his "Western Design" in 1654. But his commanders had failed him and Jamaica, the ultimate stronghold of Henry Morgan, had been his only prize. In 1695 Scotland had responded to the lure of the Spanish monopoly and had dispatched an expedition to settle in Darien; but even tenacious Scotland had been repulsed. In 1739 Sir Robert Walpole had ventured cautiously upon the War of Jenkins' Ear in response to a great public outcry. He launched two further expeditions against Panama; and then in an abrupt shift of circumstance the conflict had merged with and become lost in the War of the Austrian Succession. The elder Pitt at the height of his fame and influence had seized Cuba, Manila, and the Floridas, only to see his successors in office dis-

5. Among them were the voices of Lord Melville, Sir Evan Nepean, Sir Home Popham, Nicholas Vansittart, and, of course, Francisco de Miranda.

gorge all but the latter a year later in the peace negotiations of Paris.

The voices had alternately whispered and shrieked, yet despite two centuries of intermittent conflict the vast empire of Latin America had remained intact. England's preoccupation with the balance of power in Europe, and her initial concentration upon the possessions of France, had saved the Spanish colonies from the fate of Canada, despite the growing decrepitude of their mother country.

Why then should Pitt, embarking as he was upon another continental war, have considered projects which had been so barren of results in the past? Why should he have risked the success of the Third Coalition by the contemplation of speculative objects across the seas? There were at least two persuasive reasons. On the one side were all the doubts and risks connected with a continental strategy: the difficulty of mobilizing an effective army, the unreliability of allies, the catastrophe portended by defeat. To have committed Britain unreservedly to such a strategy, and without an alternative plan, would hardly have been in keeping either with Pitt's caution or England's interest. If a limited concentration upon the enemy were tried, and failed, surely the prospect of action and expansion in Latin America would be preferable to no action at all.

The choice was not unlike that of the gambler who, watching the spin of the wheel, decides to spread his chips over the green baize cloth. And the temptation to diversify risks and cut losses was enhanced by the existence of vested interests which Britain had accumulated in Latin America. These interests had developed even as the armed forays against Latin America had been repulsed; they had fed not upon victory but upon the internal rot which was sapping the energy of the Spanish empire. So far, indeed, had the erosion progressed by the seventeenth century that Spain had begun to bring foreign goods into Cadiz and Seville, whence Spanish merchants carried them to South America. England, not unnaturally, had come to play an increasingly important part in this roundabout trade. Following upon the War of Spanish Succession her interest therein had expanded rapidly, for she extracted from the Peace of Utrecht (1713) the coveted *Asiento* or contract to supply slaves to South America. The contract itself had hardly fulfilled expectations. The South Sea Company, organized to carry out its terms, had encountered difficulties at home in the ill-famed inflation of the South Sea bubble and covert resistance abroad from a jealous and uncooperative Spain. In 1750, indeed, after interminable difficulties and disputes, the company had actually surrendered the contract in consideration of £100,000. But meanwhile, behind its façade, there had sprung up a large and immensely lucrative contraband trade. The traffic in slaves had come to serve as a mere blind for an outpouring of English manufactures to the Spanish colonies, and by 1736 "a hitt in the Illicit Trade" was considered to be "like getting a great prize in a Lottery." [6]

Even after the company had returned the *Asiento* to Spain this commerce continued unabated; the habit of smuggling had become ingrown. But its course progressed unevenly. There was an inherent lack of stability in clandestine trade; volume and profits fluctuated violently in the face of ceaseless and not entirely unsuccessful efforts by Spain to resume her monopoly. Nevertheless, the lure of contraband exercised a considerable spell throughout the eighteenth century, and in England the feeling gained ground that the South American market might yet develop beyond that of India or the United States.

By 1804 the market seemed particularly attractive. The Industrial Revolution had already worked its magic upon English industry. Cotton, woolen, iron, and leather goods, beer and paper, porcelain and coal, were all being produced in ever increasing quantities in Yorkshire and Lancashire, the Cheviots and Wales. The age of the machine at last was under way; and yet, in the disruption entailed by war, consumption was falling far behind the vast outpouring of goods. While the productive processes grew in efficiency, the expanding influence of France made the continental market increasingly inaccessible. Economically the outlook for Britain was bleak and uninviting unless one considered, as so many did, the unexplored and elusive potentialities of Latin America.[7] In this critical period the prospect of that vast continent absorbing an infinitude of English goods was a tempting one, and to Pitt, with his habits of vacillation, almost completely irresistible.

6. George H. Nelson, "Contraband Trade under the Asiento, 1730–1739," *American Historical Review,* LI (1945), 62.

7. Perhaps "unexplored" is too loose a word. The value of English exports to America in 1805 (exclusive of the United States) was already £7,771,418. It was to rise to £18,014,219 by 1809. See Élie Halévy, *A History of the English People in 1815* (London, T. F. Unwin, 1924), p. 274.

The difficulty lay in giving substance to the vision. Certainly, with Napoleon threatening invasion and with the Third Coalition in the process of formation, England could spare but little of her collected force to pry open a new market; and if the past was any guide Spain would not open the market of her own accord. How, then, despite the golden prospects, was any more to be accomplished than in the two preceding centuries? The answer to this dilemma apparently lay at hand in the weapon of revolution. For if England lacked the power to expand and stabilize her commerce with Latin America, and Spain persisted in her refusal to lend aid and comfort to it, what was to prevent the colonists themselves, freed of Spanish dominion, from opening their ports to the benefits of British trade?

That the colonists were actually preparing to throw off the tyranny of Spain was perhaps too large an assumption. There had been rumors of dissatisfaction emanating from Latin America throughout the eighteenth century,[8] and the American Revolution had afforded substantial evidence of the ability of colonists imbued with a sense of injustice to arise and assert their independence. But neither the vague reports from the Spanish dominions nor the American Revolution proved conclusively that such a revolt would occur in Latin America in the near future. Upon its merits, therefore, the situation could hardly be classified as combustible. Yet, if the new voices at Pitt's elbow were to be believed, a condition of great inflammability could be created with the proper degree of alien encouragement. The only requirement, so the argument went, was a suitable instrument with which to set off the explosion.

England in 1804 held no dearth of *agents provocateurs;* since 1776 the incitement of revolution had become a highly honorable profession. A certain Mr. Pavia extolled the benefits to be accrued from an attack upon Mexico. William Burke, the progenitor of a number of elaborate schemes, showed a fancy for Buenos Aires. Charles Williamson, the London agent of Aaron Burr, advocated support of the former American Vice-president's shadowy schemes. The files of the Foreign Office bulged with their plots and pleas. Yet none of these persons could compete with the voluble plausibility of Francisco de Miranda.

8. William S. Robertson discusses these in his *Francisco de Miranda and the Revolutionizing of Spanish America,* published in the *American Historical Association Report,* I (1907), 197–210.

The history of Miranda is well known.[9] Born in Caracas, in the Captaincy General of Venezuela, he journeyed to Madrid as a youth and obtained a commission in the Spanish army. During the American Revolution he served in the West Indies where he deserted upon being charged with speculating in army supplies and trading with the enemy. Soon afterward, whether out of conviction or pique (it is difficult to say which), he became an advocate of revolution and began to labor for the cause of Venezuelan independence. A convincing conversationalist, a superficial student, brilliantly versed in those trivialities so dear to the heart of the eighteenth century, and a consummate prevaricator, he attracted an audience wherever he went. In England, where the topic of Latin America exercised an enduring fashion, he met with a particularly warm reception. In 1790, at the height of the Nootka Sound crisis with Spain, it even seemed that Pitt's government might adopt his plans for an attack upon Venezuela. But the crisis had evaporated, and, instead of entering Caracas as the savior of his people, Miranda crossed over to Paris and became a general in the revolutionary armies of France. His active military career, lasting as it did less than a year, was not entirely successful. After a defeat on the field and a sojourn in prison he returned to England.

Miranda remained in London almost continuously from 1798 until 1804, and during these six years he occupied himself in two directions. He elaborated and perfected his plans for the liberation of Spanish America, and he labored unceasingly to keep himself before the eyes of the English government. His efforts did not go unrewarded. Within a year of his return he obtained an annual pension of £300; influential friends began to plead his cause; and in 1803 he won an important adherent in the person of Sir Home Popham.

It would not be entirely correct to say that Sir Home brought a new luster to the cause of Latin American independence. Nor would it be correct to add that he worked for the cause out of a deep-seated affection for liberty. His motives were more mundane. Sir Home was a captain in the Royal Navy and his record, although marred by courts-martial, was a distinguished one. But there had been disappointments as well as citations. For one thing,

9. The details of his curious career may be found in William S. Robertson's painstaking biography, *The Life of Miranda* (Chapel Hill, University of North Carolina Press, 1929), 2 vols.

distinction and wealth had not proved synonymous, and to Sir Home, with his practical turn of mind, here was a defect in need of remedy. Since the discipline of the day was singularly lax he devoted his idle moments, hopefully and unsparingly, to the service of General Miranda. In that speculative game what might his remuneration not be?

Sir Home's support was valuable both for the vigor of his ways and for the extent of his influence. His creditors (and there were many) were helpful; he had insinuated himself into the confidence of Lord Melville, the First Lord of the Admiralty; and Pitt himself occasionally sought his advice upon naval affairs. There were other proselytes as well: Turnbull and Sons, merchants; Davidson, the military contractor to Lord Nelson; and Nicholas Vansittart, a future Chancellor of the Exchequer. But, in the final analysis, the inquirer must focus his attention upon Miranda and Popham, for it was to them that Pitt turned in his doubtful state of mind.

The first minister did not make his presence felt during the initial stages of the conspiracy. It was rather Lord Melville, his most confidential adviser, who took hold of Miranda's copious plans. In September, 1804, after studying their details, Lord Melville expressed the hope that the General "would not require a large force," and promised "to bring the business forward the first thing when he came to town." [10] For a month the negotiations proceeded at a leisurely pace, and then in October Pitt ventured his opinions on the subject. They were delightfully ambiguous. The heart of his conversation, which took place at a dinner with Lord Melville and Popham, turned on a question directed at Sir Home.

Suppose that you should be governor of Trinidad and that we should not have war with Spain, how could you restrain Miranda from crossing the narrow strait of Paria to the Continent and doing that which he has so long premeditated? Animated by elevated thoughts and by the noble ambition of becoming the legislator of his native land, he would wish to play in the most sublime manner the role that Washington played in North America.[11]

Popham reacted boldly. He pressed for a definite commitment instead of a question and a hint of official encouragement to the

10. Fitzwilliam to Miranda, September 24, 1804, *ibid.*, I, 272.
11. *Ibid.*, pp. 274–275.

General; and finally the diners agreed to re-examine Miranda's plans with a view toward giving them substance.

Together, Sir Home and the General quickly consolidated the latter's many schemes, and on October 14 they presented the results to Lord Melville. Their main campaign, in which several thousand English troops and a naval squadron would participate, was to originate in Venezuela, where the General anticipated a general uprising in his favor among the natives. At the same time other assaults would be mounted against such widely separated points as Buenos Aires, Valparaiso, Lima, and Panama. The strategy was diffuse and perhaps impractical; what was more, success depended in large measure upon the willingness of the colonial population to revolt, an expectation to which Miranda clung with a conviction which was the more admirable because it lacked substantial proof. But Lord Melville, who announced that he had been a convert to the objects of the plan for five years, accepted all the odd details without protest. And when Popham, thinking "like an Englishman," much to Miranda's disgust, suggested that England should retain one of the captured ports, Lord Melville vetoed the proposal and assured the General that his government would be satisfied with the liberation of Venezuela and the opportunity for trade. The interview was satisfactory in every respect but one: no concrete decisions had emerged from the conversations.[12]

Two months passed by and Miranda became impatient. In December he began to make inquiries, but Lord Melville merely replied that "whenever I am at liberty to be explicit either one way or other, there will be no unnecessary delay on my part." Despite the good wishes, the exchanges of confidence, the disarming faith of Lord Melville, and the cautious hints of Pitt, the whole machine of conspiracy seemed to be faltering to a halt.

In a sense the delay was curious. As long as England and Spain remained at peace no action was likely to be taken. But by December, 1804, the embarrassments of peace had at last disappeared, and Pitt himself by a series of strange maneuvers had brought about their removal. At first he had merely protested against the assistance which Spain was affording to France.[13]

12. *Ibid.*, pp. 277–278.

13. Spain had contracted certain obligations toward France under the alliance treaty of San Ildefonso (1796), among them the promise of an annual tribute of 72,000,000 francs. Until the spring of 1804 England had been content to see her fulfill these obligations undisturbed. See A. F. Fremantle, *England in the Nineteenth Century, 1801–1805* (London, G. Allen and Unwin, 1929), pp. 401–403.

When his protests failed of effect he recalled Hookham Frere, the British minister in Madrid. Spain responded by making evident her intention to place her fleet at Bonaparte's disposal. The threat was more than Pitt could bear. He determined, in a fit of exasperation, to deliver an authoritative rap across His Catholic Majesty's exposed knuckles. On September 18, after a meeting of the cabinet, he dispatched orders for Admiral Cochrane to blockade the Spanish port of Ferrol and seize a treasure convoy bound from South America to Cadiz.

On October 5 four frigates of the Royal Navy located and pounced upon the unsuspecting convoy. One Spanish vessel exploded and sank; the others quickly surrendered. His Catholic Majesty's knuckles had now been rapped, and Pitt lingered for a moment under the impression that the punishment would have a chastening effect. In this happy state he even permitted Spanish merchantmen in English ports to depart unmolested. But the combination of severity and petty courtesy somehow failed of the intended effect. On December 12, 1804, Spain dropped her pretense of neutrality and with great indignation declared war upon England.[14]

Never, surely, had the circumstances been more propitious for an attack upon South America. Miranda was jubilant.

The die has been cast [he announced to a friend in Trinidad], and war at last declared between England and Spain. The business that you know of has also been decided; but when will it leave here? As yet I cannot foretell with precision. I am convinced that an expedition will be delayed from four to five months at least, although I am told that it will leave sooner.[15]

The Spanish minister in London expressed different fears but similar expectations. While he could not determine the point of attack, he warned his government of possible attempts against Mexico, the Isthmus of Panama, and Buenos Aires.[16] Yet despite the war, despite the hopes of the General and the suspicions of the minister, the fortunes of the conspiracy failed to prosper. What had happened?

14. Rose, *William Pitt and the Great War,* pp. 513–514.
15. Miranda to Rutherford, December 22, 1804, Robertson, *The Life of Miranda,* I, 282.
16. Anduaga to Cevallos, January 6, 1805, Robertson, *Francisco de Miranda and the Revolutionizing of Spanish America,* p. 357.

If an explanation exists, it lies in the negotiations leading up to the Third Coalition. The news of Pitt's activities and their awkward outcome had inspired a deep concern in Russia, and in the last days of 1804 a series of disapproving dispatches began to emanate from St. Petersburg. Prince Czartoryski, the Tsar's foreign minister, "alluded to hopes, which . . . he had held out of his Catholic Majesty being inclined to join in a general co-operation against France." [17] The Tsar himself expressed a strong desire to see the conflict ended. And finally, on April 11, 1805, when the Act of Coalition was signed, not only was provision made for the accession of Spain; Russia was also authorized to use her influence in Madrid to terminate the conflict with England.[18] Under the circumstances Pitt had no choice but to refrain from widening the breach.

The effects of this decision upon Miranda were catastrophic. Pitt now displayed an ambiguity of manner such as the General, even during his long experience in English society, had never before encountered. The minister did not exactly forbid him to explore further the prospects of revolution. That would have been painful but comprehensible. Instead, he cut off all hope of immediate aid and displayed the General casually before Spain, as a mere instrument to be employed in default of her good behavior.

The menace was to penetrate with good effect to Madrid, where a threat to Spanish America provoked as great a fear as the wrath of France; but to Miranda the role of cat's-paw was intolerable. There were ties created by a mistress, two illegitimate children, and a £300 pension, but he wrote to Sir Evan Nepean at the Admiralty "that it is infinitely wiser to act by ourselves when there is no hope of succor than to act with all the aid which England can offer us, after confusion and disorder are once introduced into Spanish America." [19] In February he demanded permission to proceed to the Windward Islands for the purpose of organizing a revolution of his own. In May Pitt authorized him to leave for Trinidad, but stipulated that he should do nothing without the permission of the governor of the island.[20] Miranda promptly re-

17. Rose, *Select Despatches* . . . *Relating to the Formation of the Third Coalition against France*, p. 72.

18. Sir A. W. Ward and G. P. Gooch, eds., *The Cambridge History of British Foreign Policy, 1783–1919* (3 vols., Cambridge, Cambridge University Press, 1922–23), I, 341.

19. Miranda to Nepean, February 5, 1805, Robertson, *The Life of Miranda*, I, 283.

20. *Ibid.*, p. 285.

jected the proposition as beneath his dignity and continued to apply for a simple passport to Trinidad. After again conferring with Pitt, Nepean advised the General to remain a while longer in England, "for the political affairs of Europe were not yet in that state of maturity to commence our enterprise." [21] Miranda relented a trifle and agreed to stay, provided only that Pitt would initiate him into the more confidential aspects of British policy. But Pitt remained uncooperative, and in July Miranda, now at the end of his patience, requested a passport for the United States.

Suddenly this last request was granted, and the General happily busied himself with plans for his departure. He learned with particular pleasure that "whenever I might return to England my pension would be paid in the same terms as at present, and this ought to convince me of the sane intentions of the ministers and of the favorable opinion which they entertained of me." [22] He also understood or thought he understood or wanted to understand that Pitt wished to maintain a secret correspondence with him and actually intended to support his undertaking once he had established a foothold in South America. "This was also the opinion of my friend Vansittart," the General confided to his diary, "who assured me that he was intimately persuaded that the ministers had more hope in the outcome of the enterprize which I was about to execute in South America than in the entire European coalition." [23]

Nevertheless, further delays ensued, and not until September 2, 1805, did Miranda board the *Polly*, bound for America. On November 9 he landed in New York under the pseudonym of Mr. Martin, and on the more congenial soil of the United States began collecting materials for an attack upon Venezuela.

Behind him, in England, the ranks of his supporters were already thinning. Lord Melville, who faced impeachment for the illegal use of Treasury funds, had fallen by the wayside, and Sir Home Popham had found a more congenial task. In reality Sir Home had not actually deserted Miranda; he had merely sought some employment to keep him occupied while the General remained in the shadows. His search led him to urge upon the cabinet the capture of the Cape of Good Hope; and Pitt, who was contemplating the Trafalgar campaign, fell in with his suggestion.

21. *Ibid.*, p. 290.
22. *Ibid.*, p. 291.
23. *Ibid.*, p. 292.

Originally a Dutch colony, captured once by the English and then returned to Holland at the Peace of Amiens, the Cape was an important way station on the passage to India. In hostile hands it could be used to sever Britain's vital communications with the Orient. Pitt therefore authorized the collection of a scratch fleet to recapture the base and to Sir Home fell the naval command. There was some talk of sending his squadron to the Caribbean once the Cape had been taken, but nothing of this transpired in Popham's orders.[24] The gallant Captain later maintained, however, that when he took leave of Pitt on July 29

I had a long conversation with him on the original project of the expedition to South America; in the course of which Mr. Pitt informed me, that from the then state of Europe, and the confederation in part formed, and forming against France, there was a great anxiety to endeavour, by friendly negociation, to detach Spain from her connection with that power; and, until the result of such an attempt should be known, it was desirable to suspend all hostile operations in South America; but, in case of failure in this object, it was his intention again to enter on the original project.[25]

The conversation sank deep into Sir Home's consciousness, and he must often have pondered its import as he sailed down the lonely stretches of the South Atlantic to the Cape of Good Hope.

Pitt, on the other hand, seems to have attached little or no significance to his words. Although the departure of Miranda and Popham signified the loss of a convenient lever with which to pry Spain loose from France, he had also rid himself of a source of recurring temptation. There would be no more quaintly phrased letters from the General, no further insinuations from Sir Home; his mind was free to cope solely with the pressing problems of the Coalition. Indeed, with the disappearance of the two conspirators, the Spanish problem appeared to be vanishing as well. Russia had actually made some progress toward a settlement of England's quarrel with Madrid, and Pitt happily engaged his royal master "not to possess Himself . . . of any of the American colonies of Spain" as long as the negotiations contin-

24. Castlereagh to Pitt, July 22, 1805, John Rydjord, *Foreign Interest in the Independence of New Spain* (Durham, Duke University Press, 1935), pp. 234–235.

25. *Minutes of a Court Martial, holden on board His Majesty's ship Gladiator in Portsmouth Harbor, on Friday, the 6th day of March, 1807, . . . of Capt. Sir Home Popham* (London, Longman, Hurst, Rees, and Orme, 1807), p. 80.

ued.[26] Eventually, as a result of this forbearance, there was even to come from Madrid an offer of certain commercial concessions in Spanish America.[27] But, as with so many things Spanish, the offer arrived a trifle late. By the beginning of 1806 the Emperor of the French had upset all of Pitt's plans.

Napoleon had become increasingly restive over his enforced idleness on the Channel, particularly as the storm clouds of the Third Coalition arose in the east; and already by the summer of 1805 he had determined to abandon the invasion of England. Nelson's victory at Trafalgar, that last ray of sunshine for Pitt, must have effaced any of the Emperor's doubts as to the wisdom of his decision. Earlier, with great dispatch and secrecy he had decamped from Boulogne with the *Grande Armée;* now he moved his troops halfway across Europe and fell with spectacular fury upon the combined forces of Austria and Russia. The battle of Austerlitz, fought on December 2, 1805, smashed the Third Coalition before it got fairly onto the field.

The news of the defeat came to Pitt as a crushing blow. In one day the entire confederation, the result of two years of planning and interminable negotiations, had disappeared into smoke. Austria had surrendered to the conqueror and the Russian armies were reeling back toward their frontiers. The threat of an invasion of England had abated; but Napoleon stood supreme in Europe. Whether or not the British Isles could long remain secure in the face of such a concentration of power was difficult to forecast. Pitt, certainly, was incapable of an opinion. The breakdown of the Coalition had dashed his hopes and bruised his spirit. There was nothing left, no alternative course to which to turn his thoughts. In the depths of his despair not even the proposals of Miranda and Popham seem to have crossed his mind. Tormented by the gout, his frame weakened by a combination of port, hard riding, and an inadequate diet, he dragged himself down to Bath in an effort to recover his strength. The cure was of no avail. On January 22, 1806, broken in health and completely dispirited, Pitt died. His colleagues, bereft of their leader, resigned, and the country drifted in momentary confusion as the King sought to replace them.

26. Rydjord, *Foreign Interest in the Independence of New Spain,* pp. 226–227.
27. England was to be allowed to carry each year a certain amount of goods between Spain and Mexico, half of each cargo to be British, the other half Spanish. *Ibid.,* pp. 239–240.

Reports of the failure of the Coalition and Pitt's death traveled slowly. General Miranda had still heard nothing as he organized his revolution in New York. And halfway across the world, at the Cape of Good Hope, Sir Home Popham was equally uninformed. He had completed his mission with the capture of the Cape and was now engaged in the monotonous and unprofitable duties of a routine patrol. Both he and Miranda were in the backwaters of history; fate, it seemed, was to remain thoroughly unkind.

II

PRIVATE INTERESTS AND PUBLIC POLICY

THE death of Pitt required both a number of eulogies and the formation of an entirely new administration. The funeral orations poured forth with practiced ease—that was to be expected; but not until the King had haggled for several weeks with the various parliamentary factions did a government—known to history as the Ministry of All the Talents—finally emerge. Lord Grenville, Pitt's cousin, led the new cabinet as First Lord of the Treasury. Charles James Fox, its most illustrious member, entered the Foreign Office out of deference to the King who refused to tolerate him as first minister. William Windham, an ardent disciple of Burke, accepted the Secretaryship of War and Colonies, and Viscount Howick (the future Earl Grey of the Reform Bill) became First Lord of the Admiralty. Together with such lesser satellites as Richard Brinsley Sheridan, who had been advised "to drink less and speak the truth," [1] the ministry presented, in its array of statesmen, a brilliant façade to the world.

Its first days of power aroused the highest expectations. The Tories were in a state of virtual anarchy, and many of their leaders looked upon Lord Grenville as Pitt's logical successor. Public opinion was favorable; and even the King, beset with a large family, together with other more obvious infirmities, seemed for the moment content. But behind the brilliant façade there had sounded, from the first, a significant note of discord. The members of the cabinet agreed that Pitt's policy had lacked vigor: war expenditures had been too lavish, plans too diffuse, results too meager. [2] But they could not agree on how these evils should be remedied. Although Fox maintained publicly that England must continue

---

1. Harold Temperley, *Life of Canning* (London, J. Finch, 1905), p. 29.
2. *Historical Manuscripts Commission, Manuscripts of J. B. Fortescue, preserved at Dropmore* (10 vols., London, H.M. Stationery Office, 1892–1927), VIII, introd., x (hereafter cited as *H.M.C., Dropmore Papers*).

the war, privately he nourished hopes of eliminating all unnecessary expenditures by realizing an early peace with France.[3] Lord Grenville, on the other hand, remained faithful to his cousin's memory and advocated a more vigorous prosecution of the struggle, while Windham showed an appetite for adventure in South America. Each could find an echo of approval in society: Fox among the Whigs, Lord Grenville among the Tories, and Windham among the more articulate members of the mercantile community, who, finding it ever more difficult to trade in Europe, were agitating with a growing vehemence for licenses to export to the Spanish colonies. The divergence of opinion was hardly conducive to the effective conduct of a great war.[4]

Fox at first resolved the conflict by getting his own way. The discovery of a plot to assassinate Napoleon enabled him to enter into a correspondence with Talleyrand, who blithely encouraged his expectations of peace. But in April the negotiations reached a sudden impasse, owing to the exorbitant nature of the French demands, and Fox lamented that "to be Ministers at a moment when the country is falling, and all Europe sinking, is a dreadful situation, especially if we can make no great and striking efforts for safety." [5] The struggle continued nonetheless, and Lord Grenville, who was being urged by Windham to act in South America, pressed weakly for a campaign in the Mediterranean. A wave of inertia seemed about to engulf the cabinet; its members were floating upon a sea of indecision and discord; and then, with extraordinary suddenness, General Miranda, followed by Sir Home Popham, sailed over the horizon of affairs.

Miranda had slipped away from New York in January, 1806, in a small vessel, the *Leander*, accompanied by two hundred men. His original destination had been Venezuela, but, anticipating that his force would be inadequate to the task, he first spent two months looking for additional support in the Caribbean area. Although some few recruits and two unarmed schooners were forthcoming, the British authorities at the islands where he touched refused to lend official sanction to his activities, despite his assurance that the expedition had the "knowledge and tacit assent" of

3. *Ibid.,* p. vii. "As to France," he had told Howick, "I am obstinate in my opinion that Buonaparte's wish is peace—nay that he is afraid of war to the last degree." Fox to Howick, December, 1802, George M. Trevelyan, *Lord Grey of the Reform Bill* (London, Longmans, Green, 1920), p. 129.

4. Auckland to Grenville, March 16, 1806, *H.M.C., Dropmore Papers,* VIII, 59.

5. Fox to Grenville, April 18, 1806, *ibid.,* p. 105.

the administration in London.[6] The experience disenchanted the General, but in a desperate mood he determined to start his revolution anyway. Cruising down to the Venezuelan coast with his motley force, he attempted to land at Puerto Cabello on April 27, 1806. The attack was as bloodless as it was unsuccessful. The Spanish garrison had somehow been alerted, and after an exchange of shots lasting forty-five minutes the General fled in his flagship, leaving the two unarmed schooners to the victors.[7]

Still unabated in his zeal but hampered by this sudden reduction in his forces, Miranda sailed back to the West Indies in search of more ample means. At Barbados he seemed to have found them. Admiral Cochrane, who had been following the General's career with some interest, promised in a written agreement to support the next effort with several British ships. He also authorized Miranda to seek recruits in Barbados and at Trinidad. In return for this pledge the General promised to grant special commercial privileges to English subjects upon the establishment of his republic.

Admiral Cochrane began to suspect almost at once that the agreement was not particularly discreet and, abashed at his own boldness, he sent it off to England for ministerial approval. Miranda, on the other hand, hastened to take advantage of the bargain. Following upon a rebuff from the officer commanding the Leeward Islands, he proceeded to Trinidad where Governor Hislop accorded him a sympathetic reception and promised assistance. The years of delay and intrigue seemed about to culminate in a striking success; and Miranda delightedly wrote to Vansittart, who was now in the government, and advised him to win the support of his colleagues.[8]

The General need hardly have written his letter for informational purposes; the news of his activities had already reached London in the beginning of June and was causing considerable ferment. The mercantile community was particularly agitated. Turnbull, an old adherent of Miranda, not only wrote to plead for the office of "your Commercial European Agent as that may enable me to be of service, in promoting your views." He went further and had printed a variety of propaganda sheets which, on the assump-

6. Miranda to Admiral Sir Andrew Mitchell, February 13, 1806, in "Miranda and the British Admiralty, 1804–1806," *Amer. Hist. Rev.*, VI (1901), 518.

7. The Spaniards also captured about sixty of the General's bewildered recruits. See Robertson, *The Life of Miranda*, I, 305–306.

8. *Ibid.*, pp. 308–309.

tion that all of South America would soon be free, outlined the advantages that would accrue to the new states should they choose to trade with England. Together with Admiral Cochrane's brother, he even urged upon Lord Grenville and other influential members of the cabinet the importance of supporting Miranda.[9]

Turnbull's efforts fell short of success. From the beginning Lord Grenville had assumed an ambiguous attitude toward the entire affair. The question, he admitted was an immense one. But Miranda's expedition had been "launched by our predecessors as a matter of connivance only, without any plan for acting in consequence of it." How far, he wondered, "shall we now countenance it, or engage in it?" [10] On the whole, not very far; there were already too many other problems requiring his care. Fox had again succeeded in opening peace negotiations with France, and, while Lord Grenville did not wholly approve of the effort, he recognized the necessity of carrying the gesture through to a conclusion. To do so and at the same time to attack the possessions of Spain, which were included in the negotiations, went against his sense of honor and expediency.[11]

For once Lord Grenville found himself in agreement with his Whig colleagues; for Fox opposed any measure likely to jeopardize the prospects of peace, and Howick, having received Admiral Cochrane's agreement with Miranda, expressed grave doubts as to the wisdom of "embarking on this scheme." The cabinet assembled formally on July 15 and ratified his doubts by sending instructions

to Rear-Admiral Cockrane [sic], highly disapproving of his having taken upon himself, without instructions, to assist General Miranda by the employment of the ships under his command, and even to conclude a treaty with him; and that he should be directed to take no steps by which His Majesty can further be committed in that enterprize . . .[12]

9. Turnbull to Miranda, June 23, 1806, ibid., pp. 311–312.
10. H.M.C., Dropmore Papers, VIII, 179.
11. Lord Grenville to Fox, June 22, 1806: "Lord Yarmouth does not mention Spain, but I conclude that she is to be included in the general uti possedetis which we ask for the rest of Europe. We have the better right to ask it when we renounce for it views on the Spanish possessions in America." Ibid., p. 196.
12. Monroe to Madison, June 9, 1806, S. M. Hamilton, ed., The Writings of James Monroe (7 vols., New York, G. P. Putnam's, 1898–1903), IV, 450; Howick to Windham, July 13, 1806, Robertson, The Life of Miranda, I, 315; Minute of Cabinet, July 15, 1806, H.M.C., Dropmore Papers, VIII, 236.

Here at last was a decision; could it be enforced? While the discussions in London were going on, Miranda was feverishly assembling recruits in Trinidad; and in July he decided to try another attack upon Venezuela without the assistance of Admiral Cochrane. He set sail once more down the now familiar coast, this time with seven small vessels under his command, and actually succeeded in effecting a landing at the Bay of Coro on August 1, 1806. Again the results disappointed his expectations. No native uprising followed his appearance, the inhabitants of the area fled inland, and Miranda refrained from following. Instead he sent off to his British friends for reinforcements. The replies, all of them, were hostile; even Admiral Cochrane proved suddenly remiss. His only offer was one of secret assistance, to prevent the intrusion of enemy warships; for, from "my late accounts from home it appears that you have some warm friends in the ministry but I fear that you have also some that are not so much as I could wish." [13]

Deserted and powerless, the General lingered a few days longer upon his native soil, enjoying the empty victory. Then, on August 13, with the approach of a sizable body of Spanish troops, he re-embarked his ragged force and sailed off to the island of Aruba, there to meditate upon the folly of his allies. He heard from Cochrane again in September. The Admiral had received his instructions from home and was directed

to limit the assistance you are to receive from me, to protection from the Naval Force of the Enemy; to prevent succours from being landed; and to secure your re-embarkation in the event of your being obliged to leave the shore.

I am further directed to send by a fast sailing Vessel, full details of the situation in which the Continent of South America now stands in order that His Majesty's Ministers may finally decide as to the further measures they may take. [14]

The message was hardly encouraging to Miranda, despite the hint that the Talents still had his schemes under consideration. As he must have divined and as Turnbull explained English policy to him later,

The Irish applied to the French to come and assist them, and they would all rise to cooperate with them—but the French said, "Rise up

13. Cochrane to Miranda, July 30, 1806, Robertson, *The Life of Miranda,* I, 316–317.
14. Cochrane to Miranda, September 11, 1806, *ibid.,* p. 319.

first, and then we will come and assist you." So Mr. Grenville said, that Ministers waited till the Americans should show their disposition to come forward.[15]

Disconsolately, the General wandered from island to island, searching for the assistance which, in the face of the government's announced attitude, patently could not be rendered. After a brief interval in the main stream of history he had been relegated brusquely to the backwaters again.

But in another part of the world decisions were evolving which Lord Grenville and his colleagues found less easy to ignore or reverse. Sir Home Popham had, as events proved, lost all patience with his monotonous duties at the Cape of Good Hope. His conversations with Pitt, a knowledge of Miranda's plans, and complete and utter boredom were, in fact, impelling the Captain to try his hand at a filibustering expedition of his own. His enthusiasm became contagious; General Baird, the commanding officer at the Cape, interested himself in the project and lent him the Seventy-first Regiment under Colonel Beresford (the future marshal of Portugal), together with a few artillerymen, four guns, and a handful of dragoons.[16]

In April, 1806, still ignorant of Pitt's death but aware of the collapse of the Third Coalition, Sir Home set off for South America. Stopping at St. Helena, he wrote to London to announce his intentions to the government and then persuaded the governor of the island to lend him four hundred men—an act of generosity for which that functionary later paid with the loss of his post.[17] There followed the long voyage across the South Atlantic which ended on June 8, 1806, when Sir Home and his flotilla sailed into the estuary of the Plata.

Popham had originally intended to seize Montevideo as a base from which to commence more ambitious operations. But new intelligence caused him to alter his tactics. Buenos Aires, he now learned, was totally lacking in defenses and, what excited Popham even more, had recently become the repository for a large amount of specie from Peru. There was no other alternative; Sir Home threw caution to the winds, threaded his way up the river with

15. Turnbull to Miranda, November 20, 1806, *ibid.*, II, 1.

16. J. W. Fortescue, *A History of the British Army* (13 vols., London, Macmillan, 1902–30), V, 313.

17. Alexander Gillespie, *Gleanings and Remarks Collected During Many Months of Residence at Buenos Ayres and Within the Upper Country* (Leeds, B. Dewhirst, 1818), pp. 28–29.

the aid of a drunken pilot, and landed Beresford's regiment close to the city. On June 27 the Colonel's troops burst into the metropolis and after a perfunctory struggle forced its defenders to capitulate. On July 6 Sir Home informed the Admiralty of his exploits; on the eighth he went further and announced, in a letter to the Master of Lloyd's Coffee-house, "that the conquest of this place opens an extensive channel for the manufactures of Great Britain." [18] Several days later Beresford was able to report upon the booty seized—$1,086,208 in all—a handsome recompense for the daring of his men and surely excuse enough for their lack of orders.

Nor did Sir Home forget Miranda.

Here we are in possession of Buenos Aires [he announced to the General], the finest country in the world, and from what I see of the disposition of the inhabitants, I have no doubt if Ministers would accede to your propositions and send you here, that your plan would take as well from this side as from the other, try my friend to come out. . . . I am so occupied that I scarce know what to do first. I wish you were here. I like the South Americans prodigiously.[19]

But Sir Home and Beresford soon discovered that liking South Americans involved no necessary reciprocity. They had come as conquerors, not liberators; they had emptied the city's treasury; and in return—they had done nothing except to lower the import duties upon British goods. A restless stirring soon coursed through Buenos Aires, fanned by a small group of leaders who disliked the near and firm hand of English sea power even more than the careless oppression of distant Spain. Beresford crushed one attempt at revolt; another materialized in its place. On August 12, 1806, the entire populace of the city rose against the intruder and, while Popham cruised helplessly up and down the river, captured Beresford and his entire army.

Sir Home had received a striking lesson on the futility of ill-prepared and ill-timed filibustering expeditions. The South Americans had learned something as well. For the first time they had become suffused with a consciousness of sufficiency and self-reliance. To the smoldering discontent with their subordinate station in the Spanish empire they could now add the knowledge of

18. *An Authentic and Interesting Description of the City of Buenos Aires* . . . (London, Ohn Fairburn, n.d.), pp. 50–51, 54.

19. This letter went to Miranda's London address. See Robertson, *The Life of Miranda,* I, 323.

their ability to fend for themselves. The point was not distant when they would put this new-found knowledge to a long and eventually successful test.

But what of England? How did the Buenos Aires affair react upon the Ministry of All the Talents? The news of Popham's intentions reached London late in June. His announcement of the fall of Buenos Aires was to arrive only in September; that of Beresford's downfall was not received until January, 1807. Decisions, therefore, were regulated, in part at least, by the slowness of communications. They were also influenced by the peculiar frame of mind of the ministers and the nature of the expedition itself. The precariousness of the situation in Europe, the pressure from the mercantile community, and the fact that Popham was a British officer, acting with British troops for purely British ends: these factors forced the conclusion that, somehow, the beachhead in Buenos Aires must be treated differently from the forays of Miranda.

William Windham, upon whom Sir Home's communications from St. Helena had wrought a powerful impression, was insistent upon this point. He had been advocating just such an attempt as Popham's ever since his entry into office. He pleaded now not only for its reinforcement but also for the dispatch of other forces to seize vital ports on the eastern and western coasts of South America. Europe, he argued, no longer afforded any scope for the deployment of British power. Besides, although he did not admit this, he had promised his military secretary, Robert Craufurd, a little command of his own.[20] He had no interest, he admitted, in starting revolutions in South America; England must actually retain whatever territory she overran in order to counterbalance Bonaparte's recent continental acquisitions. Then,

with an establishment on the continent of South America, followed by a hearty support of the war in this country, the period may not be far distant, nor exceed the term to which we can afford to wait, when the power of Bonaparte may begin to totter; and if once thrown out of its balance, fall to the ground with very little struggle.[21]

Fox, still, could muster no sympathy for Windham's views. He was wholly European in outlook and pacific by inclination, intent upon his laborious and, so far, fruitless negotiations with France.

20. Windham to Grenville, June 30, 1806, *H.M.C., Dropmore Papers*, VIII, 209.
21. Windham to Grenville, September 11, 1806, *ibid.*, p. 321.

But Fox had begun to lose his pre-eminent influence in the councils of the cabinet; he was a dying man, no longer capable, even, of conducting the affairs of his own department. Although Lord Howick, who disliked Popham as much as he did Miranda, rushed to the support of Fox, the coalition came too late; the tide was setting against them. Even Lord Auckland at the Board of Trade, who had kept aloof from the earlier quarrels, was demanding some sort of policy. Trade with South America, though clandestine and difficult, had amounted to a million sterling during the past four months alone, and more and more shipping houses were applying for licenses. Surely the government must act positively in some way soon.[22]

That the government did not immediately respond to his advice was due in large measure to Lord Grenville. The first minister was by nature reluctant to settle his thoughts; he loved the ambiguity of shaded meanings; his mind, subtle and refined, rebelled at making choices. Fox's illness only fortified this inclination. He found himself saddled with all the responsibilities of the Foreign Office: there were the complicated negotiations with Talleyrand, spun out now beyond all reason, to be brought to a decorous conclusion; and there was the incessant nagging of Windham to be answered. Far from the gardens, the books, and the austere peace of his estate at Dropmore, Lord Grenville was an unhappy man; and like many intelligent and unhappy men he expressed his discontent in a series of evasive maneuvers.

He sent for Lord Castlereagh in the hope that secret orders from the previous administration to Popham might be discovered. The expectation proved groundless.[23] He then agreed, after much backing and filling, to dispatch reinforcements to Sir Home; and a small force under Sir Samuel Auchmuty was put in readiness.

July came and went, but the problem itself remained. Lord Grenville still could not decide what to do in the event that Popham's expedition succeeded. One solution he thought might be to use its fruits as a counterweight to Bonaparte's claims in the negotiations with France. Talleyrand had raised the disposition of the Kingdom of the Two Sicilies as the latest obstacle to the conclusion of peace. From the depths of his predicament Lord Grenville suggested indemnifying the monarch of that hapless country

---

22. Auckland to Grenville, September 1, 14, 1806, *ibid.*, pp. 302, 332.

23. Countess Castalia Granville, ed., *Lord Granville Leveson Gower, Private Correspondence, 1781–1821* (2 vols., London, John Murray, 1916), II, 231.

with something in South America. He might as well have shouted
to the winds; from the first Talleyrand treated the proposal with
scorn, and in the face of onrushing events it had to be discarded.[24]

Lord Grenville's freedom of choice narrowed even further on
September 12, when the official news of the seizure of Buenos Aires
finally reached London. The general reaction, after a year empty
of victory, was one of enthusiasm, cupidity, and possessiveness.
On September 20, to the tootling of bands playing "Rule Britan-
nia" and "God Save the King," an excited crowd escorted the
Buenos Aires treasure through the city streets to the Bank of
England. Popham, of course, was recalled: not only had his action
been unauthorized, he was a die-hard Tory. The Admiralty forced
him to pay his own passage home and in 1807 acknowledged his
services with a court-martial. When Sir Home returned to active
duty, he did so as a much chastened man.

The excitement unleashed by his exploits was not so easily
curbed. A fever of speculation struck the mercantile community,
and there was a wild rush to purchase goods and ship them off to
Buenos Aires. To the trading element Popham's victory came as
a godsent opportunity to dispose of the manufactures which England's factories were producing in ever increasing quantities and
which Bonaparte was making more and more difficult to sell. The
possibility of an uneasy peace with France, threatening as it
would, to shut off this golden market, declined rapidly in popularity.

If Lord Grenville was not conscious of this shift in public sentiment, he was aware of another blow: the death of Fox on September 13, 1806, which threw the cabinet into momentary confusion.
Lord Grenville had often disagreed with Fox in theory, but he
had depended upon him in fact to lend strength and cohesiveness
to the administration. Now, with Fox gone, he was alone; without
that solid and commanding presence how was he to carry on? As
he wrote in one of his frequent fits of self-doubt:

I want one great and essential quality for my station, and every hour
increases the difficulty. I can still, and could still, for a few years, as
long as my eyesight is spared to me, labour at my desk; but I am not
competent to the management of men. I never was so naturally; and
toil and anxiety more and more unfit me for it.[25]

24. Pierre Coquelle, *Napoleon and England, 1803–1813* (London, G. Bell, 1914).
p. 105.
25. Grenville to Buckingham (n.d.), *H.M.C., Dropmore Papers,* VIII, introd.,
viii.

The diverse elements of the cabinet were buffeting him about; Howick, Sidmouth, and Windham were offering advice from every side. He could discern the complexity and immediacy of the situation, yet the dead weight of responsibility left him helpless. Should he continue to bargain with France? Should he devote his energies to a vigorous prosecution of the European war? Or should he turn his back upon the Continent and take advantage of the opportunity offered by Popham? In his doubts and hesitations, in the irresolute cast of his mind, Turnbull even saw a ray of hope for Miranda.[26] But, Turnbull, as usual, was mistaken; in the final analysis the decision was not Lord Grenville's. Napoleon resolved the difficulty for him.

The Emperor had left Paris for the Prussian frontier early in September. The peace negotiations began to lag as a consequence, and although Talleyrand continued his conversations with Lord Lauderdale, the British emissary, he appeared to be doing so merely to gain time. In his doubtful state Lord Grenville recommended the inclusion of Buenos Aires on the agenda of the negotiations. England, he maintained, was entitled either to keep the city or to receive compensation for it in Europe. Talleyrand evaded the subject; he could make no commitments in the absence of his imperial master.[27] Lord Lauderdale grew disgusted, demanded his passports, and on October 8, 1806, left Paris. Six days later, at Jena and Auerstadt, Napoleon trapped and destroyed the Prussian armies. On November 21 from Berlin he decreed the exclusion of British commerce from all ports under his control. Western Europe was his; England might be ignored; only Russia was left to face him.

Lord Grenville had seemed on the verge of making up his mind before learning of these catastrophic events; but appearances were deceptive. He allowed Sir Samuel Auchmuty to depart for Buenos Aires with three thousand troops. He and Windham argued over the wisdom of replacing Beresford with Sir Arthur Wellesley, a new man recently returned from India. He even approved of an Order in Council designed to turn Buenos Aires into

26. "The influence and consequence of his [Vansittart's] party are most materially increased," Turnbull maintained, "by the death of Mr. Fox. Lord Grenville, I am sure is well attached to you, and to your cause." Turnbull to Miranda, September 17, 1806, Robertson, *The Life of Miranda*, I, 323–324.

27. Talleyrand to Napoleon, September 18, 1806, Coquelle, *Napoleon and England*, p. 132. The details of the abortive negotiations may be found in *H.M.C., Dropmore Papers*, VIII, 343–369.

a British colony. But still he debated and hesitated. "If we desist from all idea of acting on the Continent," he told Windham, on September 23, "we shall then probably reinforce ourselves still further in South America; . . ." But, he went on, "the moment of a fresh explosion on the Continent must not be lost to us." [28]

All wondering and straddling ceased upon the news of Jena and Auerstadt; Lord Grenville threw up his hands and turned his back on Europe. He found himself in good company. Windham, who had been looking with a long and singular intentness in the direction of South America, was alive with plans. Craufurd would circle Cape Horn, take Valparaiso, and, in hostile country with a handful of troops, establish a chain of military posts through the Andes and across the continent to Buenos Aires. Montevideo would be seized; there might even be assaults upon Venezuela and Mexico. The Marquess of Buckingham, Lord Grenville's elder brother, advanced a plan of his own; he urged separate attacks upon Peru and Panama.[29] Sir Arthur Wellesley found himself immersed in elaborate consultations about distant and exotic ports, and even Lord Grenville fell prey to the enthusiasm for drawing up plans. Indeed, his strategy, once formulated, proved to be the most diffuse of all. He would hold Buenos Aires and capture Montevideo. Other troops would depart from India, seize Manila in passing, and then descend upon the west coast of Mexico.

Windham became a trifle exercised over the intrusion by Lord Grenville in the military sphere and opposed the attack on Manila. The forces thus diverted could be used, he asserted, to much better advantage by the enterprising Craufurd.[30] So the discussion raged, and the plans grew in magnificence, and by the end of October a hundred ships were standing by in anticipation of the South American trade. In the same month Sir Arthur Wellesley proceeded to Deal to join his command, the proposed operations against Mexico neatly filed away in his mind. And Lord Auckland, from his niche at the Board of Trade, sang his praises of the transatlantic strategy. "The entire downfall of the Continental powers makes it more than ever necessary to advert to interests which are merely British," he announced. "I feel strongly that in

28. Grenville to Windham, September 23, 1806, *H.M.C., Dropmore Papers*, VIII, 353.

29. Although the Marquess professed to be a literary man, he saw nothing incongruous in offering Lord Grenville "my very vague and unfinished ideas respecting your South American projects." *Ibid.*, pp. 386–387.

30. Windham to Grenville, November 2, 1806, *ibid.*, pp. 418–420.

the actual predicament of Europe, the extension of our commerce is become the most efficient measure of war." [31]

The enthusiasm spread to the Foreign Office where Lord Howick was now presiding, and his dispatches reflected the influence. In reply to a plea for help from Prussia he stated bluntly:

. . . that His Majesty, having supported the great pressure of the contest against France during so many years in which Prussia has been at peace, has a right to expect that His Prussian Majesty should avail himself to the utmost of the resources of his own dominion before he can justly call upon His Majesty for pecuniary assistance.[32]

When Spain, seeing Napoleon upon the distant fields of Germany, offered at last to break her alliance with France and join hands with Russia and England, Howick curtly replied that the proposal was inadmissible.[33] The Tsar himself received even shorter shrift when in the last months of the year he appealed for aid. Three coalitions had come and gone without a semblance of success against France, replied the Foreign Secretary. There was little use now in attempting a fourth. Only Lord Sidmouth persisted in his advocacy of a European strategy; and, except when votes were to be counted, Lord Sidmouth hardly commanded an audience.[34]

One thing at last seemed certain. The government had decided to abandon the Continent in order to devote their energies to colonial enterprises. Yet, as the last months of 1806 drifted by, these enterprises failed to prosper. Craufurd finally sailed in December with orders to touch at Buenos Aires, but his was the only force to leave. A period that had commenced with frenzied activity was ending in a term of inanition. What had happened?

To begin with, Lord Grenville and Windham suddenly discovered that the means to carry out their far-flung schemes were not what they should have been. Not only was the military establishment too small, what there was of it was inefficient and entangled in red tape. The navy showed to little better advantage. The monotonous duties of blockade, carried on in rotting hulks for months on end, with no relief in sight, had sapped initiative

31. Auckland to Grenville, November 25, 1806, *ibid.*, pp. 441–442.
32. Howick to Morpeth, September 24, 1806, Trevelyan, *Lord Grey of the Reform Bill*, p. 151.
33. Rydjord, *Foreign Interest in the Independence of New Spain*, p. 241.
34. Sidmouth to Grenville, October 25, 1806, *H.M.C., Dropmore Papers*, VIII, 401.

and lowered morale. There was a shortage of vessels with which to transport troops; and Lord Grenville was crying mournfully: "How can I weed out the list of admirals? It is a list of incurables." [35]

Nor did the difficulties stop there. If plans for conquest flowed in abundance, they flowed without coordination. It was one thing to pick out points on a map and decide to attack them; it was quite another to determine how these points, once conquered, should be fitted into a general scheme of policy. Lord Holland, a most influential Whig, inquired after the government's intentions. Did they propose merely to hit, plunder, and run? Would they conquer and hold? Or had they decided to enter Latin America as liberators? [36] Lord Castlereagh in the House of Commons asked similarly embarrassing questions. Ministers, in their confusion and indecision, evaded direct replies. Even their instructions to Beresford and Craufurd were vague and tentative. Promises or commitments to the Latin Americans were to be avoided. Prospective conquests should simply be held in the name of the King.

The problem was too big, the attending difficulties too overwhelming. Rather than act decisively or even abandon this project too, the cabinet chose to envelop itself in a vast, impenetrable fantasy. Ministers mulled as in a dream over unborn but anticipated victories. They talked of solving the Catholic problem by sending regiments of Irishmen to South America. They watched with unruffled serenity as Bonaparte rode across the Polish plains in pursuit of the Tsar, and western Europe lay open to invasion. They debated the respective merits of the New World and the Old, but politely, academically, and concentrated their attention upon Mexico, Peru, Buenos Aires, and the Philippines.

Then suddenly, their shadowy edifice tumbled to the ground. On January 25, 1807, the news of Beresford's surrender reached London; and with its arrival complacency vanished. The problem was no longer one of conquering all of South America; British arms must first be vindicated by the recapture of Buenos Aires. Sir Arthur Wellesley, who had been laboring assiduously over the Venezuelan project, peremptorily abandoned his studies, for "every day affords a slighter hope that we shall be able to carry our plans into execution." [37] Windham alone objected: this new

35. *Ibid.*, introd., p. xliv.
36. Holland to Grenville, December 7, 1806, *ibid.*, p. 460.
37. Wellesley to Marquess Wellesley, February 21, 1807, *ibid.*, IX, 52.

attitude would involve the loss by Craufurd of his independent command. But Windham was overruled, and an order went out to concentrate all available forces in the Plata River area.

The government seemingly had become intent and single-minded in their purpose. Rapidly, they assembled an expedition and appointed General Whitelocke as its commander. Windham still proved difficult; he wished to give Whitelocke discretionary power to attempt a landing in the vicinity of Valparaiso. But during his absence from the War Office Lord Howick slipped in and drafted the General's orders. Buenos Aires, and Buenos Aires alone, was to be the British objective. Thus instructed, Whitelocke set off toward the end of March to retrieve his country's prestige.

The Ministry of All the Talents, having put a plan into motion at last, now collapsed, not upon the issue of its war strategy but upon that of Catholic Emancipation. In terms of parliamentary majorities there was no reason for them to go; they simply chose to challenge the King upon his most invincible prejudice and, in the face of his obstinacy, resigned. As Sheridan explained the debacle, the government "not only ran its head against a wall, but actually built a wall for the purpose of running its head against it." [38] A year of wasted opportunities, of utter futility, had characterized the rule of the Talents. Popham, with his fili-bustering, had finally forced their hand, but, even so, their response had been tardy and inept. They departed from office un-mourned, not to return for another twenty years.

General Whitelocke carried something of their strange inertia with him to South America. Upon his arrival in the Plata estuary he found Auchmuty with his three thousand men in possession of Montevideo, seized early in February. The prospects thus were encouraging. Montevideo itself bustled with Englishmen—merchants, traders, and adventurers—and off shore stood over a hundred British vessels, weighted down with goods for the South Americans.[39] With a good base from which to operate, with ten thou-

38. Sir Henry Lytton Bulwer, *Historical Characters* (2 vols., London, R. Bentley, 1868), II, 247. According to Michael Roberts the cabinet "fell with an air of nobility wholly fictitious, having engendered a storm of religious bigotry in England, having made Whig cooperation with the King for the future impossible, having connected the Catholic question with an attack on the monarchy, and having alienated that dangerous class of Irish agitators which their bill had been designed to conciliate." See "The Fall of the Talents, March, 1807," *English Historical Review*, L (1935), 76.

39. R. A. Humphreys, ed., *British Consular Reports on the Trade and Politics of Latin America, 1824–1826* (London, Royal Historical Society, 1940), p. 47 n.

sand troops at his disposal, surrounded by eager compatriots, Whitelocke seemed hardly capable of failing in his task. Yet fail he did. He mobilized his army, moved up the river, landed several regiments near Buenos Aires, and after a series of skirmishes with the defenders asked for a truce. The consequences of his request proved as humiliating to the British as they were surprising to Buenos Aires. On July 7, 1807, Whitelocke agreed to evacuate the province within ten days and Montevideo in two months. His proposal that liberty of commerce be extended to the British for four months thereafter was rejected out of hand by the local commander. Utterly disgraced, Whitelocke returned to England, there to stand a court-martial which resulted in his dismissal from the service. A sense of futility gripped not only the Talents but their agents as well.

But in South America the passage of the year marked a turning point in history. The rancor toward the English intruders hardly survived their departure. Dissatisfaction with Spanish rule became, by contrast, widespread; and the movement toward independence, already noticeable in the instinctive rebellion against Beresford, rapidly expanded. Perhaps General Whitelocke by retreating had rendered a greater service to England than he or his detractors ever imagined.

III

A FORMULATION OF OBJECTIVES

PITT had been too absorbed in the European conflict to evolve a precise Latin American policy. Lord Grenville's administration had been too divided and irresolute to enforce one. Its successors, seemingly, would hardly retain power long enough to discuss the problem. For the King, in what was felt by many to be a renewed manifestation of insanity, had turned for advisers to his old Tory friends; and in March a cabinet composed of Pitt's adherents and led by the aged and decrepit Duke of Portland had taken up the seals of office. It was a question of some interest, indeed, which would die first: the Duke or his administration. Certainly the prospects for either did not appear hopeful. The Duke was tortured with gallstones; his colleagues suffered alternately from internecine jealousy and a lack of parliamentary support. Competent observers allowed them the supreme authority only until the Whigs should reorganize their forces. Yet in varying forms the members of the Duke's administration were to govern England for the next twenty years.

The task which faced them in 1807 foretold little of so long a reign. There were defeats to be announced—at Buenos Aires, the Dardanelles, and in Egypt. And there was the lengthening shadow of Napoleon. From his Prussian triumphs the Emperor had moved against Russia. In February, 1807, the drawn battle of Eylau ensued, followed in June by a sweeping French victory at Friedland. The Tsar, deserted by his allies, abandoned the struggle, met Napoleon at Tilsit in July, and came to terms. The prospects for England, looked at in their entirety, were, to say the least, discouraging, particularly for an administration the life expectancy of which seemed measurable in terms of months. Yet, from the moment of their entry into office, the new cabinet exhibited a boldness and determination undiminished by the imminence of disaster. Tories with vigor—that was a curious and somehow engaging spectacle.

Two of the Duke of Portland's associates were particularly re-

sponsible for this new and spirited conduct of affairs. Both had
been especial friends of Pitt. Each expressed in his person a different facet of England. The first, George Canning, remains now as
controversial a figure as he was in 1807.[1] A brilliant orator, a competent poet, a practiced parliamentarian, he possessed that intui-
tive cast of mind which caught and unraveled with extraordinary
dexterity all the twisted threads of political motivation. Born in
England, but of Anglo-Irish extraction, a striking combination
of formal precision and extreme natural passion, he almost symbolized an age that was moving from the restrained classicism of
the eighteenth century into the romantic sensibility of the nineteenth. His environment, except for the earliest years, had been
aristocratic—Eton, Oxford, and the drawing rooms of great
Whig hostesses. But his mother had been an actress, he lacked a
private fortune, and despite an acknowledged brilliance he had
been patronized. The results were hardly surprising. Canning
developed a protective arrogance and a caustic wit, threw over
his Whig connections, and joined Pitt to the accompaniment of:

> *Men's* turning their coats such a practice has grown,
> That with satire 'tis vain to attack it—
> But sure till this time no example was shown
> Of a *Child* ever turning his jacket.[2]

Canning rose rapidly among his new friends; and as he traveled
upward the lash of his tongue, his superabundant energy, the
startling speed and accuracy of his judgments, inspired a general admiration and an equal distrust. When Pitt died and Canning announced with becoming gravity that he had buried his
political allegiance beside his mentor, it was unanimously agreed
that for once he had spoken the truth. But his abilities could not
be ignored, and when the Talents fell he entered the Duke of
Portland's cabinet as Secretary of State for Foreign Affairs. He
was thirty-five at the time. "We shall see," remarked Sydney Smith
in Whiggish disgust, "if a nation is to be saved by schoolboy jokes
and doggerel rhymes, by affronting petulance and by the tones

1. There is still no satisfactory biography of Canning. Temperley's *Life of Canning,* and *The Foreign Policy of Canning, 1822–1827* (London, G. Bell, 1925), deal
primarily with his politics. Dorothy Marshall's *The Rise of George Canning* (London, Longmans, Green, 1938), although professedly depicting the man himself, is
hardly more illuminating.

2. Captain Josceline Bagot, ed., *George Canning and His Friends* (2 vols., London, John Murray, 1909), I, 48.

and gestures of Mr. Pitt. When he (Canning) is jocular he is strong, when he is serious he is like Samson in a wig." And another poet fumed:

> Brush up your very best jokes, I pray;
> And though you can't speak any French, they say,
> Why, as for that matter,
> Fitz-Harris can chatter,
> And you can keep out of the way.[3]

Irritated by these attacks but for once holding rein on his temper, Canning proceeded to the business of untangling the policy of his predecessors.

His counterpart at the War and Colonial Office exhibited a more natural imperturbability and a similar though less obvious energy. Tall, handsome, and reserved, a poor speaker, slow in his responses, Viscount Castlereagh struck one observer as a "splendid summit of bright and polished frost which, like the travellers in Switzerland, we all admire; but no one can hope, and few would wish to reach." [4] An aristocrat, an Irish aristocrat, aided, indeed propelled forward by noble friends and relatives, did he not have every reason to be cold and unapproachable? Was not the task of government after all his inalienable right? And the purpose of such a government? Was it not to perpetuate the interests and comforts of his class? No doubt Lord Castlereagh thought as much, and as a result his name is closely associated with what was by present-day standards a decade of repression and misrule. But if he looked with infinite distaste upon the recurrent challenges to the aristocracy's monopoly of domestic affairs, in the realm of foreign policy he appeared to cultivate a less partisan view of the national interest. At the War and Colonial Office, unfortunately, there was little scope for this impressive balance of mind. As the months passed the impression gained ground that he was in fact conducting the affairs of his department with an invincible mediocrity. Yet despite the rumors and eventually the quarrels, it was he and Canning who provided the vigor and strength so essential to the embattled administration.

3. Temperley, *Life of Canning*, p. 69; Bagot, *Canning and His Friends*, I, 238 n.
4. Louis J. Jennings, ed., *The Croker Papers* (3 vols., London, John Murray, 1884), I, 225. Castlereagh, like Canning, lacks a "life." Perhaps the two monumental studies of his diplomacy by Charles K. Webster—*The Foreign Policy of Castlereagh, 1812–1815* (London, G. Bell, 1931), and *The Foreign Policy of Castlereagh, 1815–1822* (London, G. Bell, 1925)—explain this deficiency.

During the first six months of power there was little enough that they could do. Canning expressed a secret relief over Whitelocke's failure before Buenos Aires; it removed the last possibility of his having to follow in the footsteps of the Talents, and enabled him to focus his entire attention upon Europe.[5] But while he hastened to advise Vienna and St. Petersburg that Great Britain would resume her interest in the Continent, he lacked the military power to support this diplomatic vigor.[6] One small opportunity appeared, it is true, after Tilsit. Napoleon seemed about to include Denmark within his Continental System and add the not inconsiderable Danish fleet to his resources. Canning responded to the threat with hitherto unexampled speed. A fleet proceeded to Copenhagen; there followed a sharp encounter with the Danes; and before Napoleon could gather momentum the Danish battle line fell into English hands. Another opportunity arose in November. The angry Emperor determined to remove Portugal from the English sphere of influence, and after a series of highly colored threats he ordered his troops into the kingdom—only to have another British fleet appear before Lisbon, remove the royal family, and transport it to a new empire in Brazil. Napoleon next suggested in a now familiar gambit the resumption of peace negotiations. Canning met him with a polite and studied ambiguity that was totally different from the eager pliability of Fox. The Emperor withdrew his proposal.[7]

But success or rather resistance in Denmark and Portugal was by no means convincing evidence of a shift in the fortunes of war. Europe remained as yet a solid and impenetrable mass, and despite minor triumphs Canning had perforce to be patient while the Secretary of War and Colonies reviewed English prospects in Latin America.

Castlereagh found the situation to be little different from the familiar pattern of 1804 and 1805. There were the same faces, the same reports, the same pressures. It was almost as though Whitelocke's fiasco had never occurred. A party of independence with pro-English leanings was rumored to be active in Buenos

5. "There is an end of that expedition," he told Lord Boringdon, on September 12, 1807, "and if it were not for the loss with which the event has been attended, I am not quite sure that I should regret the evacuation; but do not say so." A. G. Stapleton, *George Canning and His Times* (London, J. W. Parker, 1859), pp. 128–129.

6. Earl of Malmesbury, *Diaries and Correspondence* (4 vols., London, R. Bentley, 1844), IV, 387–388.

7. Coquelle, *Napoleon and England, 1803–1813,* p. 165.

Aires. In London Colonel Williamson was agitating once more for British cooperation with Aaron Burr in Spanish North America; and Turnbull, ever faithful to Miranda, was busily cultivating the friendship of the new ministers. Even the Duke of Orleans had written a memorandum upon the Spanish empire and the dangers that might arise from an infiltration of French influence in South America.[8]

Castlereagh in his quiet, methodical way turned to a study of the subject. He favored a continuation of the war in Europe, of course, and expressed only scorn for the policy of his predecessors. Certainly nothing was more sterile as long-range policy than a combination of military occupation and commercial intercourse. Nevertheless—the conclusion was inescapable—a course somewhat similar in its outward aspects might still have to be pursued. The French system, by excluding all British commerce from the Continental ports under Napoleon's control, seemed to dictate an entirely new mercantile existence for England. But could such an existence be made compatible with the new colonial and economic theories, and with the possibility of Great Britain becoming engaged once more in the European conflict? Castlereagh searched the elaborate premises of his mind for an answer; he discussed the question with Sir Arthur Wellesley; finally, in May, 1807, he wrote a memorandum.

Some sort of enterprise in South America would be possible, he thought, even with the limited means at his country's disposal. Conquest was out of the question: the Talents, in their awkward way, had demonstrated that. Even a continuation of the contraband trade was preferable to such an expenditure of meager military resources. Castlereagh advocated as an alternative the creation of independent monarchies in the place of the Spanish viceroyalties, under such convenient princes as the Duke of Orleans. Independent monarchies, while preventing the dissemination of Jacobin principles, would not only enable England to destroy the commercial monopoly of Spain; they would, by attracting the loyalties of the native populations, limit the British role to that of a beneficent auxiliary. Decidedly, this was the manner in which to treat the problem.[9] The cabinet, led by the Duke of Portland,

8. Robertson, *The Life of Miranda*, II, 2; Charles W. Vane, Marquess of Londonderry, ed., *Correspondence, Despatches, and Other Papers of Viscount Castlereagh; Second Marquess of Londonderry* (12 vols., London, H. Colburn, 1848–53), VII, 334 (hereafter cited as *Castlereagh Papers*).

9. "Memorandum for the Cabinet, relative to South America," May 1, 1807, *Castlereagh Papers*, VII, 315–326.

extended their approbation, and Castlereagh began casting about for assistance. He conversed with Vansittart and Turnbull; he inquired after Miranda; finally he expressed a desire to see the General himself.

At the time of this inquiry Miranda was still in the West Indies, a disgruntled and impoverished idler, with visions of a return to London and his pension. The news of Castlereagh's interest excited him to action. On November 16, 1807, he left Trinidad on board the frigate *Alexandria;* by December 21 he was in Portsmouth with an official passport for London.

Canning received him at the Foreign Office early in January and found his "representations . . . certainly very inviting." [10] Other conferences took place; and Miranda, blossoming under this sudden civility, wrote to Trinidad to announce the imminent adoption of his plans. His first reply came in the form of a rebuke from Castlereagh, who, having learned of the correspondence, took pains to inform the General that there was no authority for such a statement.[11] His official relationships, Miranda now found, lacked the pleasant informality that had characterized them in Pitt's day. In its stead was a new and businesslike atmosphere which became particularly oppressive with the delegation of Sir Arthur Wellesley to the task of evaluating the General's schemes. For Sir Arthur, trim, hawk-nosed, and horrifyingly precise, was hardly the sort to be impressed by an elaborate constitutional structure over which an Inca, presumably General Miranda, would preside as chief of state. He preferred, rather, to discuss more mundane things, to weigh—what Miranda tended to gloss over—the chances of military success in South America. Such careful scrutiny would have been embarrassing in the extreme had Wellesley's final conclusions differed materially from those of Castlereagh. For better or for worse they did not.

". . . I am convinced," Sir Arthur wrote, on February 8, 1808, "that any attempt to conquer" the provinces of South America, "with a view to their future subjection to the British Crown, would certainly fail; and therefore I consider the only mode in which they can be wrested from the Crown of Spain is by a revolution and by the establishment of an independent government within them." [12] He was not, he admitted, particularly smitten with

10. Canning to Castlereagh, January 4, 1808, *ibid.,* VIII, 158.
11. Robertson, *The Life of Miranda,* II, 8.
12. Arthur, 2d Duke of Wellington, ed., *Supplementary Despatches and Memoranda* (15 vols., London, John Murray, 1858–72), VI, 62 (hereafter cited as Wellington, *Supplementary Despatches*).

Miranda. The excitable General never quite convinced him that the Venezuelans would revolt upon the appearance of British troops. Certainly they had not done so in response to his earlier appeals. Nevertheless Venezuela together with Mexico provided, in Sir Arthur's opinion, the regions most suitable for military operations. He drew up a detailed plan of campaign providing for the employment of ten thousand troops. With these, and with Miranda as a convenient tool, he thought an invasion could be properly begun.

Miranda, of course, was delighted. Not realizing the secondary nature of the role to which he was being assigned, he wrote to Admiral Cochrane of his progress in winning over the ministers and even hinted, with knowing indiscretion, that a detachment of troops earmarked for Sweden would be diverted to another destination.[13] In both respects he proved wrong, as matters turned out; but despite the deficiency of his prophetic powers certain events now occurred to send his hopes soaring to their highest pitch.

The events in question resulted from a decision by Napoleon to assume, overtly, the responsibility of governing Spain. The Emperor had been moving in that direction for quite some time. His troops were quartered upon Spanish territory; there was a further detachment under Junot in Portugal as well. Now if he could remove the ruling dynasty, the game was in his hands. The Emperor gained his objective by means of an elaborate plot which involved enticing the Spanish King across the French border to Bayonne and forcing him by terror to abdicate. French troops under Murat quickly occupied Madrid and crushed a slight but unexpected uprising. The heir to the throne, Ferdinand the Well-beloved, attempted to flee the country and then abdicated in his turn. On June 6, 1808, Napoleon crowned his brother Joseph king of Spain and the Indies. Even before the farce had been played out to this final act, the Emperor set in motion plans to extend his empire to South America.[14]

His activity excited a number of responses. Popham from the sidelines advised Miranda not to let the disturbances in Spain

so occupy your mind, as to divert your attention from the proper point. I wish you always success in all your activities. *** If I had

13. Miranda to Cochrane, March 18, 1808, Robertson, *The Life of Miranda,* II, 13–14.

14. The details of the Napoleonic policy toward Spain may be found in André Fugier, *Napoléon et l'Espagne, 1799–1808* (Paris, F. Alcan, 1930).

not more real sense in my little finger about the principle and policy of expeditions than many of your office friends, I would cut it off and give it to a Dutchman for a Tobacco Stopper.[15]

The General in his turn wrote jubilantly to Admiral Cochrane "that the thing is ultimately decided, according to our own wishes, and . . . I shall very soon have the satisfaction of taking you by the Hand. (Keep this to yourself.)" [16] The ponderous machinery of government, echoing his hopes, swung slowly into action. On June 4 Castlereagh ordered the Governor of Jamaica to prevent Cuba from falling into French hands.[17] Colonel Williamson and Joseph Pavia were dispatched to Mexico to incite a pro-English revolution, and quantities of inflammatory propaganda were transmitted with them for distribution in South America. On June 6 Sir Arthur Wellesley received his appointment to command an expedition against the Spanish colonies; and on the same day General Miranda drew up an elaborate memorandum in which he requested the government to tender a public dinner in recognition of his services. The day of liberation seemed at last to be at hand; all was in readiness; and then the fates gave the wheel of Miranda's fortunes another disastrous turn.

The Spanish resistance movement, so brutally repressed by Murat in Madrid, had reappeared in the provinces; and the French, to their great dismay, now found themselves faced for the first time with the phenomenon of a national uprising. Delegates of the movement, searching for assistance, appeared in England and were received by Canning, who saw in their appeal the long-awaited opportunity to come to grips with France. The cabinet hastily adopted his views.[18] On June 12 he was able to assure the Asturian delegates of England's readiness to aid them; and three days later before a rapt House of Commons he boldly announced that "we shall proceed upon the principle that any nation of Europe that starts up to oppose a power . . . the common enemy of all nations, whatever be the existing political rela-

15. Popham to Miranda, April 20, 1808, Robertson, *The Life of Miranda*, II, 15–16.

16. Miranda to Cochrane, May 5, 1808, *ibid.*, p. 16.

17. Castlereagh to the Duke of Manchester, June 4, 1808, *Castlereagh Papers*, VI, 367.

18. J. Holland Rose, "Canning and the Spanish Patriots in 1808," *Amer. Hist. Rev.*, XII (1906), 39.

tions of that nation, it becomes instantly our essential ally." [19]

Such an alteration of policy could only mean a drastic change of front in regard to Latin America; and the change was soon forthcoming. Sir Arthur Wellesley received new orders: he was to transport his troops from Cork to the Spanish coast; and then, if the situation there did not promise of success, he was to embark for the West Indies whence the effort to separate South America from Spain would be renewed.[20]

Castlereagh in another dispatch to the Governor of Jamaica canceled his earlier instructions and explained that, as "by the insurrection in the Asturias, some probability of restoring the Spanish monarchy is revived, an object of the first importance in his Majesty's mind, it is wished to suspend any measure tending to divide and therefore weaken that monarchy." [21] Canning authorized several Spanish vessels to proceed to Buenos Aires, Lima, and Vera Cruz, "for the purpose of conveying to the Spanish dominions in South America intelligence of the loyal and brave determination of the kingdoms and provinces of Spain, to resist the tyranny and usurpations of France and to maintain the independence and integrity of the Spanish monarchy." [22] Such, indeed, was the gravitation of British policy toward support of the resistance movement in Spain that all considerations of specific interest in South America appeared about to be discarded. As a result Wellesley was ordered to "facilitate, as much as possible, communication between the respective provinces and colonies of Spain, and reconcile, by your good offices, any differences that may arise between them in the execution of the common purpose." [23]

There remained still the task of acquainting Miranda with the reorientation of policy. The General had had an intimation of what was in store from the sudden inaccessibility of the ministers; but it was Wellesley who disabused him finally of all his previous hopes.

I think I never had a more difficult business [Sir Arthur recalled], than when the Government bade me to tell Miranda that we would have nothing to do with his plan. I thought it best to walk out in the streets

19. Temperley, *Life of Canning*, p. 87.
20. Robertson, *The Life of Miranda*, II, 18.
21. Castlereagh to the Duke of Manchester, June 20, 1808, *Castlereagh Papers*, VI, 375.
22. William S. Robertson, "The Juntas of 1808 and the Spanish Colonies," *Eng. Hist. Rev.*, XXXI (1916), 578.
23. Castlereagh to Wellesley, June 20, 1808, *ibid.*, pp. 579–580.

with him and tell him there, to prevent his bursting out. But even there he was so loud and angry, that I told him I would walk on first a little that we might not attract the notice of everybody passing. When I joined him again he was cooler. He said: "You are going over into Spain (this was before Vimiero)—you will be lost—nothing can save you; that, however, is your affair; but what grieves me is that there never was such an opportunity thrown away!" [24]

As usual Miranda proved an untrustworthy prophet. Sir Arthur moved from triumph to triumph and from title to title, until at last in 1813, as Marquess of Wellington, he swept the French out of Spain.

But the process was to be a long and painful one, and in 1808 the promise of the Peninsular War hardly revealed itself. Sir Arthur won two victories in Portugal and then, upon orders from superior officers, signed the Convention of Cintra, permitting the French to evacuate Portugal unmolested, and in British ships. Disgusted, Wellesley returned to London and the tortures of an official investigation. Sir John Moore assumed his command and marched boldly toward Madrid. He did not linger long upon Spanish soil. Napoleon suddenly appeared at the head of the *Grande Armée;* the British retreated and after a sharp struggle at Corunna in which Moore was slain re-embarked aboard the fleet and returned to Portugal.

The British government stuck grimly to their promise to aid the Spaniards despite this disaster. On January 14, 1809, they signed a treaty of peace, friendship, and alliance with the central junta of Seville; [25] but they also began to deviate from that single-minded policy which had been so much in evidence during the first days of the Spanish uprising. Canning continued to insist that he would not countenance any effort "to interfere in the government of the Spanish settlements in South America." At the instigation of the Spanish envoy he even arranged for the expulsion of one plotter, Aaron Burr, from England.[26] But, despite these gestures,

24. Earl of Stanhope, *Notes of Conversations with the Duke of Wellington, 1831–1851* (New York, Longmans, Green, 1888), p. 69.

25. It was upon the basis of this treaty that Canning later attempted to justify Britain's *right* to trade with the colonists. According to Dorothy B. Goebel, "British Trade to the Spanish Colonies, 1796–1823," *Amer. Hist. Rev.*, XLIII (1938), 298 n., the "treaty does not establish general commercial regulations save in the appended additional article, which provides for the establishment of trade on a reciprocal basis but makes no mention of either's colonial commerce."

26. Isaac J. Cox, "Hispanic-American Phases of the 'Burr Conspiracy,'" *Hisp. Amer. Hist. Rev.*, XII (1932), 171–172.

both he and his colleagues were asking, indeed, had been asking for quite some time: how would Spain repay the British people for their efforts on her behalf?

They had hoped, as the chief recompense, that the Seville junta would sanction England's existing contraband trade with the colonies, and make its future course smoother and more profitable. But the junta showed no inclination to take the necessary steps. Indeed, the colonists were permitted to learn, only after the greatest difficulty, that England was assisting Spain at all.[27]

In an effort to overcome the complicated Spanish scruples Canning dispatched that viceregal figure, the Marquess Wellesley, to Seville in June, 1809, to assist in the deliberations of the junta and to secure further support for the British army in the field. The Marquess carried with him instructions to "lose no opportunity of endeavoring to do away with the prejudices which exist with respect to the restrictions upon the intercourse with the Spanish possessions in America." [28] He might as well have packed bricks in his portmanteau. Pleas, arguments, and protests made no impression. At each turn the junta met him with the response that the colonies had been elevated to a status of legal equality with the mother country and nothing further need be attempted. Canning with great indignation wrote:

. . . it is obvious that if Spain were desirous of making a return for the assistance and protection which she has received, such return was to be found, not in mere phrases and professions and empty promises of impracticable and unnecessary aid to Great Britain, but in exertions and sacrifices of another and more practicable kind, . . . in opening to British commerce the ports of Spanish America, and thereby enabling this country to recruit the stock of specie which has been exhausted in the service of Spain.[29]

Righteous indignation was of equally little avail. Fume as they might, Canning and his associates were now fully committed to the Continental struggle. An awareness of the commitment, combined

27. Rose, "Canning and the Spanish Patriots in 1808," *Amer. Hist. Rev.,* p. 47.

28. Canning to Wellesley, June 27, 1809, Martin Montgomery, ed., *The Despatches and Correspondence of the Marquess Wellesley, K. G., During His Lordship's Mission to Spain* (London, John Murray, 1838), p. 189.

29. Canning to Wellesley, September 16, 1809, *Historical Manuscripts Commission, Report on the Manuscripts of Earl Bathurst preserved at Cirencester Park* (London, H.M. Stationery Office, 1923), p. 104.

with the accumulated suspicions of centuries, made Spanish officials impervious to all appeals.

But if the government were unable to withdraw from the Peninsular War they were equally incapable of renouncing their interest in South America. The colonists, whose restless stirrings were being reported with increasing frequency, must perforce be placated. Too faithful an adherence on the part of the government to a pro-Spanish policy might cause them to reject all communication with England, and, in the event of Spain's collapse, might prevent a revival of those schemes for independence under British protection. The mercantile element had also to be satisfied; and its appetite for the South American trade was becoming, if anything, more voracious. The additional danger, brought about by the consuming interest of the United States in all things Spanish, made it imperative that Great Britain should not remain behindhand in evidences of friendship to the colonies.

There existed, of course, no single means by which British policy could be regulated to meet these diverse contingencies. The United States could be, and was, warned that His Majesty's government could not see with indifference an attack upon the holdings of Spain in Florida.[30] But how could Spain, an ally, be warned? How could the colonists be appeased? And how could the British merchants be satisfied? One solution lay in the continuation of the contraband trade; another in keeping Miranda close at hand.

The General was well known to the Spanish government, and, just as in 1805, he stood as a symbol of impending revolution, always employable in default of Spanish good behavior. Nor did his potential usefulness stop there. He had widened the circle of his acquaintances in South America, with surreptitious correspondents in Caracas, Lima, and Buenos Aires. Surely his finding a refuge in England, together with the arrival of British goods in colonial ports, would suggest graphically the sympathy with which native aspirations were regarded. Or so at least government hoped.[31]

But while government were content to follow a modest program of threats, contraband, and special pleading with Spain, Miranda

30. Canning to Jackson, July 1, 1809, Bernard Mayo, ed., *Instructions to the British Ministers to the United States, 1791–1812, American Historical Association Report* (1936), III, 292.

31. Vansittart to Hodgson, January 27, 1814, Roberston, *Francisco de Miranda and the Revolutionizing of Spanish America*, p. 425. See also the conference between Sir Arthur Wellesley and Miranda, January 26, 1809, reported in Robertson, *The Life of Miranda*, II, 42–43.

persisted in other ideas. Despite his pension and a pleasant house on Grafton Street, the General revived his old habits of intrigue. The amenities of his establishment counted as nothing now against the agitations of his frustrated spirit. In the face of repeated warnings from influential friends he continued, in his multifarious South American correspondence, to advocate immediate revolution. Admiral Apodaca, the Spanish envoy in London, learned of his activities and protested vehemently to the Foreign Office. It became necessary, first, to remonstrate gently with the General, and, when that did no good, to bid him sternly to be silent. As an ally he seemed quite as useless as Spain.

For a short time, during the spring and summer of 1809, the General's intransigeance could be borne with some equanimity, for there were signs that Europe had at last lost patience with its oppressors. Austria attempted to throw off the French yoke; and while Napoleon advanced to subdue her a powerful expedition organized by Castlereagh landed on Walcheren Island. A new and decisive phase of the war appeared to be at hand, for the English effort was well timed and the way into the Netherlands lay open. But under the incompetent leadership of Lord Chatham the expedition wasted away even before its initial objectives could be attained; and the process of evacuation, in which the Royal Navy had become so proficient, commenced once again.

The most serious consequences of the Walcheren disaster occurred not on the field but within the cabinet itself, where Canning had been grooming himself to succeed the Duke of Portland. A quarrel between various factions in the government now broke into the open, and Castlereagh found himself on the verge of being ousted as a result of Chatham's incompetence and Canning's ambition. The prospect was more than Irish pride could bear. Castlereagh dispatched an elaborate justification of his conduct to the Foreign Secretary and challenged him to a duel. "I had rather fight than read it, by G—d!" exclaimed Canning upon examining the wordy epistle; and fight he did, receiving a ball in the thigh for his valor.[32]

Both men resigned their posts as a result of the duel; the Duke of Portland happily followed suit. Two weeks of whispered conclaves and complex negotiations ensued, and in October Spencer Perceval emerged to lead the reshuffled administration.

To fill the office vacated by Canning Perceval recalled the Marquess Wellesley from Spain. In many respects the choice was one

32. Bagot, *Canning and His Friends,* I, 324 n.

of desperation, for Lord Wellesley had already revealed himself as a man of innumerable and eccentric moods. At the Foreign Office his habits did not change. A truly regal indolence, an entire absence of method, and a persistent irresponsibility were the hallmarks of his work. The youthful Stratford Canning, who was striving frantically to arrange a treaty of peace between Russia and Turkey, heard from his new chief only sixteen times between the summer of 1810 and the spring of 1812. His most important instructions "related to some manuscript copies of classical works supposed to have been stored away in the Seraglio." [33]

There were moments, too, when Lord Wellesley's mind ran after unbelievably preposterous notions. His strange negotiation with Fouché—the essence of which was to leave Europe to Napoleon, seize the United States for England, and remove Ferdinand from Spain to his South American dominions—nearly overturned the government, and exposed him to lasting ridicule.[34] Yet, despite these faults, Lord Wellesley possessed hidden pools of strength and, in the tradition of Pitt, a powerful if capricious intellect. During the last months of 1809 and the early part of 1810 these resources would be strained to the utmost.

An English army succeeded during this time in establishing an uneasy foothold in Portugal; but despite the exertions of Lord Wellington (Sir Arthur Wellesley had changed his name) the Peninsular War was hardly progressing well. Nor was its cost sitting easily upon the public purse. Inflationary tendencies, impervious to tentative experiments in credit manipulation, were making their appearance. And the problem of marketing British goods was growing increasingly complex. The Continental System continued to impede trade with Europe; the embargoes imposed by the United States virtually destroyed the North American market; and a tendency to dump goods indiscriminately caused sporadic gluts, even in South America. By the middle of 1810 the confusion of mounting costs, specie shortages, and overexpanded credit had driven England into the throes of a financial panic.[35]

33. Stanley Lane-Poole, quoting from Stratford Canning's memoirs, in *Life of the Right Honorable Stratford Canning* (2 vols., London, Longmans, Green, 1888), I, 91.
34. Coquelle, *Napoleon and England,* pp. 223–233.
35. Audrey Cunningham discusses the details of the panic in *British Credit in the Last Napoleonic War* (Cambridge, Cambridge University Press, 1910), as does Eli F. Heckscher in *The Continental System* (Oxford, Clarendon Press, 1922). The value of English manufactured exports fell from £34,061,901 in 1810 to £22,681,400 in 1811. See Ward and Gooch, *The Cambridge History of British Foreign Policy,* I, 381.

Weighted down with these burdens the government now convinced themselves that only uninterrupted access to the Latin American market could support their credit and pay for the Peninsular War. As Lord Liverpool, presiding over the War Office, explained the situation to Wellington, "Our principal difficulty is about money, or rather about specie; and if any means can be found for providing for our wants in this respect, we shall, I trust, get through the campaign creditably, and perhaps brilliantly." [36]

What means of recruiting specie were there aside from continuing the contraband trade? Miranda and his plots remained, of course, but the General had lost his usefulness, even as an instrument of rebellion. The Spaniards no longer considered him as a genuine threat and merely protested the more obvious of his activities—which now included the publication of a newspaper, a flirtation with the Opposition, and a fruitless affair of the heart with Pitt's niece.

There was as another alternative the policy of asking concessions from Spain to be tried again. Lord Wellesley, in this vein, suggested that England be allowed to trade directly with South America and to garrison Cadiz, the entrepôt for colonial intercourse. He might as well have asked absolution of the pope. The Spanish Regency—a shadowy body established at Canning's instigation—responded that the authority for such a grant lay with the newly assembled Cortes. The Cortes, under the dominion of the Cadiz merchants, who still aspired after a monopoly of the Spanish American market, returned the proposal with a blunt rejection. Spaniards wanted money, arms, and supplies, not advice, and the Cortes argued with some reason that their resistance to the French constituted payment enough.[37] They calculated on this, as on other, occasions that the English army would remain in the Peninsula without concessions on their part in South America; and they calculated correctly. What they failed to realize was, first, that these concessions might originate elsewhere, and, secondly, that the British might somehow take advantage of them. Clearly the dissatisfaction fermenting in South America carried no moral for the legislators of Cadiz.

Yet the fever of discontent in that vast continent had reached a

36. Liverpool to Wellington, April, 1810, Wellington, *Supplementary Despatches*, VI, 517.
37. C. W. Crawley, "French and English Influences in the Cortes of Cadiz, 1810–1814," *The Cambridge Historical Journal*, VI (1939), 178.

point where it could no longer be restrained by such palliatives as legal equality within the Spanish empire. A belated concession of status could hardly compete with the confidence engendered by the repulse of Beresford and Whitelocke, and the knowledge of Spain's impotence. Inspired by the example of the United States, disgusted with the poverty of Spanish rule, excited by a combination of French precepts and English manufactures, the colonists were moving instead toward the goal of independence.

The first blow for the cause was struck in Venezuela where, on April 19, 1810, the citizens of Caracas unseated their Captain General and established a local junta. The residents of Buenos Aires followed their example on May 25; and in September Santiago de Chile and Mexico flared into revolt.

Two common acts characterized these rebellions. In each instance the newly formed juntas made haste to throw open their ports to the trade of friendly nations; they also swore eternal allegiance to the exiled Ferdinand of Spain. If the first act constituted a piece of outright defiance, the second served to cloak it in a useful ambiguity. The two combined made possible the argument that differences of opinion had arisen between the colonies and the mother country rather than that a revolution had actually begun. The British government, indeed, were not slow to take advantage of the argument. Lord Liverpool, upon learning of the Venezuelan uprising, announced in a public dispatch that "His Majesty feels it to be his duty according to every obligation of justice and good faith, to discourage any proceeding which may have the effect of separating the Spanish Provinces in America from the Parent State in Europe . . ." [38] But in a more confidential communication he went on to explain that the government did not intend to meddle in Venezuelan affairs. [39]

As far as the British were concerned the vagueness of the whole business was a splendid innovation; they could anticipate an untrammeled commerce with the colonies and yet avoid their treaty obligation to maintain the Spanish empire intact. It came as a genuine relief to the cabinet after months of futile pleading with Spain to let matters take their course. Ignorance, silence, and inactivity seemed for once the ideal components of policy.

38. Liverpool to Layard, June 29, 1810, William S. Robertson, "The Beginnings of Spanish-American Diplomacy," *Essays in American History,* ed. Guy Stanton Ford (New York, H. Holt, 1910), p. 240.
39. Liverpool to Layard, June 29, 1810, Robertson, *The Life of Miranda,* II, 80.

But to the Venezuelans the establishment of a local junta represented only a first hesitant step down the road to independence. Strong pro-Spanish elements still existed among and about them, and fear of the wrath of the mother country somehow dominated their councils. Instead of consolidating the internal sources of their strength, they began casting about for foreign aid and protection. And in their uncertainty they turned first to Great Britain.

Two Venezuelan agents, Simon Bolívar and Luis Lopez Méndez, arrived in London on July 10, 1810, and, after paying their respects to General Miranda presented themselves for an interview with Lord Wellesley.

The Foreign Secretary had already given some consideration to their reception; for while their presence was flattering it could hardly be counted as an unmixed blessing. It raised so many questions. If he accorded the agents a cordial welcome and encouraged their aspirations he would surely endanger the whole fabric of English relations with Spain. If he held them at arm's length he might just as surely destroy the prospects of trade with South America. The situation obviously was not of that kind in which one made definite and precise commitments. His first duty, according to Lord Wellesley's analysis, was to avoid the topic of independence altogether. But local self-government within the framework of the Spanish empire—that was an entirely different proposition. It could, if properly instituted, keep out French and American influence, assure a European orientation for the new communities, and at the same time provide a compromise between Spain's determination to retain her full sovereignty and the colonists' desire to assert their independence. Not only might local self-government serve as a basis for the settlement of mutual differences; surely in the process it could be employed to gain for England the benefits of a stable trade.[40]

Armed with these thoughts Lord Wellesley granted the Venezuelan commissioners their interview. Bolívar promptly took advantage of the occasion to launch into an impassioned plea for an English protectorate. Lord Wellesley only succeeded in damming the torrent with the reminder that the interview was not to be construed as the prelude to an alliance, much less a step toward recognition. He then launched into a lecture of his own upon the dangers of a precipitate course and advised a continuing

40. Robertson, "The Beginnings of Spanish-American Diplomacy," *Essays in American History*, p. 247.

allegiance to Spain as the best avenue to British assistance. England, he assured the two suppliants, would provide the naval power to protect Venezuela from France and secure the rights of Ferdinand. As for the difficulties with Spain herself, he would use his influence to promote the necessary reconciliation. The stream of bland and selfless words had its intended effect: Bolívar and Méndez left the Foreign Office, content to have their country's interests rest in such sympathetic hands.[41]

Lord Wellesley, no doubt, felt satisfied as well. In many respects, of course, his task had become more complicated. As long as the situation of the British armies on the Peninsula remained precarious, he must avoid alienating Spain. He had also to guard against offending the colonists. Cavalier treatment of their aspirations might mean not merely the loss of the South American trade but the spread of French or American influence. Deference must be paid to the prejudices of the mother country, and sympathy accorded to the grievances of her offspring. He must walk a tightrope between the two parties, wearing a bright impartial smile, daring not to sway too obviously to either side.

But despite these complications a great economic goal seemed within reach; and he could say, if not with entire truth, at least with spectacular conviction, that England had been but a spectator to its attainment. As such she could extend only advice or at most attempt to heal the breach between mother and daughters by an objective mediation. Either role was satisfactory, so long as the necessary commerce continued.

During this summer of swift and sudden changes even Miranda's fortunes underwent a brilliant transformation. Bolívar and Méndez had besought him to return to Venezuela; there remained only to obtain the government's permission. The General wrote to Lord Wellesley and requested the necessary safe passage; he suggested that his pension be commuted to a lump sum; he even employed the Foreign Secretary's son to plead his case. Lord Wellesley kept putting him off. The General was of no further use to England; it would be a relief to see him go. But as an old pensioner his departure in the company of Bolívar and Méndez would arouse the suspicion that the government approved of and was, in fact, lending support to the revolutionaries. Lord Wellesley eventually requested him to remain a while longer in England; and so, in September, 1810, Bolívar and Méndez set sail alone.[42]

41. *Ibid.*, pp. 242–246.
42. Robertson, *The Life of Miranda*, II, 90.

In October after receiving a draft law on the liberty of the press from Jeremy Bentham Miranda too departed. His reception in Caracas was a tumultuous one; and for a brief moment he savored the pleasures of political power. Accepted as the progenitor of Venezuelan liberty, he sat in the highest councils; and when, in 1811, the Spaniards appeared in force to suppress the junta, his compatriots appointed him supreme dictator and commander of the native armies.

But the fates had cast Miranda in the role of the eternal aspirant. Outmaneuvered by the Spaniards, with treachery and dissension on every side, the General abandoned the struggle without striking a blow. Enraged by this behavior, Bolívar and his associates turned him over to the invading troops; he was transported to Spain and consigned to rot in a prison cell. For five more years he lingered on, plotting vainly to escape the solitude. When he died in 1817 his presence was hardly missed; by that time British policy had moved into a splendidly self-sufficient orbit of its own.

IV

THE TACTICS OF DELAY

IF the year 1810 marked the crystallization of British policy toward Latin America, the conference between Lord Welles-ley, Bolívar, and Méndez was the act which symbolized the crystallization. As a result of that conference, and all that had gone before, British policy would now start toward increasing and stabilizing the Latin American trade and maintaining the fond-ness for England which the colonists had recently shown. The idea of conquest had vanished from ministerial minds; even the pros-pect of abetting colonial independence by means of armed inter-vention had lost its appeal. Six years of wrestling with the problem had convinced the members of the government that commerce, combined with assurances that Latin America would not fall prey to the influence of France or the United States, was the maximum benefit that they could extract from the situation.

The difficulty of the years between 1810 and 1814 was not so much the realization of these two objectives as it was their realiza-tion in terms of ends of even greater importance. Henceforward British statesmen were to face the dilemma of reconciling their transatlantic interests with their European commitments; and the solution did not come easily.[1] Lord Wellesley attempted to avoid and then to flee from the dilemma; Castlereagh literally impaled himself on its horns; and Canning, in achieving the recon-ciliation, made sacrifices which surely must have caused Pitt and Castlereagh to start up in their graves. But that was in 1825, fifteen years into the future.

1. American scholars have argued with some ingenuity: 1) that England was morally delinquent in delaying for so long her recognition of the Spanish American states; and 2) that she was morally delinquent in conniving at their independence behind the backs of Spain and the United States. Somehow, the argument is con-fusing. No doubt England, with a vast empire of her own, retained certain objec-tions to the recognition of colonial independence. But these scruples were rapidly losing their potency in the nineteenth century, and I very much doubt that they out-weighed other considerations of national interest. For a different explanation of British delays see below, Chaps. VI, VII.

In 1810 ministers had persuaded themselves that the struggle with Napoleon could continue only if the Latin American market remained open to British subjects; they felt equally certain that they must establish informal diplomatic relations with the leaders of the various revolutionary juntas in South America. There was a strong feeling that if they did not, the colonists would close their ports to British trade and turn to either the French or the Americans for succor. But ministers were also aware that the rulers of Spain looked with high disfavor upon any attempt to establish regular trade relations with Latin America or make contact with the revolutionary leaders. If Spanish disfavor turned to outright antagonism, there lurked the final danger that Wellington, in his desperate struggle with the French, might suddenly find himself fighting in a hostile country against insuperable odds. How, then, was the cabinet to prosecute the war? How, indeed, were ministers to reconcile the two sets of conflicting objectives?

Although dilemmas are sometimes solved they are more often avoided; and, in the matter of trade, the dilemma confronting Great Britain was immediately avoidable in two ways. The Spaniards, while hostile to a regular and legal trade by any outsider with the Latin American empire, were willing to tolerate the passage of contraband. There was little enough that they could do to stop the illicit commerce, and they recognized dimly that they accrued some benefits from its existence. Given this slight opportunity, the British were able gradually to build up a voluminous though erratic exchange of goods for bullion.[2]

They were also able to obtain a substantial outlet for their manufactures in Brazil. When Napoleon toward the end of 1807 determined to occupy the tiny kingdom of Portugal, his object was to seal off from British traders the last ports of western Europe and, thus, complete his Continental blockade. In his immediate objective the Emperor was entirely successful. A French army started for Portugal and on November 29, 1807, straggled into Lisbon. But as General Junot reached the capital, Don John, the Portuguese Prince Regent, departed with his court aboard the Portuguese fleet and proceeded to Brazil under British protection. Napoleon had deprived England of one market; but

2. For the pages that follow I am largely indebted to Alan K. Manchester, *British Preëminence in Brazil, Its Rise and Decline* (Chapel Hill, University of North Carolina Press, 1933), and Enrique Ruiz-Guiñazú, *Lord Strangford y la Revolucion de Mayo* (Buenos Aires, Bernabé y cía, 1937).

England, in her infuriating way, was already in the process of garnering another.[3]

English access to the Brazilian market depended, in the last analysis, upon Don John; and Don John's readiness to grant access stemmed from his unwillingness to go to Brazil. Despite the insanity of his mother, the ambitious promiscuity of his wife, and his own embarrassing obesity, the Prince Regent had contrived an absorbing life for himself in a convent on the outskirts of Lisbon. There, from the hilltop at Marfa, he had struggled for four years to save Portugal from the vortex of war. When finally he departed he did so with reluctance; and when he set foot in Rio de Janeiro he made clear his determination to return to Lisbon at the first opportunity. The difficulty of the situation was, alas, that Don John could not return by his own unaided efforts. Britain had arranged and supervised his voyage to Brazil; Britain alone could retrieve for him the peace and quiet of Marfa. Indeed, Don John did not even see how he could sustain himself in Brazil without foreign assistance. As the years passed he became partially reconciled to the rigors of colonial life and, in fact, occupied his time with plots to expand his empire. But even here he acknowledged his ultimate dependence upon England.

The Prince Regent's first act, upon his arrival in Rio de Janeiro, was to open Brazilian ports to the commerce of friendly nations. This precedent-shattering act completed, he proceeded to make an even greater concession. Lord Strangford, the British envoy to Portugal who had abetted Don John in his flight from Lisbon, appeared in Rio de Janeiro on July 22, 1808, with instructions from Canning "to make the Brazils an emporium for British manufactures destined for the consumption of the whole of South America." [4] Nothing loath, Don John entered into negotiations for a treaty of commerce. By February 10, 1810, Strangford had gained his objective. The Prince Regent, who had recently received a largess of £600,000 from London, signed a treaty of commerce and alliance which granted a special preference of fifteen per cent to British goods entering Brazil. What was more, the treaty, while subject to revision in fifteen years, purported to be permanent. As a reward for his generosity Don John received from England a guarantee against external aggression for all his possessions.

3. Manchester, *British Preëminence in Brazil*, pp. 65–69.
4. Canning to Strangford, April 17, 1808, *ibid.*, p. 78.

The guarantee was of little immediate use to the Prince Regent; but British traders took prompt advantage of their favorable position in the Brazilian market. Manufactured articles poured into the colony; saddles, crystal chandeliers, warming pans, and ice skates were among the items of export; and quantities of merchandise rusted, rotted, or broke on the quays of the capital. As a result of the initial enthusiasm the market became glutted and a number of British trading houses sadly closed their doors. Not until 1812 was the Brazilian trade reorganized on a stable financial basis; then, with the wreckage of speculation cleared away, four-fifths of England's exports to South America were passing through the colony's ports.[5]

No doubt a goodly proportion of the total ultimately fell into the hands of the rebellious subjects of Spain. And it did so without the fuss and bother of formal arrangements. The procedure was so simple, so innocuous, so flexible. Britain expanded her markets, the colonists benefited thereby, and the process, depending as it did solely upon the generosity of Don John, was such that Spain could take no exception. One aspect of the policy dilemma was, for the time being, on its way to a solution.

There was progress on a different front as well; for England's ability and eagerness to supply the South Americans with goods was taken as a special expression of her good will. French propaganda, or North American encouragement and example, hardly competed on equal terms in the minds of revolutionary leaders with the growing stream of English exports. If Britain needed trade in order to sustain her war effort, the colonists required English products in order to survive; and their juntas, without effective means of taxation, depended on the customs duties derived from those products to furnish the lifeblood of administration. Commerce alone assured to Great Britain an initial deference in the minds of most Latin Americans.[6]

And there were ways of increasing that deference without risking the outright antagonism of Spain. Public or private funds could change hands quietly and end up in the exchequers of the revolutionary leaders. Ministers could state confidentially that if Spain collapsed England would shield the colonists from the ambitions of France. The Admiralty, long on experience in such matters, could employ the Royal Navy—that most discreet of

5. *Ibid.*, pp. 90–97.
6. Goebel, "British Trade to the Spanish Colonies, 1796–1823," *Amer. Hist. Rev.*, p. 311.

all military engines—as a vehicle for the exchange of assurances
and the protection of commerce. The Foreign Office could receive
revolutionary agents at the side door and authorize the purchase
of arms and equipment. All these delicate attentions could be, and
were, extended as evidences of British intentions. Their cumulative
significance for the Spanish Americans was deep and abiding.[7]

As if these attentions were not enough, British diplomats succeeded in making their influence felt at the very center of Latin
American politics. And, as in the case of trade relations, Brazil
was the spearhead of the operation. The opportunity for intervention arose in this instance out of a mixture of princely motives.
Don John remained steadfast in his desire to return to Portugal;
but while awaiting that moment he began to indulge in plans for
the expansion of his empire. The result was that, while he continued to rely upon British advice and assistance, he cast an eye
longingly upon the province of the Banda Oriental.

A section of fertile land, bounded on the south by the Rio de la
Plata and on the north by the Uruguay River, the Banda had long
been a bone of contention between Portugal and Spain. Neither
the papal dispensations of Alexander VI nor the more mundane
arrangements of the Treaty of Tordesillas had resolved the controversy. For two centuries the dispute over the Banda raged
with intermittent violence until in 1777 Portugal relinquished all
title to Montevideo and the northern bank of the Plata to her more
powerful neighbor.

Spain had incorporated the Banda into the Viceroyalty of La
Plata, but at the time that Don John arrived in Brazil the province was being ruled autonomously from Montevideo by Governor
Elio. To Don John the possibilities of the situation were most
inviting. Portugal was nominally at war with Spain; so too was
England in 1808; and Spanish authority in the Plata basin was
divided between Elio and Don Santiago Liniers, the ruler of
Buenos Aires. The Banda hung like a ripe plum, and the only
question was: would England tolerate its plucking? For the next
six years Don John's actions were to depend ultimately on the
answer to that question.

Hardly had Lord Strangford arrived in Rio de Janeiro when

7. See Robertson, *The Life of Miranda*, II, 40. Liverpool to Layard, June 29,
1810, John Rydjord, "British Mediation between Spain and Her Colonies: 1811–
1813," *Hisp. Amer. Hist. Rev.*, XXI (1941), 30. Edward Tagart, *A Memoir of the
Late Captain Peter Heyward* (London, E. Wilson, 1832), p. 207. Arthur P. Whitaker, *The United States and the Independence of Latin America, 1800–1830* (Baltimore, Johns Hopkins Press, 1941), p. 75.

Don John flung the question at him. At first the envoy succeeded in maintaining a posture of neutrality. He was not averse, in principle, to seeing the Banda and the mouth of the Plata in Portuguese hands. But whether the Prince Regent could seize the province without antagonizing the Latin Americans was a matter which Strangford was in no haste to decide. For the moment he succeeded in staying Don John's hand on the ground that he lacked instructions.[8]

The respite which Strangford won in this fashion was only temporary, for the question soon reappeared in another form. In August, 1808, the court at Rio de Janeiro learned of the French invasion of Spain. The notorious Carlota Joaquina promptly abandoned her role as Don John's wife and, reassuming that of a Spanish princess, announced her intention of establishing a regency over all of Spanish America. The first objective of her campaign turned out to be the Banda Oriental, and her principal supporter was Sir Sidney Smith, commander of the British fleet on the South Atlantic station.

The reaction of the Latin Americans to Carlota's proposals confirmed Lord Strangford in the opinion that the most effective way of retaining colonial friendships was by allowing the colonists to work out their situation in their own way, without external interference. And so, with the aid of Don John, whose appetite for the Banda varied inversely with that of his wife, the envoy set himself up in opposition to the Princess' schemes. Intelligence of British aid to Spain, together with instructions from Canning, provided the strange alliance with the necessary offensive weapons. Sir Sidney Smith, who had received a jeweled sword and the promise of a dukedom from Carlota, suddenly lost his command and returned, crestfallen, to England. The Princess succumbed to the admonitions of her husband and the reproofs of Strangford. The plot, deprived of its principal architects, collapsed as quickly as it had arisen. Whatever damage had been done, Strangford attempted to repair by means of a correspondence with the governors of Montevideo and Buenos Aires. In a series of letters he gave explicit assurances of England's continued friendship, and of her unwillingness to share in the administration of their provinces.[9]

How well the envoy had done his work became evident when, in

8. Strangford to Canning, July 25, 1808, Manchester, *British Preëminence in Brazil*, pp. 117–118.

9. Strangford to Canning, August 16, 1809, *ibid.*, p. 125 n.

May, 1810, a revolutionary junta in Buenos Aires deposed the
Viceroy and appealed to Strangford for protection against Spain,
Carlota, and Brazil. The manner of the request was flattering,
indeed, but the demands themselves were difficult to fulfill. Nevertheless Strangford put his best foot forward. He advised the junta
to remain loyal to Spain, and he exerted all his influence to prevent
Don John from meddling in the Banda. On neither score did he
achieve a real measure of cooperation. Elio, the governor of the
Banda, now considered himself to be the only true representative
of Spanish authority in the area, and, instead of consolidating that
authority in Montevideo, he proceeded to blockade the port of
Buenos Aires. As a consequence, the junta of the city embarked
upon an invasion of the Banda; and, simultaneously, a revolt led
by a native, José Artigas, broke out in the province.[10]

This combination of events decreased the likelihood that the
junta of Buenos Aires would remain loyal to Spain. When Elio,
in desperation, appealed to Don John for assistance, the probability of retaining the colonists' friendship for England also decreased. Don John leaped at the opportunity to establish a foothold in the Banda, and before Strangford could bring his diplomatic batteries to bear, the Prince Regent dispatched troops to
Montevideo. In the confusion one thing seemed clear to the colonial
mind: England must be encouraging Don John's ambitions.

For three years Strangford labored unceasingly to erase that
impression. In October, 1811, he succeeded in bringing about an
armistice in the Banda. The armies of Buenos Aires and Brazil
withdrew from the province, and Artigas with his supporters fled
out of the reach of Elio who retained possession of Montevideo.
There was peace in the Plata basin for a year thereafter; then
Artigas descended on the Banda once more and the pattern of
events repeated itself. Buenos Aires entered the fray; Elio cried
for help; and Don John's troops worked their way back through
the wilderness to the rescue of Montevideo.

What was Lord Strangford to do? Seemingly, there was only
one course open, and that was to remove Don John from the
Banda. The envoy had, by this time, come to despise the revolutionary leaders of Buenos Aires, and regretted ever having en-

---

10. William S. Robertson, *Rise of the Spanish-American Republics as Told in the
Lives of Their Liberators* (New York, D. Appleton–Century, 1936), pp. 155–156.
Ruiz-Guiñazú, *Lord Strangford*, pp. 129–131. Manchester, *British Preëminence in
Brazil*, p. 127.

couraged them. Nevertheless he still regarded Latin American friendship as more important than the ambitions of the Prince Regent or the survival of Elio. Castlereagh, who had replaced Lord Wellesley at the Foreign Office in 1812, belatedly concurred in this opinion; and so Strangford bestirred himself once more to bring peace to the Banda. By a last exertion of authority he succeeded in persuading Don John to withdraw from the province. If Brazilian actions reflected British policy, here was a final illustration that this policy in no way ran counter to the professed interests of the Latin Americans.[11]

The withdrawal of Brazilian troops had a decisive effect upon events in the Banda. Freed of their presence, Artigas and his allies from Buenos Aires were able to crush out the last embers of Spanish resistance. The end was almost in sight. The allies quarreled and fell to fighting among themselves. In 1815 Artigas gained the upper hand, expelled the army of Buenos Aires, and established his supremacy in the Banda.[12]

By then Lord Strangford had departed from Rio de Janeiro, and Don John, freed of his alarming presence, was plotting once more to seize the Banda. The hunger of the Prince Regent was proving incurable, and Strangford, who had spent six years attempting to curb it, left with the conviction of failure. If the preservation of the status quo in the Plata basin constituted his principal function, his sense of futility was perhaps warranted; for Don John did return to the Banda, and Brazilian troops remained in occupation of the province for over six years. If, on the other hand, the cultivation of Latin American friendship was a primary duty, then Strangford might have counted his mission as an unqualified success. The Spanish Americans, despite the difficulties of these years, remembered the British envoy if not with affection, with respect and gratitude; and the contrast between conditions in the Plata basin before and after his departure served only to strengthen their feelings. Great Britain, they assured themselves, was and would remain their friend.

But as the network of commercial and diplomatic relations with Latin America grew in intricacy, the task of reconciling Spain to the new dispensation became ever more complex and delicate. Span-

11. Charles K. Webster, ed., *Britain and the Independence of Latin America, 1812–1830* (2 vols., London, the Ibero-American Institute of Great Britain, Oxford University Press, 1938), I, introd., 67.

12. Percy A. Martin, "Artigas, the Founder of Uruguayan Nationality," *Hisp. Amer. Hist. Rev.,* XIX (1939), 2–15.

ish leaders, although finding nothing concrete in British actions against which to protest, were determined not to allow the British position in Latin America to reach a point of stability. They were equally determined, at the first opportunity, to reassert full control over their rebellious empire. Here, in fact, was the sharpest of the two horns of the dilemma confronting British policy. Lord Strangford, by establishing trade relations with Brazil and by placating the Latin Americans, had avoided one horn; Lords Wellesley and Castlereagh addressed themselves bravely to the task of eluding this other.

That the colonial revolutions would force such an exertion upon him came no doubt as a surprise and disappointment to Lord Wellesley. Somehow the interview with Bolívar and Méndez had led him to expect a less time-consuming consequence. Indeed, his first reaction to the revolutions was that there would be no consequence at all; for, if the colonists had revolted, they still acknowledged the sovereignty of Ferdinand; and, if their political aspirations were regrettably advanced, their economic outlook was most praiseworthy. Spain, on the other hand, lay almost helpless in the grip of war, hardly capable of influencing the destinies of her dominions. His duty, so Lord Wellesley imagined, was therefore to perpetuate the slight and beneficial division between the colonies and the mother country: a regular and profitable trade would thus be assured to England.[13]

Two factors soon combined to destroy the Foreign Secretary's illusions. The embargo imposed by the United States upon trade with England, and ultimately the War of 1812, represented the first blow. American policy, following upon Napoleon's Continental System, served to reduce to a minimum the established outlets for British merchandise and make evident the need for more intensive compensations in Latin America.

The second factor, and the one most upsetting to Lord Wellesley's equanimity, was Spain's refusal to accept as final the dissolution of her colonial monopoly. While Lord Wellesley dreamed of inheriting the Spanish American market by the effortless process of default, the Regency and Cortes of Cadiz were thinking along entirely different lines. Not only had they convinced themselves that the British army was lagging in its efforts to liberate their country; they were equally positive that the Brit-

13. Sir Ernest Satow, *A Guide to Diplomatic Practice* (2 vols., London, Longmans, Green, 1917), II, 336.

ish government sought a share in the colonial trade for reasons quite foreign to the objectives of the war. They made no attempt to understand the financial difficulties in which England had become involved, nor did they try to analyze the reasons for the dissatisfaction of the colonists. Both the Regency and the Cortes contained men who passed in the currency of the times as liberals. And they had evolved certain political principles, ultimately expressed in the notorious Constitution of 1812, which, if they conferred no material benefits upon the colonists of Latin America, afforded them a large measure of spiritual consolation. Had they not decreed that Ferdinand's dominions should, with Spain, comprise one nation? Had they not permitted deputies from Latin America to sit in the Cortes? Had they not even passed certain measures to encourage industry, commerce, and racial equality among the colonists? Surely that was enough. The Regency and the Cortes turned their backs on the more material grievances of the colonial juntas and, with little regard for the Peninsular War, determined to reassert their authority in Latin America.[14]

The opportunities for reclaiming that authority were neither so poor as Lord Wellesley had assumed nor so good as the Regency and the Cortes anticipated. There were Loyalist troops in Spanish America as well as Loyalist sympathizers. The revolutionary leaders themselves remained uncertain of the degree of independence that they desired. And so between 1810 and 1814 Spain was able to exercise considerable influence abroad. Struggles with Hidalgo y Costilla in Mexico, with Miranda and Bolívar in Venezuela, and with Moreno and Belgrano in Buenos Aires, brought her frequent and heartening victories. Paraguay remained loyal until 1811; Elio held out in the Banda Oriental still longer; and almost until the end Peru stood as the impenetrable stronghold of Loyalist forces. But Spanish power was never quite sufficient for Spanish purposes. As the insurgents fought on, they were driven to ever more extreme political expedients; and instead of re-establishing her prerogatives, Spain succeeded only in heaping chaos upon disorder.

The consequences of this wild and bitter conflict bore extremely hard upon English trade. Where the Spaniards gained control, the access of foreign commerce depended upon the whim of cor-

14. Robertson, "The Beginnings of Spanish-American Diplomacy," *Essays in American History,* p. 238.

rupt local commanders. Traders risked only the most speculative
cargoes where the fighting still raged. Even where the insurgents
held sway and welcomed English goods, difficulties of repayment
sorely limited the amounts that they could absorb. In the place
of a regular and profitable commerce, flowing serenely through
the torn fabric of the Spanish empire, Lord Wellesley found
merely an irritating revival of the old contraband trade. Instead
of a helpless and acquiescent Spain, he discovered, in the Regency
and the Cortes, self-willed bodies perhaps even more determined
to retain their imperial dominions than to rid themselves of the
Napoleonic scourge. When Admiral Apodaca, the Spanish minister in London, protested against Lord Wellesley's reception of
Bolívar and Méndez, "his orders were to express pain at the turn
affairs had taken, after His Majesty's generous declaration respecting the integrity and independence of the Spanish monarchy." Spain, the envoy went on boldly,

is disposed willingly to admit the good offices of Great Britain in favor
of the inhabitants of Caracas, with a view to their reconciliation with
the mother-country. From these considerations, the Council of Regency flatter themselves that His Britannic Majesty will listen to their
just representations, and that far from establishing relations with the
revolters of America, His Majesty will assist the Spanish Government
to re-establish in Caracas the ancient order of things, in which England
is likewise interested, if as may be presumed, she desires the peaceful
preservation of her own colonies and establishment, as well as those of
His Majesty her faithful ally.[15]

Here was an extraordinary stubbornness, illogical, unreason-
able, and entirely unexpected. Revolutions in Latin America were
going off with explosive regularity; Spain lay almost paralyzed
under the heel of the French; and Wellington was retreating into
Portugal, to the Torres Vedras lines before Lisbon. Yet even under
these desperate circumstances the Regency refused to grasp at
the last remnants of colonial loyalty. Lord Wellesley simply could
not believe his ears, and for the succeeding six months English
diplomacy reflected his disbelief. He harped upon Spain's inability
to re-establish "the ancient order of things," and England's unwillingness to help her do so; and he fired off dispatch after

15. Apodaca to Wellesley, October 8, 1810, Satow, *A Guide to Diplomatic Practice*,
II, 337.

dispatch, requesting those trade concessions which, alone, would guarantee the continuing allegiance of the colonists.[16]

Henry Wellesley, the Foreign Secretary's younger brother, who now discharged the onerous and irritating duties of an English envoy to Spain, received orders, at one moment, to press simply for a reduction of duties upon British goods passing through Cadiz, and for authority to import specie directly from South America to England. At another moment his instructions authorized him to advance a million sterling to the Regency, with the promise of a million more should Spain allow the British to trade directly with the Latin American ports.[17] Toward the end of 1810 he learned to his utter bewilderment that England would content herself with the privilege of sending merchantmen to Latin America by way of Cadiz.[18] Henry Wellesley had not yet plumbed the depths of Spanish hostility and obtuseness and was inclined to accuse his own country of a shortsighted and selfish pursuit of commercial objectives at a time when the Peninsular War required her wholehearted support.[19] In a letter to Lord Wellington he complained of "petty British objects of commerce," and insisted that

unless the British government takes the decided line of discouraging the spirit which has broken forth in the colonies, and that too in the most open manner, it will create such a jealousy here as never can be got under, and will probably be the ruin of the whole cause.[20]

At first Lord Wellington was inclined to sympathize. But as the Regency adamantly rejected each British suggestion and at the same time began to treat the other objectives of the war with increasing levity, both men came to revise their views.

During this period Lord Wellesley was also undergoing a change of heart. The Spaniards had treated his supplications with

16. Marquess Wellesley to Henry Wellesley, July 13, 1810: ". . . that if Venezuela continued to refuse recognition of the Regency's authority, His Majesty's Government was, nevertheless, not disposed to renounce friendly relations with the Colony, much less to contribute to the use of force in order to compel it to admit to that authority." *Ibid.,* II, 337.

17. C. W. Crawley, "French and English Influences in the Cortes of Cadiz, 1810–1814," *The Cambridge Historical Journal,* pp. 182–183, 191 n.

18. Henry Wellesley to Viscount Wellington, August 16, 1810, Wellington, *Supplementary Despatches,* VI, 574.

19. For evidence that his government's motives were not so narrow as Henry Wellesley supposed, see Liverpool to Wellington, September 10, 1810, *ibid.,* pp. 592–593.

20. Henry Wellesley to Viscount Wellington, August 31, 1810, *ibid.,* pp. 583–584.

scorn; they had rejected his advice, ignored his warnings. The rebuffs were too much for the Foreign Secretary, and already by 1811 he had fixed one fact firmly in his mind. At the most Spain would grant only temporary concessions of her own accord. If England was to have her markets—and Lord Wellesley was determined that she should [21]—clearly, he must employ English power and influence, no longer to supplicate but to insist upon a comprehensive settlement of the Spanish family quarrel. Further dependence upon the limited fund of Spanish good sense was useless; he was prepared now to shift his ground, to admit frankly that the rebels possessed an argument, and to require Spanish recognition of their claims. His object, more specifically, was to mediate between the two disputants and, in so doing, to insist upon a measure of self-determination for Latin America.[22]

The decision in its immediate context was not particularly significant—a mere faint cloud upon the horizon, a condensation of two years of almost aimless thinking. The choice hardly signified more than a determination to stabilize a situation of economic advantage to England. But the cloud was to grow until it menaced and at last obscured the pretensions of Spain.

Lord Wellesley embarked upon his new policy with a nice sense of circumspection. He had already announced that Great Britain would not aid in the suppression of Latin American revolutions. He had pointed out, for Spanish edification, that the United States was taking an obvious and unsolicited interest in the Floridas.[23] He had, in a word, outlined all the dangers awaiting Spain if she persisted on her blind and senseless tack. Now, he lapsed into an ominous silence. England had abandoned the role of suitor; henceforward, Spain must come to her.

Lord Wellesley had not long to wait for the first Spanish advances. Napoleon was falling into difficulties with the Tsar; and

21. Lord Wellesley had come into contact "with the most eminent of the London merchants and capitalists, who have been thrown upon him, through the almost entire neglect of Perceval and Bathurst . . ." (?) to Marquess of Buckingham, September 17, 1811, Richard, Duke of Buckingham and Chandos, *Memoirs of the Court of England during the Regency, 1811–1820,* (2 vols., London, Hurst and Blackett, 1856), I, 126.

22. In March, 1811, the Foreign Office actually appointed Robert P. Staples as consul "on the banks of the River Plate," but the Buenos Aires junta at first refused to receive him. See Humphreys, *British Consular Reports on the Trade and Politics of Latin America, 1824–1826,* p. 331 n.

23. Marquess Wellesley to Apodaca, September 27, 1810, J. Fred Rippy, *Rivalry of the United States and Great Britain over Latin America, 1808–1830* (Baltimore, Johns Hopkins Press, 1929), p. 34.

by the spring of 1811 Wellington had emerged from the lines of Torres Vedras to gain the initiative in the Peninsular War. The English military engine was thus becoming increasingly independent of Spanish assistance. The policy of the United States was also assuming a less ambiguous form. On October 27, 1810, President Madison had authorized the occupation of West Florida; no one could forecast in such troublesome times the full extent of American ambitions.[24] And there was another and more significant factor: the Regency of Spain had run out of funds.[25]

The cessation of regular communication with Latin America had deprived Spain of her last source of income; for the mother country had long since abandoned the idea of supporting herself out of domestic resources. The war merely served to make evident the impending bankruptcy. As the crisis deepened Don Eusebio de Bardaxí, minister of state in the Regency, turned to Henry Wellesley for aid. His first move was to offer the revenues of Mexico as security for a loan of four million sterling. Since Spain was not enjoying these revenues at the moment, the English envoy refused to consider the proposition. When in April Bardaxí lowered his request to two million pounds, Wellesley gave him 1,500,000 pesos in the hope that the largess might stimulate action on a commercial treaty.

The Foreign Secretary reluctantly agreed to the transaction but warned his brother against a second commission of the same crime. He had succeeded at last in wringing from the Regency a plea for help that brought with it the offer of concessions in Latin America; he had not intended to let the pleader off with a kindly grant of 1,500,000 pesos. The time was ripe to press for a more comprehensive arrangement.[26]

On May 4, 1811, Lord Wellesley fired the opening gun of his campaign. "The Principles stated with regard to Venezuela," he

24. What neither Spain nor England realized was that on March 3, 1811, the Congress, in secret session, had passed this resolution: "Taking into view the peculiar situation of Spain and of her American Provinces and considering the influence which the destiny of the territory adjoining the southern boundary of the United States may have upon their security, tranquility, and commerce . . . the United States, under the peculiar circumstances of the existing crisis, cannot, without serious inquietude, see any part of the said territory pass into the hands of any other foreign power." See W. F. Reddaway, *The Monroe Doctrine* (Cambridge, Cambridge University Press, 1898), p. 9.

25. Henry Wellesley to Viscount Wellington, January 14, 1811, Wellington, *Supplementary Despatches,* VII, 45.

26. Rydjord, "British Mediation between Spain and Her Colonies: 1811–1813," *Hisp. Amer. Hist. Rev.,* p. 31.

informed his brother, "were expressly stated to you and to the British authorities in South America to constitute the general rule of conduct which it was intended by Great Britain to observe with respect to every other Province of South America." [27] He went on to justify British dealings with the colonies as necessary to keep them out of French hands, and concluded by suggesting England as a safe and honorable channel for the settlement of Spain's difficulties with her dominions. On May 11 he turned his suggestion into the definite offer of British mediation. His proposals were simple and to the point: the cessation of hostilities, a general amnesty for the insurgents, confirmation of all the concessions so far granted by Spain, and, of course, free trade with a reasonable preference for Spanish goods. To make the terms more palatable, he offered to affix an English guarantee to the final agreement.[28]

Not only was Lord Wellesley's sense of timing excellent; somehow, he managed to have his proposals blessed by the pope. It is hardly surprising, therefore, to find that the Regency gave them a friendly reception. Bardaxí went before the Cortes, presented the British terms with some grace, and confessed that they afforded the only satisfactory way of returning the colonies to Spain. A note of optimism appeared in Henry Wellesley's dispatches; he had high hopes of favorable action by the Cortes, even though he retained reservations about the prospects of free trade.[29]

His optimism soon proved to be unfounded. The Cortes, after contemplating the English proposals for a month, returned seven counterproposals which implied, in fact, that Britain should assist Spain in restoring "the ancient order of things." The body agreed to offer certain concessions to the colonists and to allow Britain to trade with them as long as the negotiations should last. But the negotiations were to last a maximum of fifteen months, to apply only to those portions of Latin America where Spanish authority had definitely collapsed, and, in the event of their failure (this was the seventh article), Britain was to support the reestablishment of that authority by force of arms if necessary.

These terms hardly provided a satisfactory basis for mediation; and Henry Wellesley said as much on July 1 in a communication

27. Robertson, "The Beginnings of Spanish-American Diplomacy," *Essays in American History*, p. 248.

28. Satow, *A Guide to Diplomatic Practice*, II, 339–340.

29. Henry Wellesley to Marquess Wellesley, June 8, 1811, Wellington, *Supplementary Despatches*, VII, 157–158.

to the Regency.[30] But the Regency, although secretly agreed, could do nothing without the consent of the Cortes. As a result the whole project became lost in a flow of argumentative dispatches until October, when the Regency put a halt to the discussions with the announcement that it proposed to send a special expedition against the insurgents. The news was almost too much for Henry Wellesley. He protested the decision with great bitterness only to learn that the Regency was not using English funds to finance the expedition and considered the preservation of the integrity of Latin America as vital as the defense of Spain. The Regency did not explain how the diversion of troops from the Peninsular War would achieve the latter objective.[31]

But if the cause of mediation did not improve, neither did the state of Spanish finances. Finally, despite the acrimonious exchanges of the summer and autumn, the Cortes turned again to England for aid. In December, 1811, that extraordinary body offered Great Britain a share of the colonial trade in return for a loan of ten million pounds. Henry Wellesley, remembering the scolding that he had incurred over the grant of 1,500,000 pesos, refused even to consider the proposal. The Regency then transmitted the offer slyly to London where it suffered a quiet and tactful demise.

Lord Wellesley himself did not participate in the funeral. Accustomed to the pomp and ceremony of India, and, with those splendors, to the corresponding powers of viceregal authority, he had failed to adjust himself to the intimate discussions and compromises of cabinet government.[32] Although he never conducted a great deal of business, the decisions which he reached he preferred to enforce without consultation. Cabinet dinners came to irk him; he attended them with decreasing frequency, and when

30. His principal argument was that, despite England's control of the seas, France could land agents provocateurs in Latin America, spread her Jacobin doctrines, and win many adherents unless the colonists were appeased. See Rydjord, "British Mediation between Spain and Her Colonies," *Hisp. Amer. Hist. Rev.*, pp. 30, 34–35, 42.

31. *Ibid.*, p. 36. See also Wellington, *Supplementary Despatches,* VII, 220.

32. "Lord Wellesley treated Mr. Perceval and other Ministers with magnificent scorn, and contempt . . ." according to Lord Holland. "Yet when, on Lord Boringdon's motion for an efficient administration, he was expected to vindicate his own motives and conduct, and to explain at large his views of domestic and foreign policy, though he had come down with mighty ostentation, dressed and decorated, as his usage was, for the delivery of a great speech, his nerves failed him entirely, and he allowed the question to go to a division without uttering one word." *The Wellesley Papers* (2 vols., London, Herbert Jenkins, 1914), II, 7.

he did he fell asleep. Finally, in March, 1812, having catalogued a whole host of grievances against his colleagues, he resigned. Fortunately the Perceval administration was able, without loss of time, to obtain Lord Castlereagh as his successor.

Castlereagh, of all the Tories, was perhaps best fitted to thread his way through the maze of problems which now surrounded the Latin American question. His experience from 1807 until 1809 at the War Office, together with a genuinely thoughtful and analytical mind, enabled him to place British interests in a larger perspective than any of his immediate predecessors. He possessed, further, a greater fund of simple patience than either Canning or Lord Wellesley. As Wellington progressed painfully up the Spanish Peninsula and as Napoleon prepared to throw himself into the wastes of Russia, this virtue, so rare among statesmen, came to serve him in good stead.

Patience, in fact, was the only effective response to the eccentricities which now constituted the policy of Spain. The British mediation offer still stood; but it floated about, wraithlike and disembodied, in the council chambers of Cadiz, a mere shadow of earlier hopes. Henry Wellesley had attempted to have new and friendlier ministers elected to the Regency. Then he had requested the elimination of the more objectionable articles of the Cortes counterproposal. But all Spanish politicians agreed upon the subject of Latin America; the new Regency hardly differed from its predecessor, and his request went unanswered.[33] Nevertheless, the situation was not entirely without hope. Wellington was far too well established before Badajoz to depend any longer upon Spanish good will; and the colonists, struggling for their existence, showed no signs of losing faith in the power and benevolence of Great Britain. Moreover, English trade with Latin America, although erratic, had not yet suffered from overt Spanish interference. Further conversations, therefore, could do no harm and might possibly result in an eventual settlement.

Once again, then, on April 1, 1812, Castlereagh renewed the offer of British mediation. His terms hardly differed from those of Lord Wellesley: England, as the mediating Power, neither could, nor would, employ force to bring about a settlement of the dispute, nor would she cease to trade with the colonies. The established trade with Latin America was the principal source of reve-

33. Henry Wellesley to Bardaxí, January 30, 1812, Satow, *A Guide to Diplomatic Practice*, II, 343.

nues for the conduct of the Peninsular War; and Mexico, over which Spain still exercised a species of authority, supplied, with its bullion, the largest portion of those revenues. Spain must therefore agree to include Mexico within the scope of the mediation. The commissioners appointed to work out the details of the settlement should, in fact, commence their labors there. Since this last suggestion ran counter to the proposals of the Cortes, Castlereagh strove to make it acceptable by including two other suggestions. The first repeated Lord Wellesley's promise of a British guarantee, should a satisfactory arrangement be concluded. The second, in a different vein, hinted that, if Spain persisted in her traditional policy of commercial exclusion, England might encourage the colonies to seek complete independence.[34]

Henry Wellesley had begun a diplomatic offensive even before Castlereagh's instructions arrived. He appeared before the Regency on April 4, announced that the English mediation commissioners would soon be on their way to Spain, and demanded that the Cortes rescind the seventh article of its counterproposal before they appeared.[35] The Regency, anxious to avoid deciding upon such a delicate subject, passed his demand, together with Castlereagh's recently arrived plan, on to the Cortes. That body, equally anxious to avoid responsibility, succeeded in burying both requests in a legislative committee for three weeks. In May the committee hit upon the ingenious expedient of forcing the Regency to decide whether or not the fatal seventh article should be withdrawn. By the time that Regency, Cortes, and committee had completed this cycle of procrastination, the British mediation commissioners had reached Cadiz, and Henry Wellesley had lost a large measure of his composure. When Pezuela, the new minister of state, informed him that the Regency would withdraw part of the seventh article but that the Spanish government still expected England to aid Spain against the colonies, Wellesley responded angrily that the offer was inadmissible and threatened to send the British commissioners back home. Pezuela took alarm at the grim tones of the envoy and hinted that he might rescind the entire article. His only condition was that England should remain neutral in the event that the mediation failed and Spain attempted to recover the

34. Castlereagh to Henry Wellesley, April 1, 1812, Webster, *Britain and the Independence of Latin America,* II, 311–316.

35. Lord Wellesley, in a moment of optimism, had appointed the commissioners in the previous October. See Buckingham and Chandos, *Memoirs of the Regency,* I, 150.

colonies.[36] Compared with the Regency's usual reluctance to make any concessions at all, here was progress indeed. But the proposal still failed to satisfy the terms which Castlereagh had laid down in April. Pezuela had made no mention of the areas to which mediation should apply, nor had he offered the proper suggestions regarding a more liberal commercial policy.

Late in May, therefore, Wellesley returned to the charge with a demand that the Regency specifically include Mexico in the mediation. Pezuela, who thought that he had succeeded in evading this subject entirely, rejected the demand point-blank and launched into a long and emotional tirade upon the generosity of Spain. She had allowed Britain to trade unmolested with the colonies and would continue to do so as long as the negotiations continued; surely that was concession enough.[37] For two weeks thereafter the two antagonists rested exhausted upon their arms, and the subject of mediation seemed to disappear from view. But in reality neither side was willing to bring the discussions to a final close, for by now the mere process of negotiation had become more significant than the original objectives themselves.

The Spaniards were at last awakening to the fact that England was more important to them than they were to England. Earlier, they would have preferred to abandon the war rather than lose their colonial monopoly; now, they discovered that, while it mattered very little whether they retired from the war, the danger of losing their colonial monopoly had increased tenfold. Thus, if they did not care to have the shipwreck of empire salvaged according to English lights, they did want to continue talking about the process of reconciliation. As long as the conversations continued, English policy would remain limited and circumspect; and so the day might come when Spain could wreak vengeance on her dissident subjects.

Castlereagh, too, was content to spin out the interminable negotiations.[38] So far they had prevented Spain from diverting more

36. Pezuela to Wellesley, Wellesley to Pezuela, May 15, 1812; Pezuela to Wellesley, May 17, 1812; Rydjord, "British Mediation between Spain and Her Colonies," *Hisp. Amer. Hist. Rev.*, p. 40.

37. *Ibid.*, pp. 41–42.

38. He was rapidly obtaining almost complete freedom in the conduct of foreign affairs. George III had lapsed into permanent insanity in 1810, and the Prince of Wales, who assumed the Regency, seemed content, for the moment, to accept the advice of his cabinet on such matters. Spencer Perceval died at the hand of an assassin in June, 1812, and Lord Liverpool, on becoming first minister, proved to be more a manager of men than a source of ideas. In the realm of policy, then, Castlereagh received little assistance and suffered from even less interference.

than a few thousand troops to her dominions; they had made somewhat easier the flow of trade; and, by the elusive hope which they
afforded, they had restrained the colonists from going to the extremity of independence. Castlereagh had hoped for more concrete
results—an agreement securing the benefits of uninterrupted commerce as well as a continuation of European and monarchical rule
in Latin America—but then, he could hardly expect miracles
when dealing with Spain. If England emerged triumphant from
the war—and in 1812 her hopes were rising—then the time gained
by talk would have eliminated the danger from France. There still
remained the United States, of course; but the United States was
involving itself in a painful and fruitless conflict with England.
The Americans would have few, if any, resources left over to devote to Latin American affairs. Talk, then, was cheap; and to all
intents and purposes it would bear riper fruit than action.

The tacit, almost unconscious, agreement between Spain and
England that disagreement should not constitute reason to dis-
continue the mediation, enabled Henry Wellesley to offer a revised
ten-point program to the Regency on June 12, 1812. His new
terms scarcely differed from the old ones; even the threats were
the same. If Spain excluded Mexico from the scope of the mediation commission, or if she rejected the proposals, England would
refuse to participate further in the negotiations.

The melodrama now proceeded along traditional lines; the
actors responded to their cues with practiced ease. Pezuela turned
the English program over to the Cortes and then lectured Wellesley upon the essential loyalty of the Spanish Americans. A limited
number of troops, he was certain, would suffice to stamp out the
isolated embers of rebellion. The Cortes wrapped itself in an impenetrable silence; days passed and no hint of a legislative decision emerged. Wellesley thereupon advised Pezuela that the time
had come "to end this painful affair" and threatened to send the
mediation commissioners home.[39] The minister of state had rehearsed his lines to perfection. He confided to the envoy that the
Cortes was debating the proposals most seriously and would soon
make known its decision. Once again, then, Wellesley bade the
commissioners delay their departure.

39. Henry Wellesley to Pezuela, July 4, 1812, Rydjord, "British Mediation be-
tween Spain and Her Colonies," *Hisp. Amer. Hist. Rev.*, p. 45. See also Wellesley to
Castlereagh, July 5, 1812, Webster, *Britain and the Independence of Latin America*,
II, 329–331.

On July 16, 1812, the Cortes, by a vote of more than two-to-one, rejected the English program. Here was the critical moment of the drama, what could have been the prelude to separation and violence. But the authors of the play were not tragedians, and they had determined upon a reconciliation with overtones of comedy. Wellesley immediately assured Pezuela that "whether the trade of America be opened or not, the Government of . . . the Prince Regent will make every exertion to assist the cause of Spain, to the utmost of their ability." [40] Pezuela reciprocated with elaborate expressions of friendship and, in his best comic vein, offered to arrange for trade concessions in Latin America in return for a loan.

But Wellesley had traveled far since the days of innocence and anger in 1810. He appreciated, particularly, that Castlereagh was attempting to do more than meet the exigencies of a wartime crisis in trade and finance or combat the dangers of French influence in Latin America. The objective of the Foreign Secretary, clearly, was hardening into a determination to destroy once and for all the old Spanish monopoly and to establish, amid its ruins, the right of England to participate regularly in the Latin American trade. To extend a loan in return for commercial concessions was to admit that Spain had something to sell. Wellesley therefore advised Castlereagh to ignore Pezuela's proposition.

Castlereagh hardly required the advice. Despite his meandering speeches in the House of Commons and the involved circumlocutions of his dispatches, he already possessed an uncommon grasp of all the diverse requirements of British policy. He might refuse a loan but he would not abandon mediation. A change of tactics might cause the colonists to assume that England had forsaken their enterprise. No doubt there would be a reaction in Spain as well. The Regency would probably take the end of mediation as a signal for greater military exertions in Latin America. He preferred to string out the negotiations, even at the expense of Wellesley's nerves.[41]

On August 29, 1812, Castlereagh sent off a lengthy dispatch to his minister, in which he justified the British position with all the

40. *Castlereagh Papers*, VIII, 268.
41. That mediation had become an end in itself, rather than a means to an end, seems clear from the following: Harrowby (?) to Castlereagh, August 3, 1812, *Castlereagh Papers*, VIII, 271; and Strangford to Castlereagh, November 10, 1812, December 18, 1812, Webster, *Britain and the Independence of Latin America*, I, 84, 87.

arguments that had occurred to the Foreign Office over the previous two years. He conjured up the specie need again; he mentioned the benefits that Spain derived from England's trade with the colonies; and he emphasized the dangers from France. Great Britain, in consideration of these facts, was prepared to renew her offer of mediation; was, in fact, willing to relent somewhat in her conditions. But, should the Spanish government continue to reject her terms, England must reserve "eventually the right of taking such steps as may deprive the enemy [France] of the means of wielding the resources of Spanish America against the safety of the dominions" confided to British care.[42] Castlereagh gave emphasis to the threat, as his predecessors had so often done before, by granting an interview to the agents of the Venezuelan junta.[43]

His action served to gain time—a vital six months—but it evoked no satisfactory response from Spain. Wellesley paraded the proposals back and forth before the Regency, only to have Pedro Labrador, yet another minister of state, tell him that the Constitution of 1812 conceded to the colonists all the favors that they could ever expect. Castlereagh's new terms, which varied from those previously offered in phraseology rather than substance, failed to penetrate the hard shell of stubbornness in which the Spanish government had now encased itself. On February 16, 1813, Wellesley finally admitted to his chief that a prolongation of the negotiations would serve no useful purpose.[44]

There is no evidence that his announcement engendered regret in the Foreign Office. The necessity for mediation was steadily growing less urgent; indeed, events on the Peninsula and in western Europe were tending to relegate the entire Latin American question to momentary oblivion. In December, 1812, Napoleon himself had admitted that the surviving remnant of the *Grande Armée* was retreating out of Russia. In July, 1813, came the news, first of the Battle of Leipzig, then of Vittoria, and in October Wellington advanced into France. Six months later the war was over. At Fontainebleau Napoleon surrendered his throne; and across the Pyrenees, on May 13, 1814, a crowd of cheering Spaniards dragged a carriage containing Ferdinand the Well-beloved from Aranjuez to Madrid, a distance of thirty miles.

42. Castlereagh to Henry Wellesley, August 29, 1812, Webster, *Britain and the Independence of Latin America*, II, 333–335.
43. Webster, *The Foreign Policy of Castlereagh, 1812–1815,* p. 72.
44. Rydjord, "British Mediation between Spain and Her Colonies," *Hisp. Amer. Hist. Rev.,* p. 48.

Peace had come to Europe; the menace of France had dissipated itself at last. Englishmen could emerge from their island fortress and move, with becoming assurance, once more about the Continent. Ferdinand VII, from the somber depths of the Escorial, could reinvoke the medieval spirit of the Inquisition and proclaim his absolute sovereignty over all the vast domains of Spain. For a moment there was tranquility, harmony, and a revival of older systems. Then the effects of the vast upheaval began to take their toll. Wartime alliances deteriorated, new loyalties arose, and conflicting interests came to the fore. As different alignments emerged, British policy toward Latin America regained its prominence and became the center of a struggle of another sort.

V

A NEW ENVIRONMENT

THERE are, between 1804 and 1814, three stages in the development of British policy toward Latin America. The first stage, between 1804 and 1810, is characterized by tentative explorations and a certain inconsistency. There is an almost total failure to define the nature, the extent, or the comparative importance of the English interest in Latin America. No doubt this failure is due in part to those considerations of expediency which dominated the thinking of the Foreign Office at the time. It is due, also, to the impersonal and unpredictable circumstance of a war which tossed up such odd personages as General Miranda and Sir Home Popham, dictated an alliance with Spain, and exploded the long train of dissatisfaction among the Spanish colonists. Only when the outlines of the European conflict become stabilized, with Great Britain committed to the Peninsula —only when the colonists embark upon their revolutionary career —does the Foreign Office begin to lay down a regular line of action. This represents the second stage.

According to Lord Wellesley British policy in 1810 had to fulfill four essential conditions. These were: to provide for the continuation of English trade with Latin America, to prevent Latin America from falling into unfriendly hands, to deter the colonists from imbibing too deeply at the well of Jacobinism, and above all to contribute to—or, at least, not detract from—the European war effort. By restoring a loose Spanish sovereignty to Latin America, through the medium of British mediation, Lord Wellesley had hoped to fulfill all four of his conditions. When he retired from the cabinet he had not even progressed to the point of having his good offices accepted by Spain.

In the third stage Lord Castlereagh, upon succeeding to the Foreign Office, found mediation to be a device which, if it settled nothing, prevented the tensions within the Spanish empire from manifesting themselves too violently for the duration of the war. Under his skilled direction mediation became, in other words, a convenient instrument for the maintenance of colonial good will, the soothing of Spanish fears, and the justification for British trade.

But could the potency of mediation last beyond the war? The termination of the Napoleonic conflict had brought certain changes in the conditions of British interest. The determination to trade with Latin America remained; indeed it increased. But now the Spanish ally was less than willing to countenance the influx of British goods. Ferdinand the Well-beloved had returned to his throne bent upon re-establishing his ancient monopoly over Spanish America. His spirit, it soon became clear, was not one easily attuned to temporization or compromise. In a more intelligent ruler fixity of purpose might have been an admirable characteristic; in Ferdinand such a trait was to bring only bloodshed and disaster in its train. The consequences of his stubbornness were indicated to him time and time again; Ferdinand only grew more obstinate. The colonies were his, and his they would remain. In this circumstance appeals to reason were of no avail; there was no reciprocal reason to respond—only an outwork of cunning surrounding a bastion of absolute and uncomprehending faith.

Of Ferdinand's mother Napoleon had remarked: "Maria Luisa has her past and her character written on her face, which is all I need say. It surpasses anything one dare imagine." The same might have been said of her son. Upon seeing Ferdinand his first wife exclaimed: "I believed that I had lost my senses." In that stocky and obtusely determined figure, upon that coarse and heavy face with its viselike mouth and immense, jutting chin, one sees the effect of those vaulting pretensions with which the Catholic Church favored her royal sons. It was the visage of a religious fanatic. Bred and confirmed in an iron faith, ignorant, superstitious, concerned for the future of his immortal soul, and terribly alone, how could Ferdinand, even in the matter of colonies, accept the transient decisions of the temporal world?

There were other difficulties as well. The downfall of Napoleon had removed one source of Jacobin infection, but another, according to British lights, still existed in the United States. Under these difficult circumstances could mediation satisfy the demand for trade? Could it combat the medieval stubbornness of Ferdinand and at the same time nullify the influence of the United States? Could mediation do more? Could it contribute to the maintenance of peace as it had subserved the purpose of war? Here were the great questions that faced the Foreign Office at the conclusion of the conflict. Of them all, the last assumed by far the most importance.

General war in the early nineteenth century had become if not completely disruptive at least highly inconvenient. Peace, by contrast, had gained in both respectability and desirability. Twenty-one years of deprivation, oppression, and conflict had aroused a yearning for tranquility, order, and predictability; and in high quarters the desire for peace expressed itself in an effort to surround victory with safeguards. In that process the Foreign Secretary of England played an especially prominent role. Indeed from 1814 until 1822 Lord Castlereagh's interest in peace governed the majority of his actions. British policy toward Latin America during this period is understandable, therefore, only against the background of Castlereagh's struggle for a concert of Europe.

Castlereagh, like his policy, represents a study in contrasts. Both his title and his birthplace were Irish, but he embodied singularly English characteristics. One of the handsomest men in an age noted for its profligacy, he remained doggedly faithful to a lightheaded and frivolous wife. Despite formidable barriers of frigidity, reticence, and inarticulateness, he could boast of such diverse and devoted friends as George IV, the Duke of Wellington, and Prince Metternich. Contemporaries and historians were to accuse him of corruption, brutality, and stupidity in domestic affairs, yet his record is that of a tolerant and ingenious Foreign Secretary.

The reasons for Castlereagh's success in foreign affairs were many and varied. As an aristocrat he partook of a stock of ideas common to his social equals throughout Europe. When he met with Alexander and Metternich, he talked a language which, even if modified by national eccentricities, they could readily understand. For while the aristocracies of Europe may have differed in many respects, they all agreed upon their right to rule. In previous years this basic agreement had not brought them together; only a violent and cataclysmic event could do that. But such an event had at last occurred. Having lived under the shadow of the French Revolution, having fought Jacobinism incarnate, Alexander, Metternich, and Castlereagh were inspired to eradicate those seeds of aggressive nationalism which had sprung up in the wake of Napoleon. Here was the evil fruit of a generation of disorder. International cooperation alone could repair the damage.

But Castlereagh, at least, was not impelled merely by narrow repressive instincts or the desire to perpetuate a particular social order. There were other and deeper springs to his actions. He had fallen heir to a peculiar mode of transacting business; he was, in a word, a parliamentarian. At forty-four he had learned all the intricate ways of that strange and wonderful world, the House of Commons. He had become, despite his difficulties as an orator, its most successful manager; and the experience had taught him the value of gradual and peaceful change. In 1814, when he moved from the restricted sphere of the wartime Foreign Office to the broad arena of European politics, he carried with him this appreciation of temperate and cooperative compromise.

Nor was that all. The familiar red coat, the tight white breeches, and the dashing jockey boots concealed an aristocrat with imaginative ideas. Castlereagh had been a favored pupil of Pitt. As early as 1804 he had participated in the discussions of the Tsar's peace plans which had been intermingled with the formation of the Third Coalition. And while it had proved a trifle early to discuss peace at that time, Castlereagh had for the next ten years constantly meditated upon Pitt's replies.[1] Essentially Pitt had contemplated these changes in Europe: the restoration to their original sovereigns of those territories conquered by France since 1792, the formation of a territorial barrier against future French aggression, the signature of a general convention for the mutual protection and security of the Powers, and finally the codification of public law so as to provide a guide for the future conduct of the participating states.[2] Here, with certain important exceptions, was the program which from 1813 to 1815 Castlereagh tried to realize.

His first concern, not unnaturally, was for purely English interests. On the Continent these were few and, to the other Allied Powers, of relative unimportance. Antwerp was to be removed from French hands and its arsenal destroyed.[3] France herself was to be excluded from the Scheldt. Holland was to become an independent kingdom, her neutrality guaranteed, as a barrier to future French aggression. Finally, the states of Italy and Spain were to

1. Castlereagh to Cathcart, April 8, 1813, Charles K. Webster, ed., *British Diplomacy, 1813–1815* (London, G. Bell, 1921), p. 1.
2. W. Alison Phillips, *The Confederation of Europe* (London, Longmans, Green, 1920), pp. 38–39.
3. Castlereagh to Aberdeen, November 13, 1813, Webster, *British Diplomacy*, p. 112.

be assured in some manner against their ancient scourge.[4] Such
were Castlereagh's principal demands. As paymaster of the coalition against Napoleon he was able to obtain them in the Langres
Protocol, almost three months before the Emperor's abdication.[5]

Outside the Continent, and particularly in Latin America,
British interests and British power were such that Castlereagh
neither wished nor required the assistance of his allies. He made
this point quite clear to Lord Cathcart in his discussion of maritime rights.

I cannot omit again impressing upon your Lordship [he wrote] the
importance of awakening the Tsar's mind to the necessity, for his own
interests as well as ours, of peremptorily excluding from the general
negotiations every maritime question. If he does not, he will risk a
similar misunderstanding between those Powers on whose union the
safety of Europe now rests. Great Britain may be driven out of a
Congress, but not out of her maritime rights, and, if the Continental
Powers know their own interests, they will not hazard this.[6]

The warning had its effect. As a result of Castlereagh's insistence the question of maritime rights was eliminated from future
discussion by the Langres Protocol. The protocol in its immediate
sense meant that the exercise of British sea power would be subject to no limitations in the peace conferences to come. By extension, the document implied that neither in North nor in South
America would Great Britain be governed by the necessity of
consulting with her wartime allies. In relinquishing the opportunity
to discuss the maritime question the Continental Powers justified
the belief that they would do likewise upon questions the settlement of which required an access to sea power.

In regard to the war with the United States Castlereagh proved
as adamant as he had been upon the subject of maritime rights.
As John Quincy Adams remarked, "We . . . very well know the
aversion which the British Cabinet felt to the idea of having their
disputes with America at all connected with the affairs of the
continent of Europe . . ." So great, in fact, was this aversion
that when the Tsar offered to mediate, Count Lieven, his ambassa-

4. Cabinet Memorandum, December 26, 1813, Phillips, *The Confederation of
Europe*, p. 65.
5. The Langres Protocol was signed on January 29, 1814. Castlereagh himself
wrote the paragraph which dealt with maritime rights. See Webster, *The Foreign
Policy of Castlereagh, 1812–1815*, p. 206.
6. Castlereagh to Cathcart, July 14, 1813, Webster, *British Diplomacy*, p. 14.

dor in London, "was told that the question with America involved principles of internal government in Great Britain which were not susceptible of being discussed under any mediation." [7] Once again the immediate sense of this injunction was clear. The quarrel between England and the United States was separate and distinct from the European conflict and therefore not subject to the intervention of the Continental Powers. Perhaps if the question arose in the future the injunction could be applied to the colonial uprisings in Latin America almost as well as it had been to the war with the United States.

Castlereagh did not publicly announce that by these maneuvers he proposed to limit the peace and the influence of the other Great Powers to the Continent. That was not his way. In consequence there could be no treaty specifically defining this limitation. But it is clear that by his reticence and by his attitude upon specific issues he expected to gain a free hand for Great Britain in all transatlantic affairs. No doubt in failing to obtain precise agreement upon this subject he was moving over treacherous ground, although in the confusion of peacemaking there is some question whether he could have won such a concession from his allies. As the matter rested, by leaving the subject shrouded in ambiguity, he acquired this negative advantage. In later years the European Powers would find it exceedingly difficult to enter upon a discussion of Latin America as a matter of treaty right.

But even while he labored to establish specific British interests, Castlereagh strove "to appease controversy and to secure if possible for all States a long interval of repose." [8] In the accepted fashion he conceived the first prerequisite of peace to be a balance of power. Now in the first decades of the nineteenth century power appeared to consist principally of land and human beings; the significance of technology and intensive industrialization had not yet been fully understood. The problem of equilibrium therefore resolved itself into the creation of territorial and demographic balances. The materials for such balances lay at hand in a strengthened Austria, an enlarged Prussia, and a reconstituted Poland. These states, lying across Central Europe, would not only stabilize that turbulent area; they would serve as counters to France, on the

7. Adams to Monroe, April 15, 1814, Worthington C. Ford, ed., *Writings of John Quincy Adams* (7 vols., New York, Macmillan, 1913–17), V, 36.

8. Castlereagh to Bagot, November 10, 1817, Webster, *The Foreign Policy of Castlereagh, 1815–1822,* p. 449.

one hand, and Russia on the other. Here was the basis of Castlereagh's peace system.

But Castlereagh was not as content as his predecessors had been to rest that system upon the deceptive security of territorial symmetries. He wished to go further and commit Great Britain irrevocably to a procedure for preserving the balance.[9] His reasons for wanting to involve England thus were quite simple. The balance of power, as he understood it, was incapable of fulfilling its peaceful function unless subjected to a conscious direction. The mechanism was neither exact nor automatic. And once placed in perfect equilibrium (if that were even possible) it could easily lose its original fluidity and degenerate into a set of antagonistic coalitions. That was one danger. There was a question, moreover, whether the Central European states could, by their own exertions, resist the pressure of a Franco-Russian combination. The addition of British power could preserve the fluidity of the equilibrium —and at the same time give to England the advantage of serving as arbiter among Central Europe, Russia, and France.

Owing to the relative freedom of an English Foreign Secretary in the early nineteenth century Castlereagh found it relatively simple to commit Great Britain to Europe. There remained, however, the task of creating an instrument that would operate the balance of power and yet keep the peace without giving the appearance of dictation. No doubt British influence itself would provide the principal tool, but Castlereagh preferred to conceal the efficacy of his lever beneath a great cooperative effort. Essentially, although with great caution, he was approaching the concept of collective security.

In order to put his schemes for European stability into effect Castlereagh had first to win the confidence and support of two other statesmen. The first of these, Prince Metternich of Austria, had exhibited an early predisposition toward England. And why should he not? As Castlereagh himself remarked: "Austria both in Army and Government is a timid Power. Her minister is constitutionally temporising . . ."[10] Austria's internal problems, he might have added, were of such magnitude that peace had become essential to her continued existence. Of this Prince Metternich was fully aware. And as a diplomat of the old school, in the tradi-

---

9. Phillips, *The Confederation of Europe,* p. 67.

10. Castlereagh to Liverpool, February 26, 1814, Webster, *British Diplomacy,* p. 160.

tion of Kaunitz, he naturally favored a revival of the balance of power to preserve the peace. As for a special device to sustain the balance—this too he supported; for such a device suggested the solution of Austria's manifold difficulties. Temperamentally averse to the institution of internal reforms—prevented, moreover, by the blindness of crown and nobility from being otherwise—he seized upon the suggested combination of the Great Powers as a means of keeping Austria's subjects and all her potential satellites in perpetual servitude. Here was hardly the great European, or even the statesman of international reaction, but rather a consummate diplomatic tactician and opportunist who, like the country he represented, remained forever barren of bold strategic concepts. European order in itself meant little to Prince Metternich; but the Habsburgs he meant to preserve.[11]

Tsar Alexander, the other statesman with whom Castlereagh had to deal, represented a different and more complicated order of intellect. The problem was, in a sense, two-dimensional. There was the rough, coarse canvas of autocracy, basic and unyielding; but painted over that surface was a coating of eighteenth-century enlightenment. As time passed the veneer cracked and fell away in places; only then did the tightly woven canvas show through.

A liberal education, foisted upon Alexander by his doting grandmother, Catherine the Great, had inspired a genuine desire to help the world as well as Russia; but desire alone provided no concrete basis for action. Instead, Alexander lived in a haze of splendid generalities. At one moment he imagined all states so homogeneously constituted that he, together with Pitt, would merely act as the nursemaids of their destinies.[12] At another, he asked cynically of the French ambassador: "What is Europe? . . . What is it, if it be not you and we?"[13] Still later, in 1813, he pictured himself as the perfect European.

But how was this Europe, of which he was the first citizen, to be constituted? Details did not particularly interest the Tsar; his mind worked upon another plane. Since 1812 he had been reading the Bible with especial care, and a study of the Apocalypse became his principal diversion. Under the effects of an increasing mystical ferment he imagined himself riding the length and breadth of Europe, obliterating evil with the bolts of his justice. In this

11. Phillips, *The Confederation of Europe*, p. 72.
12. Alexander to Novosiltsov, September 11, 1804, *ibid.*, p. 37.
13. *Ibid.*, p. 46.

curious state of mind the suggestion of some instrument to organize and maintain the peace struck a responsive chord.

The chord sounded, however, with special and ominous overtones. Alexander had been reared in an atmosphere charged with
violence. Force was an element which in philosophical moments he
deplored but which he plainly understood; a portion of his nature
throve upon military pomp and display. Faced with opposition he
instinctively appealed to the sword in order to resolve the difficulty. Here was scarcely an omen for peace, especially in an Autocrat of All the Russias, a man accustomed to having his smallest
whim obeyed. A liberal education and a benign countenance could
not wholly overcome a habit of dictatorial rule, aided and abetted
by a singular comprehension of the more obscure portions of Holy
Writ.

And there were other difficulties. Alexander, like Metternich,
was inherently conservative. What absolute ruler after all is not?
He dispensed terror and he lived in terror. He had participated
in the plot to murder his father; he knew how easily a similar plot
could be engineered against him. And despite the teachings of La
Harpe, despite a superficial examination of the Encyclopedists,
he could never repose his faith entirely in philosophic pretensions.
He could approve of liberal principles only if he and his fellow
sovereigns dispensed them. The restless stirrings of liberated Europe, exemplified by the *Tugendbund* in Germany, suggested that
he must guard against these same principles should they emanate
from the masses. With the example of the French Revolution
still before him Alexander harbored the unalterable conviction
that any and all outbursts of popular feeling must be swiftly repressed, wherever they arose. "I consider my Army as the Army
of Europe," he announced, "and as such alone shall it be employed." [14]

Within this mass of dangerous contradictions there was for
Castlereagh's purposes one saving grace. The Tsar was vain; he
prided himself upon an openness to reason. When appealed to he
would listen, and when at the center of the stage he would sacrifice
certain of his principles in order to savor the pleasures of his pre-
eminence. If Metternich would cooperate on grounds of self-
interest, the Tsar might collaborate out of vanity. The problem,
reduced to its simplest form, was this: to design an organization
for peace—an object of which Alexander after all approved—

14. Webster, *The Foreign Policy of Castlereagh, 1815–1822,* p. 142.

along lines less exalted than the Apocalypse, and to allow him to appear as its dominant member.

The task of gaining the sort of peace settlement that Castlereagh desired—a task which involved fitting Metternich and Alexander into a concert of Europe and at the same time excluding Latin America from their consideration—was not to be accomplished by means of unhurried dispatches from the closeted atmosphere of the Foreign Office. With the blessing of his colleagues the Foreign Secretary therefore proceeded to the Continent for a period of personal diplomacy.

His first encounter with Metternich, which occurred at Basel in January, 1814, proved eminently satisfactory. The two men agreed that Poland would provide the key to the future, that a balance of power was essential to the peace of Europe, and that Prussia should act as a sentinel upon the Rhine. The Tsar proved somewhat less amenable. Much to Castlereagh's annoyance he refused to commit himself upon territorial questions.[15]

But on the question of preserving the peace there was general agreement. The Grand Alliance, formed in 1813, and consisting of the four Great Powers, was already an effective instrument. If appropriately altered it could be used to enforce the terms of whatever peace settlement emerged. As the Allied armies drove Napoleon back into France Castlereagh labored assiduously to define the nature of the new agreement. Aided by the blind tenacity of Napoleon and by Alexander's fear that the coalition might collapse, he succeeded at last. On March 1, 1814, Austria, Great Britain, Prussia, and Russia signed the Treaty of Chaumont and extended the Grand Alliance for another twenty years.

I send you my treaty [Castlereagh wrote to his undersecretary], which I hope you will approve. We four Ministers, when signing, happened to be sitting at a whist-table. It was agreed that never were the stakes so high at any former party. . . . This, I trust, will put an end to any doubts as to the claim we have to an opinion on continental matters.[16]

In concluding the Treaty of Chaumont Castlereagh gained three major objectives. He committed Great Britain to Europe. By Article XVI of the treaty he defined the obligation of the signatories as the maintenance of peace and the balance of Europe

15. Harold Nicolson, *The Congress of Vienna* (New York, Harcourt, Brace, 1946), pp. 70–71.
16. Castlereagh to Hamilton, March 10, 1814, Webster, *British Diplomacy*, p. 166.

—thus assuring to the Alliance powers beyond a mere deathwatch over France. By the same token, if only by implication, he excluded the Alliance from transatlantic affairs. The combination constituted the first step toward collective security in Europe and freedom of action in Latin America.

Although the Alliance lacked precise definition—a failure which was increasingly to plague the Foreign Secretary with the years —here was a smashing triumph indeed. But Castlereagh remained dissatisfied. Before crossing to the Continent he had dreamed of securing a complete territorial settlement while the Allies lay under the threat of France. Upon his arrival in Europe he discovered that Russian and Prussian aspirations would not fuse with those of Austria even in the heat of battle. He had therefore to await the downfall of Napoleon to complete his work.[17]

The Emperor finally gave up the struggle in April, 1814. Shortly thereafter, on May 30, 1814, the victors, in the first Peace of Paris, defined the frontiers of France and created the Dutch barrier in which Great Britain was so vitally interested. But the central problem—that of establishing a territorial balance in Europe—still remained. The most that Castlereagh could obtain was a secret agreement to define the remaining boundaries at a congress in Vienna.[18]

The Congress of Vienna did not convene until the autumn of 1814. Then, despite an assemblage of sovereigns and ministers from every corner of Europe, the business of peacemaking fell into the hands of the four Great Powers, joined later by France. The settlement which these Powers achieved, whatever one may think of the methods employed, lasted with one major exception (the unification of Germany) for a hundred years. It offers an interesting commentary upon the balance of power as a foundation for enduring peace.

Castlereagh himself went to Vienna with the idea of establishing an exceedingly complex balance. Holland, supported by England, had already been established as a barrier to French aggression in the north. Spain and the Two Sicilies were to act in similar capacities to the south and southwest, while Prussia, brought up to

17. *Ibid.*, introd., p. xxxix.

18. The article in question stated that "the relations from whence a system of real and permanent balance of power is to be derived shall be regulated at the Congress upon principles determined by the Allied Powers amongst themselves." See Nicolson, *The Congress of Vienna*, p. 100.

the Rhine, would stand guard on the east. On the other side of Europe Poland was to be reconstituted in strength as a barrier to Russia. As further security against this unknown quantity, and as the linchpin in a grand balance against a possible Franco-Russian combination Austria was to be invigorated by virtual control over the Italian peninsula, while Prussia was to receive all of Saxony in compensation for the loss of her Polish provinces.

Metternich accepted Castlereagh's plans in their entirety, but first Russia and then Prussia raised objections. Alexander was agreeable to an independent Poland, provided he became her sovereign. Prussia, unwilling to disgorge any of the old Polish provinces, made innumerable difficulties over the Austrian frontier and insisted upon having the whole of Saxony in the bargain. The Congress fell into a deadlock, and the Swedish plenipotentiary wondered if its delegates would not "act like the Fathers of the Council of Nicaea, who settled the question of the Trinity with their fists." [19]

Only the most drastic maneuver served to resolve the dispute. Over the objections of his cabinet, Castlereagh, on January 3, 1815, entered into an alliance with France and Austria, designed to combat, by force if necessary, the designs of Russia and Prussia. Neither side admitted to the existence of the alliance, but knowledge of its signature spread with calculated rapidity. Neither Alexander nor the King of Prussia was willing to risk war in order to gain the full measure of their demands; and so, in an atmosphere of renewed cordiality, the Powers effected a compromise. A Poland smaller than originally contemplated reappeared upon the map with Alexander as her king. Prussia retained a certain portion of the old Polish provinces and got only three-quarters instead of the whole of Saxony. The final balance was not as symmetrical as the one that Castlereagh had wished to strike: Russia dipped too far into Central Europe. But with the Grand Alliance acting as a general council of Europe the Foreign Secretary hoped to preserve the fluidity of this other and imperfect equilibrium. The alliance with France and Austria had been a measure of expediency, designed to bring about a final settlement; he was ready to discard the treaty now, for he no longer wished to jeopardize the peace with such hard and fast alignments. A territorial balance together with the Concert—this struck him as the most efficient way to survive all

19. Phillips, *The Confederation of Europe,* p. 108.

the indefinable dangers of the future. No doubt for the freedom of action that such a system would allow in Latin America he was thankful as well.

Nevertheless Castlereagh made one further effort to put the padlock on his peace. Instead of renewing the limited treaty of January 3, as Metternich demanded, he proposed that the seven original signatories of the Final Act of Vienna should guarantee Europe's new frontiers against any Power that might choose to violate them. In principle his proposal met with general acquiescence. Gentz drew up a draft agreement, and the Tsar is said to have wept tears of joy when Castlereagh read it to him.[20] But the tears of Alexander were the only tangible result. No agreement could be reached over the location of the Russo-Turkish frontier to be guaranteed. The English cabinet, already appalled by Castlereagh's secret treaty with Austria and France, protested against any further extension of their responsibilities. Then Napoleon reappeared, and the proposal vanished in the resulting confusion and conflict.

Bonaparte's hundred days of liberty ended by serving the English cause well, for Wellington by the Battle of Waterloo won for Castlereagh that initiative in affairs formerly held by the Tsar. Before Russia or Austria could appear upon the field of battle Napoleon had lost his gamble, English and Prussian troops had occupied Paris, and Louis XVIII for the second time had been restored to the throne of France. Confronted with the brilliant accomplishments of British arms, Alexander could do little but acquiesce in the terms imposed upon France by Castlereagh in the second Peace of Paris.[21]

Although the destiny of Europe had now been cast, there remained the task of adapting Alexander's temperament to the complex mold. The Tsar, upon his arrival in Paris, had seemed alive with sentiments of peace and good will, and Castlereagh had succeeded in playing upon his regard for Legitimacy to secure support against the more objectionable of Prussia's demands upon

20. Castlereagh to Liverpool, February 13, 1815, Webster, *British Diplomacy*, p. 305.

21. "I not only deprived him of that character of being the *exclusive* protector of the King," Castlereagh related to Liverpool, "a relation in which, for the general politics of Europe, it is of great importance that he should not be permitted to place himself, but I have gradually brought him publicly to adopt all the principles of the other Allied Powers as his own, and to push them as far as it is at all clear they can be pushed without a dangerous reaction." See Phillips, *The Confederation of Europe*, pp. 134–135.

France. But Alexander's mind was "not completely sound," according to the Foreign Secretary. He "passed a part of every evening with Madame de Krüdener, an old fanatic"; [22] a mystical ferment was working in him; and in September, 1815, he laid bare his soul in the Holy Alliance. This "piece of sublime mysticism and nonsense," as Castlereagh called it, revealed for the first time the Tsar's real conception of a European Concert. Instead of relying upon a rational operation of the balance of power, he was proposing, essentially, to freeze the Continent in a Legitimist pattern. He was also proposing to maintain this ice age by an ill-defined directorate of the Great Powers. Such a proposition was horrifying enough to a British representative who believed in the value of gradual change. Even worse was the implied mandate, granted to the members of this alliance, to interfere in the internal affairs of the states of Europe in order to repress the manifestations of anti-Legitimist sentiment.

Castlereagh himself had been working for some time to give a sharper definition to the Treaty of Chaumont. Faced with the vague dangers of the Holy Alliance, he now devoted himself with redoubled energy to the defeat of Alexander's proposals and to the acceptance of his own. The most that he could do with the Holy Alliance, since Prussia and Austria had quickly bowed to the Tsar's wishes, was to minimize its importance and represent the document as a mere expression of principle without binding force. As for his own project, playing upon the Tsar's anxiety for some sort of Concert and deriving that support from Metternich which was to become axiomatic, he succeeded at last in having it adopted.

The second Treaty of Alliance, signed on November 20, 1815, had for its ostensible object the protection of Europe from further French aggression. Only because the object was so stated was the document accepted in England at all. But the treaty also contained what Castlereagh hoped would be an instrument for the promotion of European accord. Article VI provided for periodic reunions among the four signatories to maintain the peace of Europe. This was not much of an organization; its members arrogated no specific powers to themselves. They merely formalized the procedures of mutual consultation which had developed during the last year of the war. But the flexibility of Article VI allowed for a gradual

22. Castlereagh to Liverpool, September 28, 1815, Webster, *British Diplomacy*, p. 384; Castlereagh to Liverpool, September, 1815, Wellington, *Supplementary Despatches*, XI, 127.

elaboration and institutionalization of forms should the process of mutual consultation prove congenial.[23]

The Alliance Treaty of November 20, 1815, not only completed Castlereagh's peace structure; it set this postwar period quite apart from similar periods in the eighteenth century. The usual balance of power was present; but superimposed thereupon was this curious device which, while possessed of infinite possibilities, would cause no cataclysm if found unworkable. Also, the sphere of the balancing process had been limited to Europe—a defect in the eyes of some; but Castlereagh could not have wished otherwise. Given peace on the Continent, he relied upon British power to adjust affairs in the outer world without the assistance of his wartime allies. So anxious, in fact, did he grow to avoid a discussion of this outer world, and particularly Latin America, that he returned to their original owners many of Great Britain's colonial conquests. Such generosity, Castlereagh discovered, so startled the recipients that in the excess of their surprise they did not consider applying to America and Asia those principles of mutual consultation and responsibility which he was so busily imposing upon Europe.[24]

Castlereagh's colleagues in the cabinet were shocked not only by the surrender of colonial conquests; they disapproved of his other departures from traditional diplomatic practice. The business of regular conferences, of attempting to build gradually a system of interstate cooperation, instead of relying upon the naked facts of power—these aberrations struck them as unprofitable occupations for a British Foreign Secretary. The only consolations arose from the limited nature of the British commitment. According to Castlereagh England had assumed but two specific obligations. She had pledged herself to defend for twenty years the exact territorial dispensations of Vienna. She had also pledged herself to meet periodically in congress with her allies. She was not bound—upon this point Castlereagh was emphatic—to suppress internal disorders anywhere except in France.[25] Nor was she obligated to act, he might have added, otherwise than as her interests dictated in Latin America.

But Castlereagh was not content merely to fulfill these minimum obligations. Whatever he told the cabinet, and that was never a

23. Webster, *The Foreign Policy of Castlereagh, 1815–1822,* pp. 54–55.
24. Phillips, *The Confederation of Europe,* pp. 84, 86.
25. Harold Temperley and Lillian M. Penson, eds., *Foundations of British Foreign Policy from Pitt (1792) to Salisbury (1902)* (Cambridge, Cambridge University Press, 1938), p. 37.

great deal, he conceived as his first duty to infuse the new Alliance with cohesion and a sense of its great purpose.

It is of the utmost importance [he wrote to his minister at Naples], to keep down, as far and as long as possible, these local cabals which may shake the main Alliance—still indispensable to the safety of Europe. . . . We cannot be too susceptible in our minor relations to the hazards of the great machine of European safety.[26]

He must preserve fluidity above all else, if only by a cautious and calculating approach to the problems of the moment; for Castlereagh belonged to that select group of statesmen who believe that by doing their duty to the present, even without grandiose schemes, the future will take care of itself. As he explained himself to Charles Bagot:

. . . if a statesman were permitted to regulate his conduct by the counsels of his heart, instead of the dictates of his understanding, I really see no limits to the impulse, which might be given to his conduct, upon a case so stated. But we must always recollect that his is the grave task of providing for the peace and security of those interests immediately committed to his care; that he must not endanger the fate of the present generation in a speculative endeavour to improve the lot of that which is to come.[27]

In providing peace for his generation Castlereagh could be optimistic on at least one score. In 1815 there was no one state on the Continent sufficiently powerful to pursue its ambitions alone. His chief problem therefore lay in preventing the rise of any aggressive coalitions. The Grand Alliance obviated the need, ostensibly at least, for such arrangements; and within the Alliance Castlereagh could congratulate himself on controlling the balancing process. Austrian policy coincided with his own in its desire for peace, and Prussia, disgusted with the treatment meted out to her by Alexander at Paris, followed along tamely enough in Austria's path. France lay inert under the weight of the Allied armies of occupation; only Russia remained as a potential menace to the peace—and Russia was isolated within the Concert. Upon any crucial issue the Tsar could be outvoted three to one.

But there was always the question of how long the Tsar would

26. Castlereagh to A'Court, January 1, 1816, Nicolson, *The Congress of Vienna*, p. 253.

27. Castlereagh to Bagot, October 28, 1821, Webster, *The Foreign Policy of Castlereagh, 1815–1822*, pp. 376–377.

accept the opinions of the majority. In 1815 he appeared to be content with the great role assigned to him, emphasized as it was at every turn by Castlereagh and Metternich; and he took no steps to challenge the principles and limited scope of the Alliance. Peace and continued cooperation with his wartime partners still remained his principal preoccupations. Indeed, the process of being outvoted seemed not to disturb him at all, particularly as Castlereagh displayed an unusual talent for making the decisions of the majority appear to express the Tsar's opinions as well.[28] But the Holy Alliance stood as a symbol of Alexander's craving for a more inclusive and autocratic organization. Far more dangerous than the pursuit of purely Russian interests was the possibility that the Tsar would launch his troops across Europe in order to impose the sort of order which the more emotional side of his nature thought just. The prophet of the Apocalypse with half a million men at his back—this was the greatest obstacle to the type of international organization after which Castlereagh so anxiously sought.

The character and policy of Prince Metternich afforded a somewhat different hazard. The Austrian Chancellor was scarcely a mystic. Indeed, Metternich, seeing the Tsar in his own image, became convinced that the expressions of Christian brotherhood and monarchical solidarity embodied in the Holy Alliance merely concealed Alexander's more mundane desire to exert Russian influence in every part of Europe, particularly Germany and Italy. As time passed he grew increasingly obsessed with this notion. He already possessed Castlereagh's support for the broad outlines of his diplomacy; his policy of petty repressions (a truly unoriginal contribution to the preservation of the Austrian state) was functioning effectively; and the timid Frederick William of Prussia had become his most faithful coadjutor. Yet in his insecurity the Prince sought more permanent guarantees of the Austrian position. He begged Castlereagh to revive the old secret alliance of January, 1815, against Russia. When Castlereagh coldly replied that he disliked "measures of precautionary policy upon speculative grounds" and suggested that they postpone such action until faced with "a real and obvious danger," Metternich was assailed with doubts over the wisdom of relying upon a government which,

28. According to Professor Webster, "No one cared less than Castlereagh for that kind of prestige which is obtained by flaunting a diplomatic victory. When he had obtained his own way he was anxious that it should be accepted by other countries as their way also." See *The Foreign Policy of Castlereagh, 1815–1822*, p. 502

under different leaders, might refuse to follow in Castlereagh's footsteps.[29] In his uncertainty he turned to a re-examination of the Alliance. Was there here some alternate means of assuring Austrian security? As he studied the treaties and protocols he thought he saw a way. Instead of relying upon the thesis of limited liability advocated by Castlereagh, or the all-embracing interpretation which Alexander was beginning to assert, he fell upon the phrase "moral solidarity" as the correct interpretation of the obligations undertaken by the signatories of the Alliance. "Moral solidarity" would permit him to enjoy the support of Russia in any given contingency without exposing himself to the dubious pleasure of Russian troops marching back and forth across his master's domains. Also, "moral solidarity" would prevent Great Britain from withdrawing into complete isolation. Or so Metternich hoped. Thus supported, he could continue his "reforms" in Germany and Italy, protected from unwelcome military assistance and relieved of the necessity of giving more than moral support, should one of his partners fall upon evil days.

For seven years Castlereagh did battle with the vague and menacing benevolence of the Tsar and the "moral solidarity" of Metternich. And as long as there remained a lingering hope that the Concert might survive in its original form he showed conciliation in other directions. Even in Latin America he retarded the progress of British diplomacy in order to soothe the sensibilities of the Allied Powers. Despite earlier efforts to exclude that problem from their consideration he eventually became willing to concede to them at least a formal vote in its resolution. Outside the strictest confines of English interest there were few concessions that he was not prepared to make in order to establish a stable and enduring peace.

The struggle over the Alliance was a difficult and absorbing one. Its extension to Latin America resulted in complex and often obscure diplomatic maneuvers. It was a battle which, to be resolved in Castlereagh's favor, required not only understanding and sympathy but also converts and apostles. Yet tragically enough Castlereagh, in his red coat and jockey boots, entered the lists alone. He was temperamentally incapable of elucidating his purpose. His age had lived under the shadow of Napoleon; it had experienced the sudden and miraculous collapse of the conqueror. Now it

29. Nicolson, *The Congress of Vienna*, p. 254. See also Castlereagh to Stewart, May 24, 1817, Phillips, *The Confederation of Europe*, p. 155.

lingered on in frustrated anticipation of a better world, feeding upon the romantic bathos of the poets and playwrights, while the legend of St. Helena sprang up to dim the uglier aspects of the Emperor's reign and to suggest that, had he not fallen, surely the millennium would have arrived.

How could Castlereagh, the supreme aristocrat, with a tendency to make bad speeches, appeal to such an audience? All he could offer as an alternative was a painfully practical program of almost imperceptible progress. He made several efforts to explain.

If the Councils of the Sovereigns had not been brought together [he announced to the House of Commons], if they had been forced to look at their special interests through that cloud of prejudice and uncertainty which must always intervene when events are viewed at a distance . . . he was sure the councils of Europe would have been disturbed to such an extent by doubts and misapprehensions that those great exertions whose successful issue was now before the world, would never have been made.[30]

But who among his audience cared for "Councils of Sovereigns" or clouds of "prejudice and uncertainty" when confronted with the trappings of absolutism? Castlereagh sauntered down his singular path in a mood of increasing reticence, and Shelley, embittered by the massacre at Manchester, remarked as he saw him go:

> I met Murder on the way—
> He had a mask like Castlereagh—
> Very smooth he looked, yet grim;
> Seven blood-hounds followed him.[31]

Despite the indifference or antipathy of the masses, despite the determination of the English mercantile classes to pursue their interests in Latin America irrespective of the problem of peace, the question of how the Grand Alliance should be employed occupied the attention of most European statesmen from 1815 until 1822.[32] They gave their first, but by no means their most con-

30. Webster, *British Diplomacy*, introd., p. xliii.

31. "The Mask of Anarchy," *The Poetical Works of Percy Bysshe Shelley*, ed. Edward Dowden (London, T. Y. Crowell, 1920), p. 347. Actually, Shelley was at Leghorn at the time.

32. National self-determination was to the nineteenth-century liberal what world federation is to his twentieth-century counterpart. Castlereagh's advocacy of a European Concert therefore met with opposition from the most articulate section of public opinion.

clusive, answer in 1818. On September 27 of that year Castlereagh, together with the sovereigns and ministers of the other three Great Powers, met at Aix-la-Chapelle in fulfillment of their obligations under the Grand Alliance.

The Congress had been assembled primarily to determine the future state of France. With extraordinary harmony the Powers agreed to fund the French indemnity and to withdraw their occupation forces from the territory of the beaten foe. Other less significant problems were disposed of as well. But beneath the placid flow of agreements there stirred the turbulent question of the Alliance itself. Here was the real point at issue.

In the interval between the second Peace of Paris and the Congress of Aix-la-Chapelle the agents of the Tsar, led by General Pozzo di Borgo, his ambassador at Paris, had been acting with great vigor to exert Russian influence in western Europe. As time passed this pressure seemed to be directed specifically toward gaining an ascendancy over the Bourbon courts of France, Spain, and Naples with the object of introducing them into the Alliance as counters to the preponderating influence of the Anglo-Austrian-Prussian bloc. Whether the Tsar had actually authorized this diplomatic offensive is not clear; but at Aix he countenanced Pozzo di Borgo's attempts to bring Spain into the Concert. Only when Castlereagh, supported by Metternich, announced his unalterable opposition to such an expansion of the Alliance did the project fall to the ground. As yet Alexander remained unwilling to part with his wartime friends.[33]

Hardly had the sound and fury of this controversy died away when the issue arose in another form. The removal of the occupation forces from French territory involved the admission that France was an equal among the Great Powers, somehow to be fitted into the Concert. The difficulty was that the Alliance which had created the Concert also provided for the continued surveillance of France. The debates as to how the ex-enemy should be brought into the European directorate—without destroying the original purpose of the treaty—therefore raised in their train a discussion of the Alliance itself and the wisdom of subjecting it to revision.

Twice during the Congress Alexander attempted to resolve the dilemma according to his own lights. On the one hand, he proposed retaining the original Quadruple Alliance as a safeguard against France. On the other hand, he advocated a new and more general

33. Webster, *The Foreign Policy of Castlereagh, 1815–1822,* p. 121.

Concert consisting of all the signatories of the Final Act of Vienna, and having for its purpose the perpetual guarantee of Europe in its existing form.[34] Castlereagh took immediate exception to both propositions.

The problem of a Universal Alliance for the peace and happiness of the world [he told the Congress], has always been one of speculation and hope, but it has never yet been reduced to practice, and if an opinion may be hazarded from its difficulty, it never can. But you may in practice approach towards it, and perhaps the design has never been so far realized as in the last four years. . . .

The idea of an Alliance Solidaire, by which each state shall be bound to support the state of succession, government, and possession within all other states from violence and attack, upon receiving for itself a similar guarantee, must be understood as morally implying the previous establishment of such a system of general government as may secure and enforce upon all kings and nations an internal system of peace and justice. Till the mode of constructing such a system shall be devised, the consequence is inadmissible.[35]

As he had done earlier, so now Alexander recoiled before the strictures of the British Foreign Secretary. He still dared not or would not risk sacrificing the original Concert toward which, after all, he had made such a contribution. Instead, he accepted the simple alternative which Castlereagh proposed. This plan, while providing for the Quadruple Alliance, invited France to accede to the sixth article, which defined the nature and powers of the Concert. Article VI itself underwent a certain change in the general transformation—in part because of the natural English antipathy to the whole scheme, in part because of Castlereagh's desire to end once and for all the looseness of its definition. The treaties under which the new five-Power Concert would function were now enumerated. Reunions were no longer to be held at fixed intervals; they were to be called only upon the unanimous agreement of the five Powers.[36]

34. Castlereagh remarked that such an agreement would open up "to such a Power as Russia . . . an almost irresistible claim to march through the territories of all the Confederate States to the most distant points of Europe to fulfill her guarantee." Phillips, *The Confederation of Europe,* p. 170.

35. Memorandum by Castlereagh, October, 1818, *ibid.,* pp. 173–174.

36. "There is no doubt," Castlereagh explained, "that a breach of the Covenant by any one State is an Injury, which all other States may, if they shall think fit, either separately or collectively resent, but the Treaties [of Chaumont, Vienna, and Paris] do not impose by express stipulation, the doing so, as matter of positive obligation."

I persuade myself [Castlereagh explained to his colleagues], that it will nevertheless answer the practical end of keeping up a salutary impression of *surveillance*, of evincing to Europe that the Great Powers feel that they have not only a common interest, but a common duty, to attend to; and that when the occasion shall call for it the Cabinets of these Powers may thus be brought into contact.[37]

To Lord Bathurst he was even more expansive. "I am quite convinced," he wrote, "that past habits, common glory and these occasional meetings, displays and repledges are among the best securities Europe now has for a durable peace." [38]

No doubt the Congress of Aix-la-Chapelle justified Castlereagh's faith in this "new discovery in . . . European government." [39] On the one hand, while France and Russia had suggested the Latin American question as a matter for discussion, they had done so to extort concessions from the British in Europe rather than because they were interested in the problem itself. On the other hand, with the redefinition of the Concert not only had the prospects of European cooperation grown brighter; the chances of Latin America being discussed again had declined proportionately.

Only one question remained: had the Russians truly been won over to the policy of limiting the application of the Concert? Castlereagh seems to have thought that they had, and before leaving Aix he made one concession to their demands for an *Alliance Solidaire*. In the protocols of the Congress there appeared a declaration which expressed, in vague and apparently innocuous terms, many of the principles that Alexander had tried to force upon his allies in the form of a treaty. At the time the gesture seemed generous and inexpensive. But shortly thereafter the Tsar, who was moving with great élan from liberalism to reaction, affected to believe that the Powers had actually bound themselves to enforce these principles, and he accused Great Britain of pursuing an egoistic and exclusive policy.[40]

Temperley and Penson, eds., *Foundations of British Foreign Policy*, pp. 39–40. See also Castlereagh to Bathurst, November 5, 1818, Phillips, *The Confederation of Europe*, p. 176.

37. Castlereagh to Cabinet, November 5, 1818, Webster, *The Foreign Policy of Castlereagh, 1815–1822*, p. 160.

38. Castlereagh to Bathurst, October 3, 4, 1818, *ibid.*, p. 144.

39. Castlereagh to Liverpool, October 20, 1818, Élie Halévy, *A History of the English People, 1815–1830* (London, T. F. Unwin, 1926), p. 128.

40. Phillips, *The Confederation of Europe*, p. 200.

The Congress of Aix-la-Chapelle thus described the high-water mark of the Grand Alliance. In the years that followed the tide of European cooperation ebbed rapidly, and as it went out questions of Latin American policy assumed a larger place in the calculations of the Powers. The eternal Russo-Turkish dispute, the revolt of the Greeks, and in 1820 a military rebellion in Spain furnished the major tests of Allied solidarity. Latin America was merely the last obstacle, the hurdle before which the Concert balked and then collapsed.

It was the Spanish rebellion which revealed for the first time the extent of the rift in the Allied lute. Alexander, thwarted momentarily in his Turkish ambitions by the opposition of Castlereagh and Metternich, sought to bolster Russian prestige by suggesting an Allied intervention in Spain. At the same time he renewed his proposal for a treaty of general guarantee. Castlereagh responded with his celebrated State Paper of May 5, 1820, in which he expressly reaffirmed the agreements so carefully defined at Aix-la-Chapelle.

So long as We keep to the great and simple conservative principles of the Alliance [he announced], when the dangers therein contemplated shall be visibly realized, there is little risk of difference or of disunion amongst the Allies : All will have a common interest ; But it is far otherwise when We attempt with the Alliance to embrace subordinate, remote, and speculative cases of danger . . .[41]

The Spanish revolution he considered to be just such a "remote and speculative" case.

The principle [he concluded], of one State interfering in the internal affairs of another in order to enforce obedience to the governing authority is always a question of the greatest moral, as well as political, delicacy. . . . to generalise such a principle, to think of reducing it to a system, or to impose it as an obligation, is a scheme utterly impracticable and objectionable.[42]

Prince Metternich received Castlereagh's memorandum with unfeigned relief, for the thought of a Russian army marching through Germany and down into Spain, to the aid of Ferdinand the Well-beloved, had filled him with terror. He still disapproved of the narrow limits to which Castlereagh confined the Alliance (the Brit-

41. Temperley and Penson, eds., *Foundations of British Foreign Policy*, p. 55.
42. Nicolson, *The Congress of Vienna*, p. 267.

ish Foreign Secretary hardly mentioned the principle of "moral solidarity"). But Metternich was far more anxious at the moment to thwart the Tsar than to quarrel over the terms of an agreement which he still looked upon as the chief instrument of Austrian hegemony in Central Europe. In return for the support which Castlereagh had been extending to him in Germany and Italy he was only too happy to follow the British line in Spain. Prussia, as usual, followed suit; and once again Alexander found himself in a minority within the Concert. Once again, too, he accepted the decision of the majority. For the moment what else could he do?

The circumstances changed somewhat when a revolution in Naples forced the king there to adopt the dread Spanish Constitution of 1812. A moment of appalled silence ensued, and then the diplomatic activity resumed. The Neapolitan uprising was bound to have more serious repercussions than the Spanish rebellion, for it threatened the whole structure of Metternich's system in Italy. Moreover, its leaders, by adopting the Constitution of 1812, had violated certain Austrian treaty rights with Naples.

Castlereagh immediately agreed that Austria should act vigorously to put down the revolt. He in fact encouraged Metternich to do so.[43] But the Austrian Chancellor hesitated; his worst fears recurred. While the Austrian army hastened toward Naples might not a similar revolt occur somewhere in Germany? And might not the Tsar, using the Austrian action for his precedent, hasten to suppress the uprising, and thus fasten his influence permanently upon a portion of Central Europe? To Metternich's harried mind such a possibility represented the ultimate in catastrophes. Rather than risk the eventuality, however remote, he fell back upon his formula of "moral solidarity," and demanded that the Austrian advance against Naples receive the unanimous approbation of the Alliance. On the surface such a request seemed harmless; indeed, it wore an aspect of excessive deference. But, by thus making himself the instrument of the whole Concert, Metternich in effect hoped to forestall a similar move by Russia into Germany —unless she too became the instrument of the Concert. To such a move, of course, he would never consent.

Alexander immediately fell in with Metternich's wishes; he

43. For this act Castlereagh has been roundly abused, even by Professor Webster. The universal condemnation is, I think, unjust. The issue was not merely one of liberalism versus reaction, but also of a European Concert versus European anarchy. True to his principles, Castlereagh considered the latter issue the more important of the two, and made his decision accordingly.

merely insisted that, since Austrian intervention in Naples was to have the approval of the Concert, it should be preceded by a formal conference among the Allies. This seemed little enough to ask; but Castlereagh could not bring himself to support such a proposition. Overt approval of an act such as Austria contemplated might well result in the downfall of the Liverpool administration. Even more serious, approval would directly contradict those very principles of noninterference which, for five years, he had been so patiently urging. He could go so far as to agree to Austrian intervention in Naples on the grounds of special interest; but having rejected the principle of European intervention in Spain he could hardly condone it elsewhere. As he explained to the Austrian ambassador, the revolt must be treated "as a *special* rather than as a *general* question, as an *Italian* question rather than as an *European*, and consequently as in the sphere of action of *Austria* rather than of the Alliance." [44] According to Prince Esterhazy he was "like a great lover of music who is at Church; he wishes to applaud but he dare not." [45]

Metternich's timidity thus had placed him in the embarrassing position of having to choose between his two principal allies. In an effort at compromise he proposed that the Powers should merely signify their approval of the Austrian intervention in an informal conference. Castlereagh was agreeable; but Alexander insisted upon a full-dress meeting of the Alliance. He came to Troppau, in Austria, and over a cup of tea confided to Metternich that he had been mistaken in abiding by his liberal ideals for so long. "So we are at one, Prince," he admitted,

and it is to you that we owe it . . . you have correctly judged the state of affairs. I deplore the waste of time, which we must try to repair. I am here without any fixed ideas; without any plan; but I bring you a firm and unalterable resolution. It is for your Emperor to use it as he wills. Tell me what you desire, and what you wish me to do and I will do it.[46]

Metternich attempted to tell him what he wanted, but the Tsar still refused to consider the idea of an informal conference. Since he had turned reactionary at last he seemed bent upon advertising his conversion in the grand manner. Metternich gave in to his

44. Webster, *The Foreign Policy of Castlereagh, 1815–1822*, p. 271.
45. *Ibid.*, p. 326.
46. Phillips, *The Confederation of Europe*, p. 206.

new-found friend, and, with the British represented only by an unofficial observer, the Conference of Troppau proceeded. The three Eastern Powers—with France a reluctant fourth—signed a protocol endorsing the sentiments which Alexander had so resolutely advocated in 1818. Castlereagh publicly protested against the idea of the Allies setting themselves up as "the armed guardians of all theories" and refused to accept "the moral responsibility of administering a general European police of this description." [47] Alexander and Metternich ignored him, and eighty thousand Austrians marched upon Naples. As Stendhal remarked, "The Party of the candle-snuffers triumphs."

Another conference assembled at Laibach in January, 1821, to settle the terms of the Austrian occupation. Again Great Britain was represented unofficially, and again Castlereagh protested against the assumption of the prerogatives of the Alliance by the Eastern Powers. His protest was of no avail. The Alliance, so he sadly told Esterhazy, had "moved away from us without our having quitted it." [48]

Yet Castlereagh refused to believe that the Alliance had moved far. The ties of reaction between Russia and Austria were tenuous; they could scarcely hope to survive the antagonisms which separated the two countries in Central Europe and the Balkans. In 1820 his hands had been tied by the accession of George IV to the throne of England and by that outlandish monarch's desire to divorce his wife. Absorbed in the sordid business of her trial he had devoted too little time to foreign affairs. But by 1821 the Queen had died, the domestic crisis had passed, and Castlereagh could set himself to healing the breaches in the Alliance.

A combination of circumstances provided a favorable opportunity for the task. George IV decided to visit his Hanoverian kingdom; and Alexander began to press his grievances against Turkey. Castlereagh journeyed with his sovereign to Hanover where he found Metternich in a state of alarm over the Tsar's latest diplomatic offensive. There were conferences; both men agreed that if Alexander went on to use the Greek revolt as a means of raising the entire Eastern Question he would expose Europe to "the most awful dangers." [49] They decided to attempt once again

47. Nicolson, *The Congress of Vienna*, p. 268.
48. L. A. Lawson, *The Relation of British Policy to the Declaration of the Monroe Doctrine* (New York, Columbia University Press, 1922), p. 49.
49. Castlereagh to Sir Robert Gordon, October, 1821, Phillips, *The Confederation of Europe*, p. 222.

to thwart the Tsar by means of the Concert. The basic power pattern of the Alliance reasserted itself; and Castlereagh left Hanover in the hope that the damage of Troppau and Laibach might now be repaired.

From London he bombarded the Tsar with notes, arguing that Russia could not consistently oppose revolution in western Europe and at the same time support Greek independence in the East. His arguments, together with evidences of renewed Anglo-Austrian cordiality, appeared to take their effect. Once again Alexander restrained himself: the magic of the Concert still seemed to work a spell.[50]

But this triumph was to be followed by a final catastrophe. The Powers had decided to assemble another congress in the autumn of 1822; their agenda consisted of the Eastern Question, the Greek and Spanish revolutions, and the Spanish American colonies. Lord Castlereagh took the utmost pains to prepare himself for the test, for he hoped, by the force of his personality and the revival of his voting majority, to return the Concert to its original purpose. The time for the Congress approached; elaborate instructions materialized; final cabinet discussions ensued. Then, with appalling suddenness, Castlereagh vanished. With him, in wild disorder, went the last remnants of his dream.

50. Castlereagh to Sir Charles Bagot, December 14, 1821, *Castlereagh Papers*, XII, 445.

VI

THE DILEMMA REVIVED

IF the history of the Grand Alliance stamps Castlereagh as a statesman of the highest order, the record of his Latin American policy reveals even more clearly the transcendent nature of his genius. For while conceiving it his primary duty to endow Europe with an enduring peace, Castlereagh could never forget what England considered to be her separate and vital interests. The reconciliation of such a general purpose as peace with the insistent and often contrary demands of domestic politics is a task from which most statesmen shrink, and few emerge with credit or dignity. For Lord Castlereagh the reconciliation was made more difficult by the lack of sympathy in Great Britain for his peace program. Yet somehow he succeeded in advancing the British interest in Latin America without openly violating the conservative principles of the European Concert. To those accustomed to the somewhat less urbane methods of the twentieth century his diplomacy comes as a distinct and not unwelcome surprise.

The reconciliation of a Latin American policy with the vigorous prosecution of the war had proved a painful but, on the whole, successful affair. The termination of the contests in Europe and North America did not make any easier a repetition of that success. On the one hand, the need for a determined and clear-cut statement of British objectives had become more pressing. Castlereagh could no longer ignore the fact that with each passing day the allegiance professed by Spanish America toward Spain was decreasing in significance. Nor could he ignore the prospect of this vast mass of potential power severing its last ties with Europe and swinging into hostile hands. Admittedly the danger of French competition had temporarily subsided, and the colonists still looked upon Great Britain as their most reliable friend; but in the absence of overt British assistance the reinvigorated democracy of the United States might well attract their wavering loyalties. As a conscientious guardian of his country's interests Castlereagh could not risk the possible consequences of such a shift in the balance of power. Nor could he risk the anger of the English mercantile interests who, faced with the reviving competition of the United States and Europe, clung tenaciously to their South American markets.[1] For in the elaborate nexus of British trade lay the foundations of British power.

On the other hand, several obstacles prevented the Foreign Secretary from making that clear-cut statement of British policy which the facts of the domestic and Latin American situations suggested. While the pressure of the mercantile interests increased rapidly and the Whigs clamored with all the vehemence of a party long in opposition for governmental support of the colonists, neither group appreciated the real risks that such an isolated course would involve. Perhaps it is true, as the Whigs maintained, that Castlereagh was temperamentally incapable of condoning liberty. But whatever his private sentiments (and they were never quite so reactionary as his liberal detractors would have us believe) they rarely interfered with the execution of what he considered to be a truly national policy.[2] As shall appear, he had no real objection to Latin American independence, providing independence was equated with stability, was characterized by a strong pro-British orientation, and did not conflict with his European commitments. In this last proviso lay the nub of his difficulty.

As a part of his peace structure Castlereagh had included a treaty of alliance with Spain, signed in July, 1814. To seal the bargain Spain had extracted from him a promise not to extend aid or comfort to the Latin American insurgents. For her part she had agreed to concede to Great Britain a share in the colonial trade—should the economic monopoly ever be abolished.[3] The English pledge, admittedly, had as little practical significance as Ferdinand's assertion of all his ancient rights over the colonies; but a real danger lay elsewhere. Thwarted by Great Britain in every effort to exercise those rights Ferdinand might take his grievance to the Grand Alliance.

Now Castlereagh had gone to a great deal of trouble, and some expense, to avoid a discussion of non-European matters with his allies, and the Alliance Treaty of November 20, 1815, specifically

1. Halévy, *A History of the English People, 1815–1830,* p. 6.
2. For his views on the liberal movement see Castlereagh to Bentinck, May 7, 1814, Webster, *British Diplomacy,* p. 181.
3. Charles K. Webster, "Castlereagh and the Spanish Colonies," *Eng. Hist. Rev.,* XXVII (1912), 80.

mentioned Europe as the area of their competency. But no specific rule prevented them from examining transatlantic questions in the future; indeed, they could argue with some plausibility that the disposition of the Spanish colonies intimately affected the interests of Europe. If under the circumstances Great Britain should encourage the insurgents in South America and Ferdinand should appeal to the Legitimist prejudices of his brother sovereigns, how would Castlereagh justify his country's conduct? By flouting his own creation, by rejecting the advice and assistance of the Alliance? Hardly, since his principal preoccupation as Foreign Secretary was to enhance that body's prestige. Clearly, whatever policy he devised must be based upon such principles that Ferdinand would take no offense, or, in taking offense, would find little balm for his sensibilities within the precincts of the Alliance.

Faced with these problems—with the task of reconciling so many demands, antagonisms, and ideals—Castlereagh resorted to a defensive strategy. For three years he did almost nothing except to conceal his inactivity behind clouds of notes, insinuations, and tactical sorties. It was a masterly display of busy procrastination.

The situation in Latin America aided him immeasurably. The cause of the colonists was not progressing brilliantly. Spain had recovered a semblance of her authority in Chile and Colombia, Peru still remained loyal, and Buenos Aires was rent by internal faction.[4] As a result the insurgents, becoming increasingly desirous of British friendship, welcomed gestures where, if more successful, they would have demanded deeds.

The diplomacy of Spain proved equally helpful. Had she immediately taken her quarrel with the colonists to the Alliance or had she insisted publicly upon the cessation of British trade, Castlereagh might have surrendered his ambiguous positions. But as long as there remained a faint hope of success by other means, boldness was banished from Spanish plans.

Now hope is a commendable emotion, but in the breast of Ferdinand the Well-beloved it was to have the most disastrous results. For as the hope of ultimate victory increased, so too did the fear that the prize would slip from his hands. Driven forward by the prospect of regaining complete control over his dominions, thwarted by his inability to do so alone, and tormented by the thought that

4. Dexter Perkins, *The Monroe Doctrine, 1823–1826* (Cambridge, Harvard University Press, 1927), p. 42.

another Power might intervene in a hostile sense, Ferdinand turned blindly to Great Britain for assistance. In so doing he played directly into Castlereagh's hands.

The first Spanish overture appeared in November, 1815. Ostensibly it offered Great Britain special privileges within the Latin American market should she succeed, by mediation, in re-establishing Ferdinand's authority over the colonies. Actually the note invited the use of English force toward that end.[5] On December 20 Castlereagh rejected the overture. As a disinterested Power Great Britain must not favor either side in the dispute. Nor could she accept special privileges from either party. Her duty was to follow the neutral course which she had defined for herself in 1810. Pointing out that he had never requested special commercial privileges, Castlereagh went on at last to offer British mediation upon the terms which he had already twice advanced in 1812.[6]

Although acceptance of those terms would have resulted in a settlement entirely satisfactory to British interests, Castlereagh must have known beforehand that Spain would not accord them a favorable reception.[7] Why then did he make the gesture? Seemingly he accomplished several purposes thereby. He indicated to the colonists the interest with which Great Britain continued to view their cause. He revealed to the world at large the reasonable nature of the English position. And although Spain quickly rejected the terms, he left the United States puzzled as to the exact nature of his intentions.

This last result was, of course, one to which Castlereagh attached a particular importance. He was determined, on the one hand, to remove as many as possible of those irritations which had contributed to the War of 1812: this strategy was as much a part of his general peace policy as the Concert of Europe. He was equally determined, on the other hand, to prevent the substitution of American influence for that of Great Britain in the Spanish colonies. Despite its rejection by Spain, the offer of mediation suggested to the representatives of the United States that an aggressive bid for Latin American friendship would bring them into collision not only with Great Britain but with the entire European

5. Vaughan to Castlereagh, November 16, 1815, Webster, "Castlereagh and the Spanish Colonies," Eng. Hist. Rev., pp. 80–81.

6. Castlereagh to Vaughan, December 20, 1815, Webster, Britain and the Independence of Latin America, II, 346.

7. Webster, "Castlereagh and the Spanish Colonies," Eng. Hist. Rev., pp. 89–90.

Concert.[8] Castlereagh spared no effort to make the impression a lasting one.

To a certain extent he was aided in this object by John Quincy Adams, the American minister in London. Despite a diplomatic experience unparalleled in the annals of United States foreign relations—Adams had represented his country at the Hague, in Berlin and St. Petersburg, and at Ghent—despite an extraordinary perceptiveness and a tactical skill equal to that of Castlereagh, the American was subject to a strong emotional bias. He did not, he positively could not, like the British. His dislike extended itself particularly to British statesmen. After meeting with Castlereagh he judged the latter's deportment as "sufficiently graceful" and his person as "handsome." His manner, however, "was cold, but not absolutely repulsive." [9] In time Adams became convinced that Castlereagh was snubbing him. Taking note of a letter received from the Foreign Office by Count Fernan-Nuñez he remarked acidly: "I expected some such answer as this, and remark in it, principally, the politeness and complacency of the manner, which is in a style very different, when addressed to the Spanish Ambassador from what it is in similar cases when addressed to me." [10]

Encumbered with such dislikes and suspicions, Adams had some difficulty in arriving at a correct estimate of Castlereagh's policy. He sensed that England wished to keep Spain impotent; but at the same time he suspected that she wished to suppress the colonial insurrections. The apparent irreconcilability of these objects only persuaded him further of the subterranean nature of British motives.[11] When early in 1816 the rumor circulated that Spain had ceded the Floridas to England, his impression of duplicity gained ground. He went for an interview with Castlereagh and bluntly inquired about the rumor.

You will find nothing little or shabby in our policy [Castlereagh told him]. We have no desire to add an inch of ground to our territories in any part of the world. We have as much as we know how to manage

8. *Ibid.*

9. Charles Francis Adams, ed., *Memoirs of John Quincy Adams* (12 vols., Philadelphia, J. B. Lippincott, 1874–77), III, 205.

10. *Ibid.,* p. 421.

11. Adams to Monroe, January 22, 1816, Ford, *Writings of John Quincy Adams,* V, 488–489.

. . . Do you only observe the same moderation. If we should find you hereafter pursuing a system of encroachment upon your neighbors, what we might do defensively is another consideration.[12]

Such an assurance, followed as it was by an implied threat, did little to dispose of Adams' misconceptions about the objectives of British policy. What could he think, after all, when at one moment an Order in Council prohibited the export of arms and ammunition to the insurgents, while at another Lord Castlereagh announced that the government "were taking all measures in their power to increase the commerce with South America . . . "?[13] Although the Foreign Secretary preserved his invariable urbanity and showed in a remarkable number of instances an unusual susceptibility for purely American interests, his circumspection in regard to Latin America, his declared willingness to mediate the dispute, and his veiled warnings—these things drove Adams to the conclusion "that any extraordinary interest shown on the part of the United States towards the South Americans would unavoidably indispose in the same degree the British Government against them."[14]

This, of course, was exactly the conclusion that Castlereagh wished Adams to reach. The year was now 1816. Spain, so far, had been frustrated; the United States lay paralyzed; yet England's position of ostensible neutrality rested upon such fair and logical grounds as to avoid the reproaches of the Allies. It was an exceedingly pleasant state of affairs. What was more, it gave the colonists the time needed to reorganize their forces against Spain. With a diplomatic stalemate in Europe and North America, who could doubt what their ultimate destiny and predilections would be?

But the best of both worlds could not be enjoyed forever. A dim consciousness of the policy being pursued by Great Britain was dawning in Madrid, and in October, 1816, Spain made a determined effort to break the stalemate. Count Fernan-Nuñez once again sounded Castlereagh on the possibility of British mediation, cautiously avoiding all mention of the usual terms as he did so.[15]

12. Adams, *Memoirs of John Quincy Adams,* III, 290–291.

13. Entry of March 11, 1816, *ibid.,* III, 308; Adams to Monroe, April 30, 1816, Ford, *Writings of John Quincy Adams,* VI, 21.

14. Conversation with Mr. Del Real, May 7, 1816, Adams, *Memoirs of John Quincy Adams,* III, 353.

15. Conde de Fernan-Nuñez to Castlereagh, October 17, 1816, Webster, *Britain and the Independence of Latin America,* II, 348.

Castlereagh with equal care avoided any reply whatsoever on the grounds, as he told Sir Henry Wellesley, that

the Court of Madrid wishes to drive the British Government into a peremptory negative, and upon that refusal to found some change either in the system of its political relations in Europe with a view of procuring support against their revolted colonies, or in their South American policy, finding the other hopeless in point of success.[16]

Silence, while only a temporary expedient, avoided driving Spain to either extreme; moreover it served to gain time. For Ferdinand lingered on under the impression that silence might after all give consent; while the possessive manner with which the United States was treating the Floridas inspired a growing sense of helplessness and dependence. Fernan-Nuñez returned to the charge again in January, 1817, offering to institute a more liberal colonial policy in return for what he euphemistically referred to as armed British mediation.[17]

This time there could be no evasions. Castlereagh retorted with a reaffirmation of the cardinal points of English policy: abolition of the monopoly system and a refusal to aid Spain with force. In so doing he ended whatever hopes Spain had entertained of finding sympathy in England. He also complicated the process of procrastination. But he could hardly complain. Almost two years had elapsed; British trade with Latin America was increasing; and the colonists were once again resurgent. The Republic of La Plata had declared its independence, Colombia was in full revolt, and San Martin was toiling across the Andes to liberate Chile. Time was upon Castlereagh's side.[18]

Even Ferdinand the Well-beloved had come to this conclusion and before Fernan-Nuñez met with the final rebuff he began to intrigue with the Russian ambassador in Madrid, in an effort to obtain the assistance which England denied to him. The intrigue as such signified little. The plans that developed involved giving Russian naval support to a Spanish expedition against South America in return for the cession of the island of Minorca. The whole project lacked the official sanction of the Tsar and was based upon the strange assumption that the battered Russian fleet

16. Castlereagh to Sir Henry Wellesley, December 20, 1816, Webster, "Castlereagh and the Spanish Colonies," *Eng. Hist. Rev.,* p. 83.
17. *Ibid.*
18. *Ibid.;* Perkins, *The Monroe Doctrine, 1823–1826,* p. 42.

could materially change the fortunes of Spain. What mattered was that the intrigue suggested a willingness on the part of Russia to undermine her Allies' interests, and it heralded the approach of that moment when the colonial question would come before the Concert.[19]

To Castlereagh, therefore, the project possessed an importance out of all proportion to its immediate significance. He promptly wrote to the Tsar and warned that an action such as the one contemplated in Madrid might bring about the collapse of the Concert. Since Alexander still set great store by the Grand Alliance he responded generously to Castlereagh's note and ordered Tatistchev, his ambassador, to put an end to the plotting. When Ferdinand himself responded to this rebuff by suggesting a Russo-Spanish attack upon Portugal, the Tsar in horror agreed to sell a portion of his fleet—on the condition that Ferdinand discard this last mad design. The bargain was struck; eventually the Russian ships arrived in Spain. There was much pomp and ceremony, and then the vessels were discovered to be unseaworthy.[20]

Despite this contretemps Ferdinand continued his restless search for aid. In the spring of 1817 he received a measure of encouragement from Pozzo di Borgo, the Tsar's ambassador in Paris, who urged him to present his case to the Allied Conference of Ambassadors which was meeting in Paris to supervise the occupation of France. Pozzo himself had no particular interest in contributing to the solution of the Spanish American question. His motives were less exalted. He had become thoroughly tired of being outvoted by the Austro-British combination within the Alliance; he was anxious to end his isolation; he wished to start a dispute inside the Conference of Ambassadors and perhaps drive a wedge between Castlereagh and Metternich. His tactics almost succeeded.

On July 2, 1817, the plot was sprung when Count Fernan-Nuñez, brought over especially from London, stated the Spanish case before the assembled ambassadors. His appeals to the principle of Legitimacy, and the grim picture which he evoked of the terrors of revolution, caused a sympathetic stirring among his audience. Although the Austrian and Prussian envoys lacked instructions, they joined in according the Spanish plea a favorable reception. Only Sir Charles Stuart, the British ambassador, re-

19. Vaughan to Castlereagh, November 28, 1816, Webster, "Castlereagh and the Spanish Colonies," *Eng. Hist. Rev.*, p. 85.
20. Webster, *The Foreign Policy of Castlereagh, 1815–1822*, pp. 93–95.

fused to be stampeded into approval. He insisted on postponing
any further discussion of the subject until he had consulted with
his government. In vain Fernan-Nuñez, supported by Pozzo,
stormed and argued; Sir Charles stood firm.[21]

His attitude met with instantaneous approval at the Foreign Office. Castlereagh realized that he could not procrastinate forever;
the Tatistchev intrigue had already afforded him an ominous insight into the future. He could no longer expect to retain the colonial question indefinitely as a matter of private discussion between
Great Britain and Spain on the one hand and Great Britain and
the United States on the other. Eventually, upon the stubborn
insistence of Ferdinand, the whole subject was going to reach a
broader audience. And in reaching that audience it was bound
to be discussed, at least by Russia, in a sense contrary to British
interests. Under these circumstances, and at the very least, Castlereagh was determined to postpone a general examination of the
question as long as possible. And when he could wait no longer,
he was equally determined to have the examination conducted on
premises of his own choosing.

If the plot in Paris did not provide him with the opportunity
to select those premises, neither did it necessitate any thought of
retreat. The whole business had been too hastily conceived to
breach the British defenses. Instead of discussing the substance
of the question Castlereagh therefore attacked the fashion in which
it had been broached.

I cannot too strongly represent to you [he informed Sir Charles
Stuart] the importance of making the Spanish and all other Governments feel that the allied ministers are limited in their functions to the
execution of the late treaties and to such special duties as their courts
may think fit to impose upon them, but that it neither appertains to
them to originate discussions on other subjects, nor to become a channel of general reference to their courts upon subjects foreign to their
immediate duties . . .[22]

Metternich likewise received a communication upon the folly
of the Russians and Spaniards, together with a suggestion that
the Austrian envoy in Paris be instructed to mend his manners.
Castlereagh's efforts met with immediate and heart-warming suc-

21. Webster, "Castlereagh and the Spanish Colonies," *Eng. Hist. Rev.,* pp. 85–86.
22. Castlereagh to Sir Charles Stuart, August 21, 1817, *ibid.,* p. 86 n.

cess. Sir Charles Stuart rested grimly upon his original refusal to consider the Spanish project; the Austrian ambassador, upon being prompted from Vienna, joined him; his Prussian colleague followed suit; and Pozzo di Borgo once more found himself in a minority of one. As a consequence Fernan-Nuñez and his proposal quickly dropped from view.

But Castlereagh was not content with this triumph, complete though it proved to be. He had resented the secret agitations of the Tsar's agents, and he now decided to make a sortie of his own —to state the British case on the colonial dispute openly, and force Russia to emerge from behind her screen of intrigue. On August 20, 1817, he circulated among the Powers an elaborate summation of his position. The patent inability of Ferdinand by his own exertions to recover his authority over the colonies was discussed with obvious relish; the general logic and specific purposes of the British mediation offer were reviewed. Finally, Castlereagh expressed a willingness to share the burden of settling the dispute with his Allies—providing, of course, the British terms served as the basis of their intervention.[23]

Austria responded admirably to the memorandum. "Prince Metternich is of the opinion that the Mediation should be ostensibly" undertaken by the Alliance, Castlereagh learned, "but conducted in fact by Great Britain as their organ and upon such terms as she wishes to propose . . ."[24] Prussia expressed similarly flattering sentiments. Even the pariah, France, admitted "that the extensive Colonial relations of Great Britain must give a weight to the interference of that Court, which neither France nor any other Power can in the present situation of the world pretend to assume . . ."[25]

Only Russia appeared to challenge the English position. In a vague and wordy countermemorandum she suggested that instead of force some sort of commercial coercion be used to bring the colonists back to their original allegiance.[26] Spain herself, to whom Castlereagh had sent a special exposition of the British case (together with a threat of counteraction should she continue her secret plotting), replied by making known her complete unwillingness to accept any of the British conditions.[27]

23. Foreign Office Confidential Memorandum, August 20, 1817, Webster, *Britain and the Independence of Latin America*, II, 353–357.

24. Gordon to Castlereagh, October 2, 1817, *ibid.*, p. 4.

25. Stuart to Castlereagh, September 8, 1817, *ibid.*, p. 94.

26. Russian Memorandum of November 29, 1817, Webster, "Castlereagh and the Spanish Colonies," *Eng. Hist. Rev.*, pp. 88–89.

27. Sir Henry Wellesley to Castlereagh, October 5, 1817, *ibid.*, p. 88.

In one respect Castlereagh's sortie had proved eminently successful. Russia had been forced to make an open statement regarding Latin America; hereafter her agents would encounter difficulties in ascending the winding stairs of the Escorial to intrigue in the dim and scented apartments of Ferdinand. The Concert with all its elaborate diplomatic formalities was now the forum to which Russian views must be brought; and the Concert—or at least the majority of its members—presently favored the British program. The stalemate, the precious stalemate, would thus continue. Only one flaw showed: the danger existed that, with the Concert paralyzed, the United States might attempt to exert its own influence in Latin America.

This danger had been haunting Castlereagh for quite some time. During the first week of June, 1817, he had in fact gone to great lengths to dispel from the mind of Adams any suspicion that Great Britain or her Allies had relaxed their efforts to solve the troublesome dispute.[28] In response to queries from the American minister he continued to hold forth the possibility of a mutually cooperative and congenial solution, while promising with irritating condescension to see that the United States was treated upon a basis of equality with the Powers of Europe in any prospective markets. When Adams returned to the United States in the summer of 1817 to assume the duties of Secretary of State in President Monroe's cabinet, Castlereagh pursued him with an offer of British mediation in the Spanish-American quarrel over the Floridas, and implied once again that a final settlement of the colonial affair was about to be undertaken.[29]

The cloud of insinuations contrived to win for the Foreign Secretary another respite from the United States. Although Adams and President Monroe quickly rejected British intervention in the Floridas question, they took pause at this sudden display of concern for Spanish interests.[30] In April, 1818, Charles Bagot, the British minister in Washington, reported jubilantly upon their reluctance to recognize any of the insurgent Latin American states.[31]

28. Entries of June 1, June 7, 1817, Adams, *Memoirs of John Quincy Adams,* III, 551, 561.

29. Castlereagh to Bagot, November 10, 1817, Webster, *Britain and the Independence of Latin America,* II, 489. For Castlereagh's intent regarding the proffered mediation between the United States and Spain see Castlereagh to Bathurst, October 31, 1817, *H.M.C., Report on the Manuscripts of Earl Bathurst,* p. 441.

30. Entry of March 30, 1818, Adams, *Memoirs of John Quincy Adams,* IV, 72.

31. Bagot to Castlereagh, April 7, 1818, Webster, "Castlereagh and the Spanish Colonies," *Eng. Hist. Rev.,* pp. 93–94 n.

This was comforting news indeed, since the principal threat to British prestige in Latin America would probably result from the prior recognition of the insurgents by another Power. But Adams, with his diamond hardness, was hardly likely to remain paralyzed forever in the face of mere insinuations. As time passed he grew stronger in the conviction that all was not as well within the Concert as Castlereagh implied. The Foreign Secretary had promised to keep him informed about the progress of the impending settlement, yet Bagot, in response to his repeated queries upon the subject, danced back and forth in an agitated and embarrassed silence.[32] From other sources Adams learned of the British memorandum of August 28, 1817, and of the querulous Russian reply. Sensing that the United States might soon act without risking the united displeasure of Europe, he carefully began to scout the diplomatic terrain. At the instigation of President Monroe he suggested to his minister in London that the moment was not far distant when the United States and Great Britain might cooperate with great profit to regulate the destiny of Latin America.[33] Having let fall this interesting proposition, he went on to instruct his representatives in Paris and St. Petersburg, as well as in London, to hint at the possibility of unilateral recognition by the United States.[34]

Adams was now thoroughly on the alert, but in so testing the sentiment of the Concert he tended to overplay his hand; for, as the American ministers scattered their hints, a faint frightened shudder coursed through the chancelleries of Europe, and the Great Powers reacted by drawing together to meet the projected menace. Even Castlereagh, learning of the contemplated recognition, became convinced of the necessity to hazard a more speculative and positive course. He foresaw that he must shift the incidence of his policy and strive to win unanimous Allied acceptance of the British position in the Latin American controversy. If he was to prevent the Concert from scurrying panic-stricken to the aid of Spain, if he was to erect a more formidable obstacle to the implied aims of the United States, he must assume the offensive at last.

In embarking upon a positive policy Castlereagh could draw

32. Entry of June 25, 1818, Adams, *Memoirs of John Quincy Adams*, IV, 103.
33. Bagot to Castlereagh, June 29, 1818, *Castlereagh Papers*, XI, 458.
34. Adams to G. W. Campbell, June 28, 1818, Ford, *Writings of John Quincy Adams*, VI, 378–379.

both encouragement and inspiration from the curious fate that was overtaking Spain and Portugal in their tedious conflict over the Banda Oriental. Since 1815 Artigas, the revolutionary leader, had ruled undisturbed over the Banda; and since 1815 Don John, the Portuguese Prince Regent, had been seeking ways of ousting him and attaching the coveted territory to Brazil. The departure of Lord Strangford from Rio de Janeiro afforded Don John the spiritual comfort of being allowed to formulate his own ideas; the release of thousands of well-trained Portuguese troops from Wellington's army and their transportation to Brazil provided him with the means of implementing his views.[35]

Despite the radical views of Artigas—he believed strongly in democracy—it was not easy to conceive of him as a threat to Brazil. But when the Provinces of La Plata proclaimed their independence at Tucuman in the summer of 1816, Don John, by an extraordinarily free association of ideas, decided to protect his frontiers against the radicalism of his tiny neighbor. Late in 1816 Portuguese troops returned to the Banda Oriental, and on January 20, 1817, Montevideo fell before their onslaughts. Buenos Aires, occupied with its own internal difficulties, was powerless to intervene and accepted the *fait accompli* with temporary good grace. But Spain greeted the news of the Portuguese coup with a mixture of frustration and blind rage. Completely incapable of exercising her sovereignty over the Banda, she nevertheless clung to all her prerogatives with a fanatical zeal. The Spanish minister in Rio de Janeiro protested to Don John with angry vehemence. In Madrid Ferdinand the Well-beloved fumed impotently and then in the spring of 1817 took his wounded pride to the Grand Alliance.

There were, apart from Ferdinand's own feelings, several reasons why the Concert should consider the question of the Banda. To begin with, Spain was both willing and able to attack Portugal in retaliation for Don John's seizure of the Banda. The original quarrel thus had a definite interest for Europe. Secondly, Great Britain, by reason of her guarantee of the integrity of Portugal, was liable to be drawn into the dispute as a belligerent. What was perhaps most important, the threat to the peace clearly outweighed any special interest that Great Britain might have in the fate of the Banda. Castlereagh was therefore willing to allow the Allies to attempt a general mediation.

35. Manchester, *British Preëminence in Brazil,* p. 138.

The Concert as a whole undertook the task in March, 1817; but it was Castlereagh who regulated the sequence of events from a decorous position just off stage. He had no way of dictating the course of Spanish policy; that dubious distinction was shared by Ferdinand and an extremely frivolous providence. But upon Portuguese policy he could and did exert a direct and decisive influence. Don John soon learned to his dismay that in the absence of a satisfactory explanation of his conduct in the Banda the British guarantee of Portugal would be abrogated. Shortly thereafter Castlereagh turned the thumbscrews a trifle tighter. Don John was informed that he might lose the aid of his British advisers and officers in both Portugal and Brazil. Then with the pressure at its height Castlereagh offered an avenue of escape. Don John must dispatch full powers of negotiation to an envoy in Europe; in regard to the Banda Oriental he must depend entirely upon the advice and guidance of his friends.[36]

Thoroughly cowed by the British tactics Don John acceded hastily to the British suggestions. Castlereagh thus kept the guarantee, which had its uses, and at the same time assured himself of full control over the Portuguese side of the Banda negotiations. He needed nothing more.

A year passed. In May, 1818, the Allied Conference in its collective wisdom, and with much blunt prompting from the Duke of Wellington, announced its solution to the dispute. The restoration of Artigas had never received the slightest consideration. Instead, the Portuguese were to continue their occupation of the Banda until replaced by Spanish troops; Don John was then to receive a monetary recompense for his troubles.[37]

The envoy of Don John, with Castlereagh looming in the background, accepted the Concert's terms. But much to the disgust of the Continental Powers Spain refused even to consider them. She had received no material aid from the Allies; she could not recruit sufficient loyal troops to garrison the Banda. She therefore preferred to leave Don John upon the ground (without however admitting his right to remain there) rather than to risk the return of Artigas and his revolutionaries or a new invasion by Buenos Aires. The negotiations continued futilely into 1819, causing the Duke of Wellington to lose all faith in the Alliance as an instrument of mediation. Eventually they resulted in Don John staying

36. *Ibid.*, pp. 142–143.
37. *Ibid.*, p. 146. See also Wellington, *Supplementary Despatches,* XII, 587.

with approval where he had entered with such disfavor—ensconced securely in the Banda Oriental.[38]

The chief importance of this affair to Lord Castlereagh during the spring of 1818 lay in the fact that it finally opened the eyes of his Allies not only to the extent of Spain's presumptions but also to the difficulty of coming to any arrangement whatsoever with her. Where previously he had dreaded their intervention, he now saw ways in which collaboration could be made useful. The Allies, with the Banda experience and the intransigeance of Spain fresh in their minds, would be the more liable to see the merit of his old proposals for the settlement of the whole Latin American dispute. If they went further and actually accepted these proposals —as Castlereagh hoped they would—several beneficial results could follow. The Allies themselves would be committed to support the British position in the dispute. Either Spain would assent to their mediation—at most a very doubtful proposition—or she would reject it, leaving the situation no worse than before. In either instance the colonists would be left with the impression that Great Britain had striven to assist them. And the United States, faced with the closed ranks of the Concert, might be discouraged from acting independently. The stalemate, so favorable to British interests, would thus continue while the Latin Americans worked out their own salvation.[39]

In striving for these results it was imperative that Great Britain should appear disinterested. Here, as elsewhere, Castlereagh wished to avoid the impression of forcing his views upon the Concert. He therefore waited cautiously until the unraveling of events should make his change of tactics appear natural and unobjectionable.

As matters fell out, he had not long to wait. The spring of 1818 found the Allied Powers preparing to meet in congress at Aix-la-Chapelle. Spring also found Spain reduced to a state of terror by the veiled insinuations of the United States. In March Ferdinand appealed to England to prevent the ultimate catastrophe of American recognition—an appeal which Castlereagh sternly rebuffed.[40] In June the Spanish monarch retreated a step and requested the mediation of the Concert upon terms vaguely similar to those so

38. Webster, *Britain and the Independence of Latin America,* I, introd., 68–69; Manchester, *British Preëminence in Brazil,* pp. 147–149.

39. For evidence of this attitude see Castlereagh to Bathurst, October 26, 1816, *Castlereagh Papers,* XI, 308–309.

40. Castlereagh to Sir Henry Wellesley, March 27, 1818, Webster, "Castlereagh and the Spanish Colonies," *Eng. Hist. Rev.,* p. 91 n.

often laid down by Great Britain. This time, sensing an opening for his own scheme, Castlereagh equivocated. He put Spain off with the demand for a more precise statement of her proposed concessions; and then in interviews with Richard Rush, the American minister in London, and in letters to Charles Bagot, he boldly informed the United States that negotiations for a final mediation had gotten under way. When Castlereagh embarked for the Continent once more, he felt reasonably confident that his remarks would afford Adams a temporary pause.[41]

At Aix-la-Chapelle the Foreign Secretary scored his greatest diplomatic triumphs. Not only did he obtain a redefinition of the Grand Alliance; he induced the entire Concert to accept the British mediation plan for Latin America. The labor was a difficult but rewarding one. He had first to defeat the attempt, made by Ferdinand and supported by Russia, to introduce Spain into the Congress. After he had surmounted this obstacle he had to make palatable to all the Allies the logic upon which since 1810 Great Britain had based her Latin American policy.

He broached the subject with characteristic caution toward the end of October. His suggestions ignored the practical consideration that Great Britain alone possessed the power to enforce any Allied decision, and concentrated on the technical difficulties involved in five-power mediation. These turned out to be enormous. In order to preserve the unanimity of the Concert, prior agreement on terms first would have to be reached. Then, in order to give the intervention of the Alliance its deserved weight, one man would have to be selected to act as its agent. Nevertheless, the first difficulty could be overcome if the Allies would accept the British terms; and that unique individual, the Duke of Wellington, might conceivably serve as the mediator.

At first Castlereagh's suggestions did not evoke a response; the other Powers were too concerned with the intricacies of French reparations. Indeed, Spain, now excluded from the Congress, let it be known that she would accept no limitation on her freedom

41. Richard Rush, *A Residence at the Court of London* (London, R. Bentley, 1833), pp. 273–274, 295–298. Rush to Adams, July 25, 1818, W. R. Manning, ed., *Diplomatic Correspondence of the United States Concerning the Independence of the Latin-American Nations* (3 vols., New York, Carnegie Endowment for International Peace, Oxford University Press, 1925), III, 1444. Castlereagh to Bagot, August 8, 1818, Webster, *Britain and the Independence of Latin America*, II, 491.

of action, and Castlereagh half expected to see the whole matter dropped.[42]

But in November the Russians, together with the newest member of the Concert, France, became alarmed over the possibility that the United States, allied with the Latin American insurgents, might attempt to reintroduce Jacobin principles into Europe. In order to forestall such a disaster, they brought out a series of proposals which left Spain the hope that force might yet be employed to further her cause.[43]

The care with which Castlereagh had constructed his peace treaties now justified itself at last; his answer to the Franco-Russian proposition stemmed from an irrefutable logic. With sudden and extreme bluntness he pointed out that only Great Britain could provide the force necessary to aid Spain, and he castigated Russia for counteracting English influence in Madrid "without substituting anything in its room but false hopes, which must end in final disappointment, after a serious loss of valuable time." From this point he proceeded to emphasize the moral principle which forbade the Alliance to intervene in the internal affairs of another state. The Powers, he announced flatly, "were not entitled to arbitrate or to judge between His Christian Majesty and his subjects, and as a consequence not competent to enforce any judgment directly or indirectly; that we could only mediate or facilitate but not compel or menace . . ." [44]

The Russian and French plenipotentiaries receded slightly from their original position in the face of this blast. They suggested substituting a commercial boycott for force as a means of coercing the colonists. Castlereagh only manifested disgust over their patent unwillingness to face the facts of the case and resorted to the extremity of a personal interview with the Tsar. The appearance of unanimity within the Concert still outweighed all other considerations with Alexander, and rather than alienate Great Britain he bowed to Castlereagh's arguments. Spain found herself confronted at long last with an entirely unsympathetic audi-

42. Castlereagh to Bathurst, November 2, 1818, Webster, *Britain and the Independence of Latin America,* II, 58–62.

43. Whitaker, *The United States and the Independence of Latin America,* p. 260; Charles K. Webster, "Castlereagh and the Spanish Colonies," *Eng. Hist. Rev.,* XXX (1915), 637.

44. Castlereagh to Bathurst, November 24, 1818, Webster, "Castlereagh and the Spanish Colonies," *Eng. Hist. Rev.,* pp. 634–635.

ence. The Foreign Secretary could now write to Lord Liverpool that "we have taken up our ground upon principles so fair in themselves, yet so repugnant to all the past prejudices of Spain, that either we get rid of the negotiation *in limine*, or we bring Spain to occupy our ground." [45]

To bring Spain "to occupy our ground" was, of course, an impossible task. Sir Henry Wellesley, still marooned in Madrid, refused even to make the effort. He planned to take no initiative himself and, should Spain approach him for aid, he proposed merely to recite the terms of mediation agreed upon by the Alliance.[46] The Tsar was more sanguine. He ordered his ambassador to press upon Ferdinand the advantages of accepting the mediation of the Concert. As a result Tatistchev fell into disgrace and in 1819 bade farewell to Madrid. Ferdinand refused to listen even to the advice of his confessor and resumed preparations for a giant expedition against Spanish America. On their part, the Continental Powers came to understand the impossibility of doing regular business with Spain, and there were no further reports from Madrid of foreign intrigues against Great Britain.

As far as Latin America was concerned, the fruits of the Congress of Aix-la-Chapelle could be counted as rich and plentiful. The Alliance, by accepting the British terms of mediation, had temporarily neutralized itself. The insurgents had gained more time to complete their work; they had also been treated to an edifying example of British influence subtly at work in their behalf.[47]

Nevertheless, Castlereagh had decreased his own liberty of action by admitting the right of the Concert to participate in any prospective mediation. For the Concert, while disgusted with Ferdinand and no longer willing to extend aid to him, was equally reluctant to see Great Britain encourage the forces of revolution—even in South America. Since Castlereagh had made the colonial

45. Castlereagh to Liverpool, November 26, 1818, *Castlereagh Papers,* XII, 90.

46. Sir Henry Wellesley to Castlereagh, February 4, 1819, Webster, *Britain and the Independence of Latin America,* II, 375. "I am assured," Wellesley maintained, "that M. de Lozano de Torres, who is now the King's principal adviser, is ignorant even of the geographical positions of the countries which form the principal objects of the negotiations with Portugal and the United States, and it may be doubted if the King himself is much better informed upon the subject." Webster, *The Foreign Policy of Castlereagh, 1815–1822,* p. 227.

47. So pleased was Lord Liverpool that he began to advocate recognition of the insurgent states. See Liverpool to Castlereagh, November 9, 1818, Wellington, *Supplementary Despatches,* XII, 823,

question one of general consideration, the spirit of the Alliance required that he do nothing thereafter without first consulting and obtaining the assent of the Powers. As a result he was reduced to inching his policy forward, moving quietly and circumspectly so as to avoid suspicions and accusations of ill faith. From 1819 onward recognition seems to have been Castlereagh's goal; but his European obligations forced him to move in that direction with great caution, and only as the opportunities for progress presented themselves.

During the months following the Congress of Aix-la-Chapelle Castlereagh contented himself with a defense of his policy in Parliament and with an effort to strengthen Great Britain's neutrality laws. As early as 1817 the Prince Regent had warned his subjects not to participate in the revolutionary contests. The warning had proved singularly ineffective. In May, 1819, the government therefore brought forth the Foreign Enlistment Act, which made it an offense not only to enlist in Great Britain for foreign service but also to enter foreign service at all. The bill passed through Parliament after a violent struggle, but its subsequent history shows that the government had no intention of enforcing its provisions. Lord Cochrane, the hero of several sea battles and one hot engagement upon the London stock exchange, sailed for Chile unopposed; troops under a certain Colonel English embarked without molestation for service in Venezuela; and in Ireland General Devereaux established headquarters at a hotel in Dublin, paraded about the streets in a uniform of his own design, and boldly recruited men for Bolívar's armies under the eyes of the local constabulary.[48]

A neutrality of such ambivalence served several purposes. It afforded Castlereagh a convenient refuge from carping Spanish complaints; there, after all, was the Foreign Enlistment Act as evidence of his good intentions. Also, it prevented his Allies from accusing Great Britain of a relaxation of principle; she had manifestly done her best to conform. At the same time it enabled a large number of Wellington's Peninsular veterans to exchange the embarrassments of poor relief for the glory of emancipating Latin America. Such nobility required no excuse at all.

Other and more subtle ways of enlisting the gratitude of the

48. Rush to Adams, August 24, October 5, 1819, Manning, *Diplomatic Correspondence*, III, 1457, 1458–1459. See also A. Hasbrouck, *Foreign Legionaries in the Liberation of Spanish South America* (New York, Columbia University Press, 1928).

insurgents also came to mind. The fate of the Chilean agent in London was typical. In an unofficial interview with Lord Castlereagh he learned to his pleasure that Chilean vessels would be admitted to English ports and

that Sir Thomas Hardy, who was appointed to command the squadron destined to act in the South Seas, was charged to attend to British interests in that quarter, and would be the medium of any communications necessary between his own Government and the authorities in Chile, and thus exercise, in effect, consular functions.[49]

So, beyond the horizon of Spain and his Allies, Castlereagh began to construct the delicate network of permanent political relations with Latin America.

Unfortunately there was still the United States to be reckoned with. Not until the middle of October, 1818, did Adams learn of the Concert's intention to mediate between Spain and her colonies. Then he was not particularly impressed.

It is our true policy to let this experiment have its full effect [he confided to his diary], without attempting to disturb it, which might unnecessarily give offence to the allies; and after it shall have failed, as fail it must, and as England certainly must know it will, we shall then be at perfect liberty to recognize any of the South American Governments without coming in collision with the allies.[50]

In December he evinced his contempt for the whole procedure by proposing to acknowledge the insurgents in cooperation with Great Britain—a cooperation "not of formal compact, but of common good understanding." [51] And in January, 1819, he wrote to Richard Rush and advised that the President would soon recognize the independence of Buenos Aires. He qualified this bold statement, however, with the phrase, "if no event occurs that would justify postponement." [52]

Adams made it evident, with this cautious insertion, that he still hesitated unilaterally to take the ultimate step of recognition. His prudence was motivated in part, no doubt, by fear of what Europe might do in retaliation. The uncertainty surrounding the set-

49. Richard Rush, *A Residence at the Court of London*, 2d ser. (2 vols., London, R. Bentley, 1845), I, 201–202.

50. Adams, *Memoirs of John Quincy Adams*, IV, 167.

51. *Ibid.*, pp. 186–187. See also *Castlereagh Papers*, XII, 99.

52. Whitaker, *The United States and the Independence of Latin America*, pp. 264–265.

tlement of the Floridas dispute also gave him pause. Although the treaty, ceding vast stretches of territory to the United States, was signed on February 22, 1819, it was not finally to be ratified by Spain until 1821. To recognize the Latin American colonists while Ferdinand still withheld his signature from the document did not strike Adams as an intelligent way of advancing American interests. But perhaps the determining factor was the personal repugnance which, independent of all other circumstances, Adams felt toward venturing such a step. The situation in Latin America remained cloudy; no stable governments had yet arisen amid the ruins of the Spanish viceroyalties; and there were too few manifestations of what the Secretary of State considered to be true republican virtues. In the final analysis Adams was quite willing to wait a while longer before recognizing, especially since his great political rival, Henry Clay, was pressing for a more precipitate course.[53]

It is doubtful that Castlereagh would have changed his tactics even if he had been aware of Adams' conservative views. As long as the United States remained a potential rival in Latin America he felt duty-bound to place a limit upon its influence. Despite the basic similarity of views shared by the two countries a trickle of misinformation and misrepresentations continued to issue from the Foreign Office. When Richard Rush suggested a concert of action in February, 1819, Castlereagh announced that Great Britain still hoped to bring about a reconciliation between Spain and her colonies.[54] Late in March he finally confessed to Rush what was already well known: that Spain had rejected all offers to settle the dispute; but still he insisted that British policy had not changed. Although he sought to placate the United States on every other question— he even urged Spain to ratify the Floridas Treaty—in regard to Latin America Castlereagh endeavored to convey the impression that Europe might yet intervene.[55]

In September it seemed that the Foreign Secretary's evasions might reap their reward at last. The first crack in the façade of Allied indifference and neutrality appeared, and Castlereagh learned that France had shown an interest in placing one of the

53. *Ibid.*, pp. 273–274.
54. Rush, *A Residence at the Court of London*, I, 1–6. Castlereagh told Prince Esterhazy that he was trying still to convey the impression that Europe might yet intervene. See Webster, "Castlereagh and the Spanish Colonies," *Eng. Hist. Rev.*, p. 637.
55. Rush, *A Residence at the Court of London*, I, 39–40, 167–168.

Spanish princes upon a throne in Buenos Aires. Although he could muster little enthusiasm for the scheme itself—he felt confident that Ferdinand would never accede to it—the proposition nevertheless opened the way for further discussions of the whole Latin American question among the Allies. Since the autumn of 1818 he had cautiously avoided suggesting any new plans for the solution of that question; he had not wished to lay himself open to the charge of self-interest. But now that France had undertaken the first step, he felt that the moment had arrived to attempt something more realistic than the outworn efforts to mediate the dispute.[56] Formal conversations were about to get under way among the Allies, and then a military revolution swept over Spain.

The troops assembled by Ferdinand for his expedition against Spanish America had already revolted once in July, 1819. On January 1, 1820, they embarked upon a new and more successful insurrection. Led by two colonels, the rebels proclaimed their adherence to the Constitution of 1812 and marched northward from Cadiz. Their progress was everywhere triumphant. Madrid rose in anger against Ferdinand, and in the spring that wayward monarch swore unconditional allegiance to the hated Constitution. Byron, with more than a touch of poetic license, marked the act as the beginning of "the first year of freedom's second dawn." Wellington, who had suffered more from the Spanish liberals than his erratic compatriot, remarked in a calmer vein: "Their colonies must now be considered as lost." The general tendency in England was to look upon the revolution as a not unusual expression of the manifest instability of the Latin race.[57]

But to the Autocrat of All the Russias the uprising represented far more than that. Alexander had by now discarded his liberal pose. Constitutions were anathema; he was frankly and unabashedly reactionary; and his reaction was as sincere and fanatical as his erstwhile liberalism. The Tsar was convinced that the Spanish revolution posed a threat to the entire structure of European society. He immediately pressed for a congress to deal with the menace; and Castlereagh had to reveal to the world for the first time, in his State Memorandum of May 5, 1820, the ideological difference which had been plaguing the Alliance from the start. He was able, with Metternich's support, to prevent Alexander

56. Castlereagh to Sir Henry Wellesley, September 24, 1819, Webster, "Castlereagh and the Spanish Colonies," *Eng. Hist. Rev.*, pp. 637–638 n.
57. Wellington to Beresford, February 12, 1820, *ibid.*, p. 639.

from marching across Europe to the aid of Ferdinand. But scarcely had he resolved this crisis when another, more immediately relevant to the Latin American question, arose in its stead.

Owing to a violent quarrel among the ruling factions in Buenos Aires it became known in the summer of 1820 that the French government, instead of attempting to provide a throne for one of Ferdinand's many progeny, had actually tried to force the Bourbon Prince of Lucca upon the colonists. The plan not only revealed a deep-seated hostility to Great Britain; it also indicated an active desire on the part of France to extend her influence to Latin America. The latter possibility was, of course, intolerable. Although the plot had failed, the reaction of English public opinion and government was immediate and extreme. Castlereagh promptly demanded explanations of France.[58] Sir Charles Stuart, the British ambassador in Paris, carried the attack even further and observed to the French Foreign Minister:

. . . that an uncalled for attempt to prove the *right* of France to enter into a negociation of this nature is not calculated to inspire much confidence on the part of the Allies, because any justification of the reserve maintained towards other Powers upon this occasion may, without misrepresentation of his intentions, be considered to indicate a disposition to abandon the principle which connects the chief States of Europe, and to separate the interests of France from those of the Alliance.[59]

Castlereagh, in an unfamiliarly belligerent mood, now sent openly for the Colombian agent in London and informed him of Great Britain's willingness to consider the recognition of any colony that adopted monarchical institutions.[60]

It seemed, in truth, an auspicious moment in which to act independently of Europe. France had set the precedent with her blundering intrigue. The Allies were defiantly gathering at Troppau in spite of Castlereagh's strictures upon the local nature of the Neapolitan revolt. In the United States the House of Representatives had at last adopted a resolution favoring the recognition of the Latin American states. A similar resolution had been presented to the House of Commons. But Castlereagh remained faith-

58. Castlereagh to Stuart, July 5, 1820, *ibid.*, p. 638.
59. Stuart to Castlereagh, July 24, 1820, Webster, *Britain and the Independence of Latin America*, II, 105–107.
60. Webster, *The Foreign Policy of Castlereagh, 1815–1822*, p. 425.

ful to his concept of the Alliance and refused to fly in its face.

Moreover, a whole series of domestic crises had arisen to stay his hand. George III, after a reign, often shadowy, of sixty years, had died in January, 1820.[61] To the throne succeeded the incredible George IV, who immediately discarded his latest mistress, Lady Hertford, and proceeded with an attempt to divorce his wife upon grounds of adultery. The first act decreased Castlereagh's influence at court; the second absorbed his whole time and energy. As the divorce trial got under way, it turned into a political contest. The Opposition and the London crowd sided with the Queen, and Castlereagh, who remained faithful to his royal master, became the most unpopular minister in England. For days at a time he was forced to hide away at the Foreign Office in order to escape the hostility of the mob. Canning, who in 1816 had joined the cabinet in a subordinate capacity, resigned at a crucial moment because of a former intimacy with the Queen. A plot to assassinate the entire cabinet was thwarted, but thereafter Castlereagh made a habit of going about armed. As the tensions mounted Lord Liverpool, usually dignified, took to leaping over sofas in after-dinner society, and Wellington remarked hoarsely to Countess Lieven that "We should have thrown up the whole thing twenty times over if Castlereagh and I had not represented to our colleagues what the general consequences would be if we resigned." [62]

Throughout the summer of 1820 the strange spectacle of a royal divorce trial unfolded; and as the defendant calmly played backgammon in the House of Lords, Castlereagh fought desperately in the Commons to hold his Tory majority together. At last, in November, the farce played itself out. The government withdrew its bill of charges against the Queen, and relieved wits now prayed:

> Gracious Queen, we thee implore,
> Go away, and sin no more;
> But if that effort be too great,
> Go away—at any rate.[63]

61. According to Countess Lieven, there was "something poetic in the picture of this old, blind king wandering about in his castle among shadows, talking with them; for he lived his life among the dead—playing on his organ and never losing his serenity and his illusions." Peter Quennell, ed., *The Private Letters of Princess Lieven to Prince Metternich, 1820–1826* (New York, E. P. Dutton, 1938), pp. 11–12.

62. Countess Lieven to Prince Metternich, June 15, 1820, *ibid.*, p. 43.

63. Bagot, *George Canning and His Friends*, II, 107 n.

Infuriated, George IV retreated into sulkiness, contemplated changing his ministers, and reluctantly received his favorites, "lying at full length in a lilac silk dressing-gown, a velvet nightcap on his head, his huge bare feet (for he had gout) covered with a piece of pure silk net." [64] Not until 1821 was Castlereagh able to devote his full energy to the mounting duties of the Foreign Office.

Perhaps the most remarkable result of this confusion was not the inaction of the British government but the paralysis which overcame the United States. Adams had kept himself fully and gleefully informed of Castlereagh's difficulties, but he still remained a prey to the old fears and suspicions of England.

The British Government [he wrote to President Monroe], just now have their hands so full of coronations and adulteries . . . high treasons and petty treasons, pains, penalties, and paupers, that they will seize the first opportunity they can to shake them all off; and if they can make a question of national honor about a foothold in latitude 60°40′ upon something between rock and iceberg . . . and especially a question with us, they will not let it escape them. . . .

The idea [he went on], of having a grave controversy with Lord Castlereagh about an island latitude 61°40′ south is quite fascinating.[65]

As for Latin America, with the Floridas Treaty still unratified by Spain, he saw no reason to risk his handiwork by recognizing the insurgents. Besides, he could muster no real sympathy for their cause.

As to an American system [he remarked], we have it, we constitute the whole of it; there is no community of interests or of principles between North and South America. Mr. Torres and Bolívar and O'Higgins talk about an American system as much as the Abbé Correa, but there is no basis for any such system.[66]

Nevertheless he was ready to edge up to recognition, and in April, 1821, he informed the new British minister, Stratford Canning, of his willingness not to suggest but "to receive any proposal from Great Britain" on the subject.[67]

64. Countess Lieven to Metternich, June 12, 1821, Quennell, *The Private Letters of Princess Lieven*, pp. 136–137.
65. Adams to Monroe, August 26, 1820, Whitaker, *The United States and the Independence of Latin America*, pp. 296–297.
66. Entry of September 19, 1820, Adams, *Memoirs of John Quincy Adams*, V, 176.
67. Stratford Canning to Castlereagh, April 27, 1821, Webster, *Britain and the Independence of Latin America*, II, 492–493.

It is doubtful whether Castlereagh would have considered such a proposition even at the nadir of his fortunes. By 1821 his prospects had improved sufficiently to ignore it completely. The King had become reconciled to his ministers; the conferences upon the Neapolitan revolt, from which England had so defiantly abstained, were now gone by; and in October Castlereagh had joined with Metternich to take the first steps in rehabilitating the Grand Alliance. The Foreign Secretary was thus able to turn his attention more fully to Latin America.

The situation there was such that the re-establishment of Spanish authority had become well-nigh impossible. The Provinces of La Plata had long been free of Spanish troops. In June, 1821, Bolívar had secured the independence of Colombia with his striking victory at Carabobo. In July San Martin had entered Lima, bringing the revolution to Peru, the most loyal of Spain's South American provinces. And in August General O'Donoju, the acting Viceroy of Mexico, had signed a truce with the insurgent forces in that province and virtually recognized their independence.

Mediation, with Spanish sovereignty as a *sine qua non*, was obviously out of the question either as a practical solution to the dispute or as a means of further encouraging the pro-British sentiments of the colonists. Both the logic of events and the dictates of national interest now made imperative an acknowledgment of their status. Mercantile groups in all the great cities of England were bombarding Parliament with petitions for the establishment of regular political relations with the insurgents. The Opposition happily took up the cry. And from Paris Zea, the Colombian agent, threatened retaliatory measures unless diplomatic representatives were exchanged.[68]

By the spring of 1822 Castlereagh knew that the days of procrastination and intricate defensive measures were over at last. He must take some concrete step to acknowledge Latin American independence, yet his progress must be designed so as not to alienate the Alliance. He had already warned Spain that recognition was imminent. As a result of the Hanover meeting with Metternich he could count upon the usual support from Austria and Prussia—providing his policy did not challenge too seriously their conservative principles. But now that he was about to advocate positive action, a stalemate within the Concert no longer sufficed. The

68. Stuart to Castlereagh, April 11, 1822, Webster, "Castlereagh and the Spanish Colonies," *Eng. Hist. Rev.*, p. 641.

veto which he had exercised implicitly for six years and which Austria and Prussia had supported must somehow be exchanged for unanimity among the five Great Powers, if the Alliance was to survive.

Russia no doubt held the key to united action by the Concert, but Russia represented a most difficult object of persuasion. Alexander, finding himself thwarted once more in the Eastern Question by the Austro-British combination, had resumed his campaign to have Ferdinand restored to full and untrammeled sovereignty over Spain. A policy of refusing him this dubious pleasure while at the same time asking him to approve the recognition of the Latin American insurgents, did not promise a great deal of success. But judging from past experience the Tsar could be brought to accept even the most distasteful decisions provided he first found himself completely isolated within the Concert. Instead of risking a head-on collision with Russia, Castlereagh therefore chose the more circumspect method of initially concentrating his diplomacy upon France.

French support was important not only to embarrass Alexander into agreement. Since the revelation of the De Lucca conspiracy it had become expedient to put an end to French ambitions in Latin America by containing them within a more comprehensive plan of British origin. To accomplish this delicate maneuver Castlereagh reached into his files and extracted the scheme which he had first considered in 1807—that of independent monarchies.

A sufficiently strong royalist sentiment still flourished in Latin America to give such a scheme some chance of success. Moreover, since kings were indigenous to Europe, their transplantation to Latin America would not only arrest the dissemination of republican principles; it would insure both a European orientation and a sharp reduction in the influence of the United States. Most important of all, the creation of independent monarchies, while appealing to the conservative principles of the Alliance, would be an enterprise most difficult for France to reject. For was that not, after all, what she herself had proposed in 1819?

During April and the first days of May Castlereagh undertook to negotiate along these lines with Chateaubriand, the French ambassador in London. He explained casually enough that he was not overly anxious to recognize the revolutionary governments. But, he went on to say, circumstances were forcing him to dispatch commercial agents to Latin America to protect British trade, and to acknowledge the insurgent flags when they appeared in British ports. Chateaubriand listened sympathetically. Castlereagh then suggested that France and Great Britain might cooperate to establish a series of monarchies in Latin America and provide them with European princes. Chateaubriand was enthusiastic and immediately urged the project upon his government. His words carried no weight.[69]

The French government was at that moment rent by two factions. The Count de Villèle, the leading figure in the cabinet of Louis XVIII, favored strengthening the monarchy by stimulating the French economy. The opportunity to expand trade through access to the Latin American market, even in cooperation with Great Britain, struck him as an eminently suitable means to that end. But Villèle was opposed by a powerful group at whose head stood the King's brother, the Count d'Artois. This coterie was equally convinced that the only way to obliterate Napoleon's memory was by equaling his military triumphs, and it was already intriguing to free Ferdinand from the shackles of the Constitution of 1812 by force of French arms. Since Castlereagh's overture obviously was not consistent with the restoration of that illustrious monarch to all his former prerogatives, the ultraroyalist faction succeeded, on May 13, 1822, in having it rejected.[70]

If Castlereagh was disappointed by this rebuff he showed no outward signs of chagrin. The establishment of monarchies in Latin America no doubt struck him as the best solution to the long and tedious conflict, but the rejection of the plan by France at least permitted him to say to the Alliance that he had exhausted every avenue of compromise before acting independently.

The news that reached London early in May was certainly of an order to encourage independent action. The United States had begun to recognize the former colonies of Spain; Adams had finally taken the fatal step. Yet such was the impression left by Castlereagh's diplomacy that the Secretary of State hastened to explain the step away.

We trust it will not be considered, even by the British Cabinet, a rash and hasty measure at this time [he told Rush]. Should the subject be mentioned to you . . . you will remark that it was not understood or intended as a change of policy on the part of the United States nor

69. *Ibid.*, pp. 642–643.
70. *Ibid.*, p. 643.

adopted with any desire of turning it to the account of our own interests. Possibly no one of the proposed diplomatic missions may be actually sent before the next session of Congress.[71]

American recognition, presented in this dim light, appeared less as a menace than as a positive boon to Castlereagh. In addition to the obvious inability of Spain to exercise even the remotest control over her former provinces, he could now point to the action of the United States as an incentive for the Alliance to stabilize the situation by somehow following suit. What better way than recognition could there be, after all, of counteracting the dreaded spread of republican influences?

When Spain protested against the American step in an official note to the Powers and promised to attempt some sort of reconciliation with her colonies, Castlereagh prodded her to produce a concrete and liberal plan of action. When the fulfillment of this request proved beyond the limited capacities of the Escorial, the Foreign Secretary took the opportunity to state his final position.

His Britannic Majesty [he announced coldly], would not act with the candour and explicit frankness which he owes to his Ally, the King of Spain, were he not, under present circumstances to warn him of the rapid progress of events, and of the danger of delay. His Catholic Majesty must be aware that so large a portion of the world cannot, without fundamentally disturbing the intercourse of civilised society, long continue without some recognised and established relations; that the State which can neither by its councils, nor by its arms effectually assert its own rights over its dependencies so as to enforce obedience, and thus make itself responsible for maintaining their relations with other Powers, must sooner or later be prepared to see those relations established from the overruling necessity of the case, under some other form.[72]

His undersecretary, Mr. Planta, was more explicit.

If I were to describe our line [he told Stratford Canning], I should say it would be one of as little *overt act* as possible, but one of securing to our subjects all the commercial advantages enjoyed by any other nation with the South American Provinces. For this object we shall insert a clause in one of our acts of Parliament, I believe the Naviga-

71. Adams to Rush, May 13, 1822, Webster, *The Foreign Policy of Castlereagh, 1815–1822,* p. 427.
72. Castlereagh to Onis, June 28, 1822, *ibid.,* pp. 432–433.

tion Act, to permit and protect this trade . . . But we shall make as little fuss about it as we can, and reason and defend the matter with Spain as absolutely required from us under the circumstances.[73]

Mr. Wallace of the Board of Trade on May 20 introduced to the House of Commons a bill providing for the admission of insurgent vessels to British ports. The bill quickly passed; but as might have been foreseen, it failed to satisfy the general appetite for political relations so sharply stimulated by the prior recognition of the United States. Petitions favoring prompt action poured into Parliament from the great manufacturing centers; the Colombian agent, Mr. Zea, lately arrived from Paris, even received a testimonial dinner in London with his grace the Duke of Somerset in the chair. Finally, on July 23, the Opposition took up the cry and during a noisy debate in the House of Commons urged a course of recognition upon the government. They were rebuffed as usual; Castlereagh refused to be hurried. His only admission was that "the whole was purely a British question, uninfluenced by foreign Powers and resting only upon the law of nations, and the character of generosity and prudence, which he trusted this country would ever maintain." [74]

Did this statement mean that Great Britain had cut herself adrift from the Concert, at least in regard to Latin America? Rush, a reasonably acute observer, thought as much. Indeed, Castlereagh himself had said almost as much. Mr. Zea reported to the American on an interview in which the Foreign Secretary had maintained "that Great Britain would not carry her consideration for Spain so far as to postpone too long her rights of acting as she might think fit . . ." [75] Yet, despite the mounting pressure, despite the soft words to Zea, Castlereagh continued to seek the cooperation of the Allies. He pointedly informed the Austrian and Prussian ambassadors of the rapid progress of the revolutionaries, he confided to Count Lieven his intention to send commercial agents to Latin America, and he described the course of his abortive negotiations with France. As a result, the Russian ambassador painted for his superiors in St. Petersburg an almost pathetic picture of Castlereagh—caught, as it were, between the inexorable pressure of the commercial classes (which for nearly ten years he had ig-

73. Planta to Stratford Canning, May 11, 1822, *ibid.,* App. G, p. 584.
74. *Ibid.,* p. 433.
75. Rush to Adams, July 26, 1822, Manning, *Diplomatic Correspondence,* III, 1472.

nored) and the adamant attitude of the Concert.[76] No doubt, at the moment in question, that was the kind of portrait that Castlereagh desired. He himself had already graphically illustrated the futility of negotiating with Spain, both in the Banda Oriental mediation and at Aix-la-Chapelle. For seven years he had kept faith with the Alliance; for at least three more he had done its members the honor of confiding in them. Now, surely, they could hardly object to the action of an old friend in protecting a set of British interests which had become sanctified by prescription.

The case for recognition was almost complete. Castlereagh added a last artistic touch by circulating his Spanish note of June 28 among the Allies, with the remark that "the approaching meeting at Vienna will afford me an opportunity of fully explaining to the Allied Cabinets the sentiments of His Majesty's Government upon this important question." [77]

He had been laboring over the agenda of the Congress since early in 1822; for this was to be his supreme personal effort to bring the Alliance back to those principles which he had so carefully formulated in 1815 and 1818. He anticipated that the three great problems that would confront the Concert would concern Turkey, Spanish America and Spain, and that volatile geographical expression, Italy. If the desire for unanimity still exercised its spell over the Tsar and if he could be granted some small satisfaction upon the first and last subjects, Castlereagh hoped to win Russian acquiescence to the British solution of the Spanish American question.

Castlereagh's final ideas as to what that solution should be may be found in the instructions which he prepared for himself. "The whole," he noted succinctly, "may be regarded rather as a matter of time than of principle." He was willing to discuss the moment and type of recognition with his Allies, but it is clear that he regarded some sort of recognition as essential in any event—even if Great Britain had to act alone.[78] The task, admittedly, was monumental; and Castlereagh alone possessed the knowledge, the skill, and the patience to see it through to a successful conclusion. Yet even he faltered and fled before the test.

76. Lieven to Nesselrode, June 10, 1822, Webster, *The Foreign Policy of Castlereagh, 1815–1822*, App. F, pp. 578–579.

77. *Ibid.*, p. 433.

78. Arthur, 2d Duke of Wellington, ed., *Despatches, Correspondence, and Memoranda of Field Marshal Arthur, Duke of Wellington, K. G.* (8 vols., London, John Murray, 1867–80), I, 286 (hereafter cited as Wellington, *Despatches*).

Early in June he had suddenly and inexplicably confided to an acquaintance that "he was sick of the concern, and that if he could well get out of it would never get into it again." [79] The momentary depression apparently passed. Lord Sidmouth dined with him at Cray on August 2 and found him cheerful and vivacious. Four days later, at a cabinet meeting, "he laid before his colleagues the instructions he had drawn up for himself, dealing with the matters to be discussed at Verona. He expounded them with all his usual wisdom and clarity of mind." [80] But on the eighth there was a sudden and terrifying change. A friend, noticing an unusual taciturnity, remarked, "I hope . . . you are looking forward with pleasure to your continental trip; the journey, I think, will be of use to you and you will have the satisfaction of renewing several of your former diplomatic acquaintances." Castlereagh passed his hand wearily across his forehead and replied slowly: "At any other time I should like it very much, *but I am quite worn out here,*" with his hand still upon his forehead, "quite worn out; and this fresh responsibility is more than I can bear." [81]

The following day Wellington discovered him in a state bordering upon incoherence—suffering from a persecution complex, hallucinations, fits of deep melancholy, and bursts of tears. The Duke called Dr. Bankhead, who promptly bled the patient, pronounced him much improved, and escorted him down to Cray. The course in bleeding continued; and then on the morning of August 12 Castlereagh slipped into his dressing room and with a small penknife slashed his throat. As the terrified Bankhead rushed to the door, he murmured, "let me fall upon your arm; it is all over," and collapsed to the floor, with blood spurting wildly from a severed artery. He died almost instantly.

The funeral [Wellington noted] was attended by every person in London of any mark or distinction of all parties, and the crowds in the streets behaved respectfully and creditably. There was one exception at the door of the Abbey, which showed that even upon such an occasion the malevolence of the Radical Party could not avoid displaying itself. Those who misbehaved there, however, were few in number, were evidently employed for the purpose, and were ashamed of showing themselves.[82]

79. Temperley, *The Foreign Policy of Canning*, p. 25.

80. Countess Lieven to Metternich, August 13, 1822, Quennell, *The Private Letters of Princess Lieven*, p. 192.

81. Hamilton Stewart to Lord Stewart, August 20, 1822, Webster, *The Foreign Policy of Castlereagh, 1815–1822*, pp. 484–485.

82. Wellington, *Despatches*, I, 263.

A great European had passed from the scene, leaving only Alexander and Metternich to carry on his example according to their own strange lights. The liberal world rejoiced, and Byron, wandering restlessly through Italy, stopped to write an epitaph:

> Oh Castlereagh! thou art a patriot now;
> Cato died for his country, so didst thou;
> He perish'd rather than see Rome enslaved
> Thou cutt'st thy throat that Britain may be saved! [83]

83. "Miscellaneous Poems," *The Complete Works of Lord Byron* (Paris, A. and W. Galignani, 1835), p. 902. Byron, in a more scurrilous vein, wrote:

> Posterity will ne'er survey
> A nobler grave than this;
> Here lie the bones of Castlereagh:
> Stop traveller, and . . . .

VII

THE HIGH COSTS OF SUBTLETY

FOR ten years Lord Castlereagh had been the principal orna-
ment of the Liverpool cabinet. Virtually singlehanded he
had devised and executed the foreign policy of his country.
As leader of the House of Commons he had borne the brunt of the
many attacks upon the government and had been responsible
for the passage of its unpopular legislation. Lounging on the
Treasury Bench, garbed in the familiar hunting coat with its
bright brass buttons, wonderfully handsome and serene, invariably
courteous and good-tempered, a trifle inarticulate, he had seemed
a living symbol of all that was strong and permanent in the Tory
party. His sudden disappearance left a void which could not be
filled by any of his colleagues. After the initial shock had passed
it was suggested that Wellington should become Foreign Secretary, with Robert Peel as leader of the House of Commons. But
Lord Liverpool, conscious that his administration had exhausted
the credit gained for it by the Duke's military victories, quickly
rejected the proposal. He had determined to infuse new blood into
his cabinet.

Only one man possessed the abilities necessary to replace Castlereagh and sufficient popularity to strengthen the government.
That man was Canning. But was he available? His long and singular career, meandering, as it were, from the Foreign Office to obscurity, and from an embassy in Lisbon and a subordinate place
at the cabinet board back again to obscurity, seemed about to
culminate at last in the governor-generalship of India.[1] Canning
himself seemed to crave this final, stately oblivion. Fame, he whispered, was a squeezed orange. The King appeared to insist upon
exile. On no account, he declared, was Lord Liverpool to "impede
the arrangements which are already settled respecting India, as

---

1. Huskisson protested that Canning's "peculiar quality of Parliamentary elo-
quence ought not to be exported to India like the skates and warmingpans were to
Buenos Ayres." Croker to Peel, August, 1822, Bagot, *George Canning and His
Friends*, II, 125 n.

it is my decision that they should remain final and unalterable." [2]

A majority of the cabinet opposed the inclusion in their ranks of a man whom they considered to be treacherous, unstable, ambitious, and above all, plebeian. Even the Whigs, wandering in the Parliamentary wilderness, objected. Brougham, himself an opportunist, referred to Canning as "the joker," and made quips about his gout and irritability.[3] Creevey expressed the opinion that he was "as rotten as a stewed prune, or words to that effect." [4] Hobhouse in a vicious speech accused him of having "talents without character." [5] Byron, who remained tentatively sympathetic, had already taken note of his temper and pride. "So Canning and Burdett have been quarrelling:" he remarked, "if I mistake not, the last time of their single combats, each was shot in the thigh by his Antagonist; and their Correspondence might be headed thus, by any wicked wag.

> BRAVE Champions! go on with the farce!
> Reversing the spot where you bled;
> Last time both were shot in the . . . ;
> *Now* (damn you) get knock'd on the head!" [6]

John Wilson Croker, however objective, was equally unkind.

His genius is a bright flame [he noted]. It is liable to every gust of wind and every change of weather; it flares, and it flickers, and it blazes, now climbing the heavens, now stifled in its own smoke, and of no use but to raise the wonder of distant spectators, and to warm the very narrow circle that immediately surrounds it.[7]

Lord Liverpool nevertheless persevered in his efforts to bring this strange man into the government; and the Duke of Wellington, haunted by his eternal sense of duty, suddenly came to the support of the first minister. As the crisis deepened and the administration drifted ever closer to dissolution, opposition to the appointment collapsed—its leaders consoled no doubt by the ru-

2. George IV to Liverpool, August 17, 1822, C. D. Yonge, *The Life and Administration of Robert Banks, Second Earl of Liverpool* (3 vols., London, Macmillan, 1868), III, 195.

3. Brougham to Creevey, September, 1822, Sir Herbert Maxwell, ed., *The Creevey Papers* (London, John Murray, 1933), p. 392.

4. Creevey to Miss Ord, September 15, 1822, *ibid.*, p. 391.

5. Halévy, *A History of the English People, 1815–1830*, p. 156.

6. Bliss Perry, ed., *The Complete Poetical Works of Lord Byron* (Boston, Houghton Mifflin, 1905), p. 237.

7. Jennings, *The Croker Papers*, I, 219.

mor that Canning would be less troublesome inside than outside
the cabinet. The King himself surrendered unconditionally to this
argument during the first week in September, and Lord Liverpool at once opened negotiations with Canning. On the fifteenth,
successor to the whole heritage of Castlereagh—as Secretary of
State for Foreign Affairs and leader of the House of Commons—
Canning arrived in London. With him there dawned a new era in
British diplomacy.

The first object of Canning's consideration was the Grand Alliance. He did not approve of it now, and he had opposed it from
the first. In 1818, while Castlereagh was at Aix-la-Chapelle, he
had confided to Lord Bathurst that such a system

of periodical meetings of the four great Powers, with a view to the
general concerns of Europe,—[was] of very questionable policy . . .
it will necessarily involve us deeply in all the politics of the Continent,
whereas our true policy has always been not to interfere except in
great emergencies, and then with a commanding force.[8]

Such meetings, he felt sure, would also decrease the possibility
of Great Britain being enabled to play the balance of power according to her specific needs and interests. The conferences of
Troppau and Laibach merely confirmed him in this conviction.
Where Castlereagh had been prepared to forget the occurrences
of 1820 and 1821 in order to perpetuate his scheme, Canning was
determined to use the moral strictures of the Eastern Powers as
the excuse to bring about its destruction.[9]

In this determination Canning accurately reflected the tradition of the eighteenth century. He had no use for "Areopagus, and
the like of that . . ." War constituted a natural and inevitable
portion of human relationships: he almost gloried in the admission.
The function of the statesman therefore consisted of a species of
contest with other statesmen—a contest of rigid interests in which
each country would be strengthened at all costs, and the inevitable
postponed as long as possible.[10]

In postponing the inevitable for Great Britain, Canning depended upon his ability to manipulate the balance of power, as to
a certain extent had Castlereagh. But whereas Castlereagh had

8. Bathurst to Castlereagh, October 20, 1818, *Castlereagh Papers*, XII, 56.
9. Webster, *The Foreign Policy of Castlereagh, 1815–1822*, p. 499.
10. Canning to Granville, December 6, 1826, A. G. Stapleton, *George Canning and His Times*, p. 541.

hoped to maintain the fluidity necessary to such a manipulation by bringing the Powers together and concealing the balance behind the imposing façade of the Concert, Canning rejected such a system as conducive to the very coalitions which his predecessor had wished to avoid. Rather than cater any longer to such dangerous abstractions as "moral solidarity," he preferred to encourage each Power to pursue its own interests quite independently of any common purpose. And he preferred to rely upon his own skill and intuition—combined with the power of Great Britain—to intervene at the proper moment, and upon the proper side, when the pursuit of those interests seemed about to threaten a general war.[11]

If Canning's first ambition was to shatter the Concert, his second objective was to recognize the Latin American states. The economic arguments for so doing impressed themselves upon him with some strength, for, as the parliamentary representative of Liverpool, he had become particularly responsive to the doctrines of laissez faire. Latin America must be brought into the family of nations so as to give unrestricted scope to British trade. But that was not the only reason. There were strong political motives as well. Canning, like Castlereagh, apparently labored under the impression that the new states would develop into militarily influential Powers. Attached to Great Britain by ties of friendship, they could thereafter be used both as counterweights to the United States and as reserves to be thrown into the European balance should he find himself in need of additional power there.

To a certain extent Canning was assisted in his first objective by the failure of Lord Liverpool's cabinet to appreciate fully what Castlereagh had been attempting to do.[12] But whereas its members had trusted Castlereagh, they looked upon Canning with rank suspicion. For over a year all his proposals were to meet with their most stubborn and implacable opposition. It was not only that policies such as the proposed recognition of Latin America disturbed Lords Westmoreland, Sidmouth, and Eldon upon principle. The mere fact that those policies should emanate from Canning sufficed to arouse these aged gentlemen to a counterpolicy of obstruction. Even before he appeared upon the scene, they had

11. Bathurst to Castlereagh, October 20, 1818, *Castlereagh Papers,* XII, 56.
12. The doctrine of collective responsibility had not yet been fully developed as an integral part of cabinet procedure. As a consequence, individual ministers possessed far more liberty of action than is now the case. The cabinet was still a collection of more or less independent sovereigns, who depended for coordination upon the initiative of the first minister.

flung down the gage of battle and had challenged his authority over foreign affairs by appointing the Duke of Wellington to Castlereagh's place at the Congress of Verona.

No doubt the Duke was the Englishman best qualified to represent his country in the councils of the Allies. His prestige and experience were enormous. His reputation for impartiality was unrivaled. All Europe had made a habit of asking his advice. To his utterances there was attributed a special wisdom; he had become a sort of oracle, precise and conveniently articulate. But had he, with all his extraordinary talents, become a diplomat as well?

When the Duke left London in September he was armed with Castlereagh's instructions but he lacked Castlereagh's ideas. Accustomed either to command or obey, he found it exceedingly difficult to enter into the limbo of compromise. The Duke was inclined by instinct and training to judge issues on their individual merits rather than upon their interrelationships. He lacked the quality of perspective. This purblindness had proved an asset upon the battlefield; in the gossamer web of Allied diplomacy it caused the Duke to go astray. Wellington had fallen into the error of accepting the Alliance as an accomplished fact. It was obvious and almost palpable and he saw no reason to pamper it. His only duty, now that the Alliance had been established, was to prevent it from being operated in an outlandish fashion. He apparently failed to realize that opposition or even indifference might not only prevent the adoption of a particular policy but also destroy the Concert itself. Nor did his colleagues seem to appreciate that in selecting the Duke they might be furthering Canning's basic objectives.

In accordance with his instructions, Wellington stopped at Paris to discover the attitude of the French government toward the revolutionary regime in Spain.[13] Villèle received him and proved not only charming and equable but extraordinarily frank. He barely attempted to justify the presence of one hundred thousand French troops along the Spanish frontier. He merely assured the Duke of his own reluctance to use them, even for the purpose of rescuing Ferdinand. What he failed to explain, and what the Duke failed to realize until it was too late, was that the Count d'Artois had replaced Villèle in the confidence of the King. Yet the omission was important; for, in spite of Villèle's apparent objections, the French troops were rapidly being maneuvered into positions from which to launch an invasion of Spain. There remained, in fact, only the task of securing sole credit for the ex-

13. Wellington, *Despatches*, I, 286.

pedition to the French monarchy without, however, incurring the wrath of the Alliance.[14]

Essentially the whole Congress of Verona revolved about this puzzling question. The Duke arrived in Verona early in October. A host of adoring young ladies immediately surrounded him; he took tea with Marie Louise; his health improved rapidly. In a burst of self-confidence he assured Canning "that nothing will be done here in regard to Spain which will be at all inconvenient to you." [15] The world was roseate, the young ladies grew increasingly attractive, and then on October 20 his serenity was shattered. The Congress met, and the French representatives in that august assemblage immediately proceeded to depict the Spanish Constitutionalists in the most sinister terms. They played upon the danger to which the example of revolution exposed the throne of Louis XVIII. Finally they proposed that as Austria had upheld Legitimacy in Naples, so France should be permitted to rescue Ferdinand in Spain.[16]

According to French lights the initial reaction of the Allies was not entirely satisfactory. The Tsar was inclined to go too far. He not only acquiesced in the high purpose of France but actually offered to further it with one hundred thousand Russian bayonets. Metternich, on the other hand, was not inclined to go far enough. As a compromise he suggested an assertion by the Concert of its "moral solidarity"—a parade of threats and suspended diplomatic relations instead of the use of force. In the melee of disagreements the French proposal seemed doomed to defeat. Then Wellington spoke his mind.

The Duke did not believe in the dangers of ideological contagion. He had, moreover, received instructions from Canning which forbade him to support any kind of intervention in Spanish affairs, moral or otherwise.

If [Canning had written], as I confess I see reason to apprehend, in the late communications both from Paris and Vienna, there is entertained by the Allies a determined project of interference by force, or by menace, in the present struggle in Spain, so convinced are His Majesty's Government, of the uselessness and danger of any such interference—so objectionable does it appear to them in principle, and so utterly impracticable in execution—that, if the necessity should

14. Wellington to Canning, October 4, 1822, Phillips, *The Confederation of Europe*, pp. 250–251.
15. Wellington, *Despatches*, I, 304.
16. Temperley, *The Foreign Policy of Canning*, pp. 65–66.

arise, or (I would rather say) if the opportunity should offer, I am to instruct Your Grace at once frankly and peremptorily to declare, that to any such interference, come what may, His Majesty will not be a party.[17]

Wellington, in obedience to his instructions and his sensibilities, therefore rejected each one of the Allied proposals. Metternich, the Tsar, the French envoys, all pleaded with him in turn. Shuffling through his papers, increasingly reticent, the Duke remained adamant. Europe appeared about to witness the dissolution of the Concert.

But at this juncture Metternich resolved to salvage something from the mounting wreckage. He did not approve of the proposed French action, although he himself had set the style for it at Troppau. In the main he preferred those principles of nonintervention which Castlereagh had repeatedly stated, so long as his own hegemony in Central Europe remained undisturbed. But Castlereagh was now gone; a "malevolent meteor" presided over the Foreign Office; he could no longer count upon British support. He stood before the Tsar, alone, weak, and more than a trifle disturbed. Under these circumstances a rump alliance without Great Britain, but with the means of controlling Alexander, seemed better than no alliance at all.[18] Since the Duke proved completely unmovable Metternich fell in with the original French plan. Prussia promptly joined him. The four Powers, with the Tsar in reluctant agreement, drew up a series of protocols which provided for concerted diplomatic action by the Alliance and authorized France to act on their behalf should force be needed against Spain.

The Duke, who had been excluded from these meetings, protested against each agreement as it emerged from the council chamber. His protests were ignored. He approached each of the four Powers and solicited its recognition of the Latin American states. He obtained only well-phrased evasions, and a lecture from Chateaubriand, in return.[19] Finally, on November 30, 1822, disillu-

17. *Ibid.*, p. 65.

18. Wellington to Canning, November 22, 1822, Wellington, *Despatches*, I, 565–568.

19. "You may rely on it," Wellington told Canning, "that nobody here either knows or cares anything about these questions of colonies or colonial policy, excepting as far as they may find in our conduct in them some ground for finding fault with us, and on which they may detract from our high character, and depreciate us in the opinion of the world." Wellington to Canning, November 19, 1822, *ibid.*, pp. 544–545.

sioned and disgusted, the Duke left Verona for Paris. With his departure, Great Britain surrendered her seat at the Concert. Had the Concert dissolved as a consequence?

Canning, out of touch with the decisions of Verona though he was, felt relatively sure that it had. Perhaps better than the Duke he had divined the motives of France: that she was bent not on cooperating with but upon using the Alliance. The professions of moral solidarity and unity of purpose which Alexander and Metternich were intoning left him at once amused and unperturbed. To complete the carnage of Verona it remained only to expose the hollowness of their pretensions.

Meanwhile Canning busied himself with preparations for the recognition of the Latin American states. In his own mind there was no need to justify such an act; it was obviously a requirement of the national interest. The chief difficulty facing him was that of making recognition palatable both to his colleagues and to Europe. The majority of Lord Liverpool's cabinet, veterans in one way or another of the Napoleonic Wars, held revolution in as great abhorrence as did the Tsar. They had looked in another direction as long as Castlereagh directed affairs; he, after all, had been a gentleman and an aristocrat. But this new man with the flowing eloquence and the searing wit was something quite different. Whatever he proposed must undergo their most critical scrutiny. Canning understood that he would need all his ingenuity and eloquence to circumvent them.

As for the Continental Powers, it was not precisely their approval that he sought. Rather was it their immobility—the immobility, let us say, that would result from the collapse of the Concert. And their inability at some later date to use his action as a precedent for policies in Europe inimical to English interests. In other words he must base his recognition upon grounds difficult even for the Continental Powers to gainsay, and he must declare himself at a moment when their talent for cooperative retaliation had become exhausted. The first and most obvious step in such a game was to demonstrate—as Castlereagh had so frequently demonstrated—the impossibility of bringing Spain to reason.

In September Canning began methodically to complain of the sporadic Spanish interference with the Latin American trade of Great Britain. In October he remarked ominously

that if England forebore to prejudge the question of a possible amicable settlement between Spain and her ancient Colonies . . . she did so, in the complete understanding and on the condition distinctly admitted by Spain, that her trade with those Colonies should be free and unmolested . . .[20]

In November he announced in a reasoned memorandum to the cabinet that since Spain was no longer carrying out her share of the bargain (which, if it ever existed, had never been reduced to writing), he must dispatch a naval expedition to the Caribbean to prevent further attacks upon British commerce. That such an expedition must cooperate with the insurgent authorities in Latin America to accomplish its purpose, that such cooperation must lead in turn to some sort of understanding with them—these things he hardly doubted. That the entire maneuver might result in the establishment of regular diplomatic relations—this he did not say; but what fruits might the future not yield? [21]

To protect himself from the accusation of traveling too fast, to exhibit his extraordinary patience, Canning at the same time took another and even more familiar step. On November 30, 1822, he offered Spain the services of Great Britain as mediator in the Latin American dispute.[22] He went on, having made this pleasant and meaningless gesture, to deny to France and the United States that he harbored territorial designs upon any of the colonies. In the privacy of the Foreign Office he also drew up a list of the consuls to be sent to Latin America. The stage was being set, and events in Europe were rapidly approaching the ripe state of confusion which Canning needed in order to act.

French policy during December left the impression that the final scene might be played even sooner than Canning had anticipated. When Wellington reached Paris from Verona he found Villèle apparently bent upon avoiding intervention in Spain. To all intents and purposes the rump Alliance was collapsing under the weight of British displeasure and its own internal discords. Canning seized upon the occasion and offered to mediate between France and Spain—no doubt hoping to evoke further evidences of disunity by this gesture. The move, much disliked by Welling-

---

20. Canning to A'Court, October 18, 1822, Webster, *Britain and the Independence of Latin America*, II, 390.
21. Cabinet Memorandum by Canning, November 15, 1822, E. J. Stapleton, *Some Official Correspondence of George Canning* (2 vols., London, Longmans, Green, 1887), I, 51–57.
22. Canning to A'Court, November 30, 1822, Webster, *Britain and the Independence of Latin America*, II, 399–400.

ton, appeared to have its effect.[23] While Russia, Prussia, and Austria signed a circular dispatch announcing their intention to withdraw their envoys from Spain, France held back. The Duc de Montmorency rejected Canning's offer of mediation on December 24—but on the plausible ground that the differences between France and Spain were not sufficiently serious to warrant British intervention.[24] And on the following day this most powerful advocate of collaboration with the Alliance resigned as Minister of Foreign Affairs, to be replaced by the exuberant Chateaubriand. At the same time the Spanish government learned that the French ambassador in Madrid would not be withdrawn. Here, indeed, was confusion twice confounded.

As the currents of European politics became more disorderly Canning happily turned his attention back to Spain. "Let Spain do us justice fully and handsomely" in Latin America, he explained, "and so enable us to behave towards her with that singleness of conduct" as her protector in Europe "which is as much our desire, as it is her interest, that we should pursue." [25] The Spanish government, terrified by the multitude of pressures, had already entered into negotiations with the colonists for the recognition of their independence. It now became even more pliant, promising to withdraw all restrictions against trading with Latin America and give satisfaction for those English ships which had been captured while engaged in the trade. Confronted with this extraordinary *volte-face*, Canning found it necessary to suspend his decision to send out consuls.[26]

But were these Spanish gestures sincere or brought on merely by the European crisis? Would Spain, moreover, make it clear to Latin America that Great Britain had inspired them? This last point was particularly important; and so there went off to Sir William A'Court, the British minister at Madrid, a singular dispatch. If the Spaniards misconstrue us, Canning wrote,

if they evince mistrust instead of thankfulness, and deny to us the means of satisfying England upon points of English interest; they may depend upon it, that the sins of American Spain will not only

23. Canning to Wellington, December 6, 13, 1822, Wellington, *Despatches,* I, 626, 650–651.

24. Duc de Montmorency to Wellington, December 24, 1822, *ibid.,* p. 667.

25. Canning to A'Court, December 3, 1822, A. G. Stapleton, *George Canning and His Times,* p. 387.

26. A'Court to Canning, December 24, 1822, Lawson, *The Relation of British Policy,* p. 98.

enable but compel us to remain not only neutral, but indifferent to the fate of Spain in Europe.[27]

In other words it was no longer enough for Spain to accept the inevitable; she must acknowledge the assistance afforded by Great Britain in removing the scales from her eyes. Otherwise—the threat was clearly implied—Canning would recognize the independence of the colonies without further reference to her feelings.

That Canning already felt free to do so without further reference to Europe goes almost without saying. He knew surely that no single Power could stop him; and the Alliance, in its disordered state, how could it retaliate? It was, he assured his ambassador in St. Petersburg, split "into three parts as distinct as the constitutions of England, France, and Muscovy." The shabby business of subordinating British interests to its whims had ended. Villèle, he announced happily, was a minister of thirty years ago—

no revolutionary scoundrel: but constitutionally hating England, as Choiseul and Vergennes used to hate us—and so things are getting back to a wholesome state again. Every nation for itself, and God for us all. Only bid your Emperor [Alexander] be quiet, for the time for Areopagus, and the like of that, is gone by.[28]

Yet as the new year dawned Canning's conviction somehow failed to be borne out by the facts. Spain, to be sure, remained submissive, her liberal government humbly willing to do his bidding. But France suddenly commenced to lend a half-hearted allegiance to the Alliance, while the Eastern Powers, faced with the secession of Great Britain, struggled bravely to maintain an unbroken front. Faithful to the Verona agreements, Prussia withdrew her ambassador from Madrid on January 9, 1823. The following day Austria and Russia did likewise. On January 18, after a decent interlude of silence, Chateaubriand ordered the French envoy to join the diplomatic exodus.[29]

From Canning's point of view the parade of ambassadors was ominous enough; but there was worse yet to follow. On January 28 Louis XVIII in a speech from the throne announced that the situation in Madrid had become intolerable. Unless Ferdinand the Well-beloved were set free "to give to his people the institu-

27. Canning to A'Court, December 29, 1822, A. G. Stapleton, *George Canning and His Times,* p. 389.
28. Canning to Bagot, January 3, 1823, *ibid.,* pp. 369–370.
29. Temperley, *The Foreign Policy of Canning,* pp. 77–78.

tions they cannot hold but from him," French troops would march to his rescue.[30]

Instead of finding confusion and paralysis, Canning beheld the shocking, the incredible, spectacle of the rump Alliance, in apparent good order, bearing down upon Spain. Now was hardly the time to recognize colonies; he must first devote his energies to staving off this new expression of the Concert's will—French intervention. In January he pleaded with Chateaubriand: "Negotiate at least before you invade. Leave the Spanish revolution to burn itself out within its own crater; you have nothing to apprehend from the eruption, if you do not open a channel for the lava through the Pyrenees." [31] In February he warned the Count d'Artois of the animosity aroused in England by the French King's speech. Pressing hard on the weak link of the Alliance he announced in the same month increases in Great Britain's naval strength. France continued her preparations to invade. Canning lifted the long-standing embargo upon the export of arms to Spain—and to Latin America. The Eastern Powers responded by assuring France of their support in the event that Great Britain should depart from her neutrality. By the middle of March the diplomatic contest had resolved itself in their favor. Canning could count upon only limited support from the country; the King and the cabinet had opposed him at every turn in the struggle.[32]

It was an infuriating and frustrating experience. Canning's intelligence indicated that France was using the Alliance merely as a shield to ward off outside intervention, that her ambitions were purely French in scope. The manner in which she had delayed all her maneuvers, acting each time a step behind the Eastern Powers so as to flaunt her independence of them, certain expressions of the Count d'Artois and Villèle, the communications of Sir Charles Stuart—all these things confirmed him in the accuracy of his estimate.[33] But here was the rub: he could muster no support for a firmer policy. The façade of the Alliance appeared too im-

30. *Ibid.*, pp. 77–78.
31. W. P. Cresson, *The Holy Alliance: the European Background of the Monroe Doctrine* (New York, Oxford University Press, 1922), p. 114.
32. Harold Temperley, "Canning, Wellington and George the Fourth," *Eng. Hist. Rev.*, XXXVIII (1923), 210.
33. Stuart to Canning, January 30, 1823, Lawson, *The Relation of British Policy*, p. 65; Stuart to Canning, February 10, 1823, E. J. Stapleton, *Some Official Correspondence*, I, 78.

posing, and a majority of the cabinet, abetted by the King, were actually wishing success to French arms. On March 21 he reluctantly confided to the French chargé d'affaires that Great Britain would be neutral in the impending conflict. Ten days later he announced the decision in an official memorandum. He could add only, and somewhat lamely, that England would take up arms were France to make her occupation of Spain permanent, were she to invade Portugal, or were she to try appropriating any part of the Spanish colonies.[34] The final result was a sad climax to his earlier protestations about the disunity of Europe.

The French government welcomed Canning's statement, ignored his conditions, and proceeded with its plans. The Duc d'Angoulême had already left Paris for the frontier to assume command of the armies. On April 6, 1823, for the second time in two decades, French troops invaded Spain. Upon this occasion they met with only token resistance and the invasion quickly developed into a triumphal parade. In vain Austria, Russia, and Prussia sought to share in its direction. Although Villèle reluctantly agreed to the establishment of an Allied control council in Paris, its decisions had no effect upon the conduct of the war. The French armies simply advanced too swiftly. By May 24 they were in Madrid. On June 11, as they progressed southward, the harried Spanish government with Ferdinand in tow fled from Seville to Cadiz, there to make a last futile stand. To all intents and purposes the conflict was over; the power and glory of French arms had been vindicated. There remained only to liberate Ferdinand— an annoying but necessary task. It was for this purpose, after all, that the war had been fought.

In England Canning made the best of a most embarrassing situation. He was by turns boastful, defiant, and sarcastic. To an old friend he admitted that he had "had an itch for war with France, and that a little provocation might have scratched it into eruption; but fortunately the better reason prevailed, and I look back upon the decision with entire and perfect self-congratulation." [35] On April 15 he appeared before the bar of the House of Commons and in a burst of calculated confidence unparalleled in the annals of English diplomacy read off a series of secret com-

34. Canning to Stuart, March 31, 1823, Perkins, *The Monroe Doctrine, 1823–1826*, pp. 58–59.

35. Canning to Frere, August 8, 1823, Gabrielle Festing, ed., *John Hookham Frere and His Friends* (London, J. Nisbet, 1899), p. 257.

munications that had passed between Great Britain and the Alliance. The House wildly cheered the liberal sentiments which he had expressed.[36] To the French chargé d'affaires he remarked sardonically: "Be yours the glory of victory followed by disaster and ruin, be ours the inglorious traffic of industry and an ever-increasing prosperity." [37] The words of Burke rose to his lips: "The age of chivalry is gone; and an age of economists and calculators has succeeded." On April 30, 1823, he announced:

We determined that it was our duty, in the first instance, to endeavour to preserve peace, for all the world; next to endeavour to preserve peace between the nations whose pacific relations appeared most particularly exposed to hazard; and, failing in this, to preserve at all events peace for this country.[38]

The House of Commons rewarded these sentiments with an overwhelming vote of confidence—372 to 20; and Princess Lieven hastily explained to her brother that:

The English public is beginning to display a little common sense; what is more to the point, an appreciation of its own interest—the first consideration with the English. They will not spend a shilling on those interesting Spaniards, the objects of their good wishes.[39]

What Princess Lieven failed to understand was that this vote of confidence, while expressing the peaceful inclinations of the country, also endowed Canning with new strength in dealing with his colleagues. The Tory majority was responding to his scintillations as Lord Liverpool had hoped it would; but in so doing it had sounded the death knell to the influence of that aged triumvirate, Lords Eldon, Sidmouth, and Westmoreland. Faced with the alternative of destroying the cabinet or acquiescing in the policies of the Foreign Secretary, they grudgingly chose to remain in office. Henceforward, despite their protests and delaying tactics, Canning was to become his own master in the realm of foreign affairs. He told Bagot quite bluntly that since April 30 and the vote of confidence "I have had pretty much my own way; and I

36. Charles K. Webster and Harold Temperley, "British Policy in the Publication of Diplomatic Documents under Castlereagh and Canning," *The Cambridge Historical Journal*, I (1924), 164–165.

37. Halévy, *A History of the English People, 1815–1830*, p. 173.

38. Hansard, *Parliamentary Debates*, N.S., VIII (1823), 1480.

39. Lionel G. Robinson, ed., *Letters of Dorothea, Princess Lieven during Her Residence in London, 1812–1834* (London, Longmans, Green, 1902), p. 64.

believe you may now consider my politicks as those of the Government, as well as of the Country." [40]

But what was he to do with this new-found freedom? The events of the three previous months had dealt a grievous blow to the prestige of Great Britain. The Alliance, so cavalierly defied at Verona, had moved on majestically without her. Indeed, as Spanish resistance crumbled before the onslaughts of the French, the pretensions of its members seemed actually to increase. By April Canning was already hearing of their intention to find some way of restoring Ferdinand to his Latin American dominions. Was this the opportunity that he had thought to find in January and which had so quickly eluded him? Could it be possible that the Concert was at last preparing to assume a responsibility far beyond its physical capabilities? He could forestall the plot immediately, of course, simply by recognizing the Latin American states, as the United States had done a year earlier; but that would only drive the Continental Powers closer together. The wiser course seemed first to allow the Allies to overextend themselves—challenge them to do their worst—and then, having exposed their collective impotence to the world, defy them by the act of recognition. Surely, if the spectacle were staged with sufficient finesse, the Alliance would expire of mortification. [41]

The scheme possessed only one notable defect: he could not operate all the levers alone. The Allies, led by France, having finished with Spain, would certainly attempt to determine the destinies of the revolutionists in Latin America; and, since this would be tantamount to a direct challenge to England, a passive attitude would just as certainly be impossible. Yet if Canning denounced the Allies by himself, they might ignore him even as they had in January, persist blindly in their plans, and bring about the very war that he wished to avoid. A denunciation, in order to be effective in this charged and uncertain atmosphere, must come with such éclat, with such an imposing show of force, that the Allies, convinced of its sincerity, would stop—would in fact

40. Canning to Bagot, July 14, 1823, Bagot, *George Canning and His Friends,* II, 180. As early as May Canning had told the French chargé d'affaires that his position was safe both in Parliament and in the country. See Temperley, "Canning, Wellington and George the Fourth," *Eng. Hist. Rev.,* p. 212.

41. While this conjecture appears to offer the most plausible explanation for Canning's actions during the summer and autumn of 1823, Harold Temperley only hints at it, and then, curiously enough, in *The Unpublished Diary and Political Sketches of Princess Lieven* (London, J. Cape, 1925), p. 84, rather than in *The Foreign Policy of Canning.*

retreat from the scene in complete disorder. Such a denunciation plainly required at least the momentary support of another Power in order to lend that touch of conviction which Great Britain's actions alone would lack. For that support Canning turned to the United States.

The moment seemed highly propitious; after an interval of almost a year Adams himself was evincing a renewed interest in some sort of negotiation with Great Britain. He had, in fact, become aware of the growing differences between Canning and the Alliance and no doubt wished to profit from them by demanding a settlement of all issues left outstanding from the War of 1812. But Stratford Canning, the British minister in Washington, interpreted the Secretary's intentions in a broader and more optimistic sense. In March he reported upon the satisfaction with which Adams "viewed the course adopted by His Majesty's Cabinet in the present crisis of European Affairs . . ." [42] In May he told Canning:

The course which you have taken in the great politics of Europe, has had the effect of making the English almost popular in the United States. The improved tone of public feeling is very perceptible, and even Adams has caught something of the soft infection. . . . On the whole, I question whether for a long time there has been so favorable an opportunity—as far as general disposition and good will are concerned,—to bring the two Countries nearer together. [43]

Finally, on June 6, 1823, Stratford was able to write that

Instructions . . . are preparing for Mr. Rush . . . to negotiate a Convention with His Majesty's Government, principally on the subject of Slave Trade and Colonial Intercourse, but also with the view of conferring, and, if possible, of establishing a common understanding, on several points affecting the interests of the two Countries. [44]

What more could Canning ask? He had already initiated certain steps of his own to prepare the American minister in London for such a rapprochement. Rush suddenly found himself subjected to toasts flattering to the principles of Jeffersonian neutrality, to

42. Stratford Canning to Canning, March 27, 1823, Public Record Office, London, F.O. 5, Vol. 176 (Photostats from the Library of Congress).
43. Stratford Canning to Canning, May 8, 1823, Perkins, *The Monroe Doctrine, 1823–1826*, p. 60.
44. Stratford Canning to Canning, June 6, 1823, Public Record Office, London, F.O. 5, Vol. 176 (Photostats from the Library of Congress).

dinner parties, charades, copies of parliamentary oratory, and other special attentions.[45] But, as was only natural, Canning preferred to have the first overtures in this game originate in the United States. Whatever the bargain he had to strike in order to obtain American cooperation would thereby cost him the less. With a rare patience he waited and wrote up a series of instructions to guide a commission of inquiry to Mexico.

Rush did not receive his instructions from Adams until July 29. Then he waited for eighteen days, studying the topics of negotiation, before he requested an interview with Canning. The interlude must have been a painful one for the Foreign Secretary. The French were speeding toward Cadiz; Ferdinand would soon be free and the Allies at liberty to embark upon more elaborate schemes. The question of Latin America was already stirring in both Paris and Vienna. Clearly, if the United States was to be brought into the field against the Alliance, an agreement as to terms must be reached with some dispatch.[46]

The tension finally eased when on August 16 Rush appeared at the Foreign Office. Almost inevitably, after certain preliminaries, the topic of Latin America came to the fore. Rush introduced the subject with the remark "that should France ultimately effect her purpose in Spain, there was at least the consolation left that Great Britain would not allow her to go farther and lay her hands upon the Spanish colonies, bringing them too under her grasp." Canning seized the opportunity with what must have been a barely concealed impatience and proceeded to elaborate his own ideas upon the matter. He immediately recommended Anglo-American cooperation as a remedy to the Continental menace. Not, he explained, "that any concert in action under it could become necessary between the two countries, but that the simple fact of our being known to hold the same sentiment would . . . by its moral effect, put down the intention on the part of France . . ."

A mixture of interest and suspicion constituted the reaction of the American minister. On the one hand, cooperation with Great Britain to protect the Latin American states from aggression, might, aside from its intrinsic value, serve as the preliminary to

45. See R. Therry, ed., *The Speeches of the Right Honorable George Canning* (6 vols., London, J. Ridgway, 1836), V, 50–51. Rush, *A Residence at the Court of London*, 2d ser., II, 79–81. Whitaker, *The United States and the Independence of Latin America*, pp. 435–437.

46. Canning had had the opportunity in June to come to an agreement with France over the colonial question, but, since this did not fit in with his own plans, he chose to ignore it. See Perkins, *The Monroe Doctrine, 1823–1826*, p. 116.

an agreement upon other outstanding issues. On the other hand, cooperation on this particular issue could cause his country infinite embarrassment. For the United States, having recognized the Latin American countries, would be bound in all good faith to honor its pledge; while Great Britain, having so far avoided the first obligation, would be free at any time to ignore the second. In an effort to avoid the dilemma Rush therefore urged Canning to bring Great Britain upon the common ground of recognition with the United States before entering into any cooperative enterprise.

But recognition was the last rather than the first step that Canning wished to take. His policy was intercontinental; his object was to destroy the Alliance; and the best way of accomplishing his purpose was to allow the Concert to try to intervene in Latin America. Premature acknowledgment of the new states might spoil the whole game. He therefore retired behind a smoke screen of ambiguities in his response to Rush, implying as he went that he was actually moving in the direction of recognition. The long and exhausting interview ended upon this inconclusive note.[47]

Nevertheless Canning refused to be disheartened, and for the remainder of the month he labored with unceasing ingenuity to penetrate the American defenses. On August 20 he sent Rush the draft of an agreement which, if it did not bind Great Britain to recognize the Latin American states, would at least preclude their transfer to the sovereignty of any other Power.

For ourselves [said Canning disarmingly], we have no disguise.

1. We conceive the recovery of the Colonies by Spain to be hopeless.

2. We conceive the question of the Recognition of them as Independent States, to be one of time and circumstance.

3. We are, however, by no means disposed to throw any impediment in the way of an arrangement between them, and the mother country by amicable negotiation.

4. We aim not at the possession of any portion of them ourselves.

5. We could not see any portion of them transferred to any other power with indifference.[48]

On August 23, while at Liverpool, and having learned of French plans to settle the fate of Latin America in a congress, Canning again wrote to Rush and suggested concerted action. Two days

47. Rush to Adams, August 19, 1823, Manning, *Diplomatic Correspondence*, III, 1475–1477.
48. Canning to Rush, August 20, 1823, *ibid.*, pp. 1478–1479.

later he went even further. At a dinner for the more prominent of his former constituents—a dinner to which a minor American diplomat, Christopher Hughes, had been carefully invited—Canning made a startling and dramatic speech. The United States and Great Britain had forgotten their dissensions, he announced; "the force of blood again prevails, and the daughter and the mother stand together against the world." [49]

None of his maneuvers evoked an entirely satisfactory response. Although Rush, for his part, expressed a warm desire for Anglo-American cooperation, he continued to insist upon the necessary precedence of British recognition.[50] Unwilling to make this concession and thus remove the opportunity for the Alliance to over-extend itself, Canning seemed to give up the fight. On August 31 Rush heard from him again.

What appears to me . . . the most advisable [Canning explained], is that you should see in my unofficial communication, enough hope of good to warrant you in requiring Powers & Instructions from your Government on this point, in addition to the others upon which you have recently been instructed & empowered; treating that communication *not* as a proposition made to you, but as the evidence of the nature of a proposition which it would have been my desire to make to you, if I had found you provided with authority to entertain it.[51]

Had the conversations come to an end? The first two weeks of September passed in silence. Rush confided to both Adams and President Monroe his deep distrust of Canning's motives. The Foreign Secretary, for his part, contemplated the steady progress of French arms against the dying embers of Spanish resistance, conversed with his cousin Stratford Canning, recently returned from his servitude in Washington, and on September 18 once more summoned Rush to the Foreign Office. As before Canning painted the ambitions and designs of the Alliance in the darkest colors and pleaded with the American to join in a concert against them. He had, he said,

the strongest reasons for believing, that the cooperation of the United States with England . . . afforded with promptitude, would ward off altogether the meditated jurisdiction of the European powers over the

49. Temperley, *The Foreign Policy of Canning,* p. 129.
50. Rush to Canning, August 27, 1823, Manning, *Diplomatic Correspondence,* III, 1483.
51. Canning to Rush, August 31, 1823, *ibid.,* pp. 1485–1486.

affairs of the new world. Delay this cooperation . . . and the day might go by; the progress of events was rapid; the evil might come on.

Rush was not to be moved. He repeated his condition that Great Britain first recognize the independence of the new states. Canning rejected the proposal and again the interview ended without result.[52]

Canning called Rush to his home at Gloucester Lodge for a final scene on September 26. This time he resorted to subterfuge and implied that the American chargé d'affaires in Paris had received new instructions which, when they reached London, would surely authorize Rush to cooperate with him. Rush was not impressed. Canning then asked if he would assent to the original English proposals on a promise by Great Britain of future acknowledgment of the Latin American states. Rush was emphatic in his negative. His refusal put an end to the entire negotiation. At the close of the conversation, according to Rush, "Canning expressed his desire, that in informing my government of his communications to me, I would treat them as entirely confidential, as well the verbal as the written; the more so if no act resulted from them. That no act will result from them," Rush concluded, "is my present belief." [53]

In this dismal judgment the American minister was entirely correct. Canning, having reached a state bordering upon desperation even before the final conversation, had already embarked upon an entirely different maneuver. The elaborate edifice of his diplomacy was collapsing about him, and the time left in which to rebuild was rapidly diminishing. Instead of allowing the Alliance to stumble into an untenable position and then covering it with ridicule by means of an Anglo-American declaration, he was being driven back into that isolated position which he had occupied with such discomfort during the January crisis over Spain. Was he to permit a repetition of that pattern, risk defiance from the Allies led by France, and find himself challenged to a war? Or were there variables in the new pattern of which he could yet take advantage? Certainly there was one important difference. Where, in the earlier contest, he had allowed the lines of disagreement to be clearly drawn before interposing his good offices between France and Spain, now he might salvage something if he could act before the Alliance took up a new and equally intractable position.

52. Rush to Adams, September 19, 1823, *ibid.*, pp. 1487–1493.
53. Rush to Adams, October 2, 1823, *ibid.*, pp. 1494–1495.

Canning's first thought had been to send a note to France, repeating in far sterner tones his warning of March 31 against European interference in the affairs of Latin America.

The alternative [he explained to the Duke of Wellington] is between giving fair notice of what we intend, in time to prevent collision, or waiting till we are called upon to speak out with all the Allies leagued against us. . . . Our way out of this complication is to act for ourselves before the Congress have decreed (as they will do) that the colonies shall be recovered for Spain, and that France, backed with the "moral force of the Alliance," shall be the instrument of their recovery.[54]

When the Duke advised against this defiant gesture, Canning reluctantly agreed to explore the subject first with the French ambassador in London.

The conferences between Canning and the Prince de Polignac lasted nine days, from October 3 to October 12, and resulted in an astounding diplomatic success for Great Britain. As they progressed Canning uncovered two interesting facts. Polignac was not only willing to forswear intervention in Latin America for his government; he was positively anxious to bring England into a congress upon Spanish American affairs. Here was tremendous luck, and Canning hastened to take advantage of the revelations. On October 9 he donned his most winning smile and persuaded the Prince to agree to a memorandum which, while pledging France not to intervene "by force or by menace" in Latin America, failed to commit Great Britain to a congress. The language upon the latter point was engagingly ambiguous. Canning promised that England would not stand in the way of any reasonable effort to settle the differences between Spain and her colonies. But he also stated that "England could not go into a joint deliberation upon the subject of Spanish America upon an equal footing with other Powers, whose opinions were less formed upon that question, and whose interests were in no way implicated in the decision of it." Finally he added to the confusion by implying that he might not attend a congress at all unless the United States too were invited. With this variety of statement Polignac had to be content.[55]

54. Canning to Wellington, September 24, 1823, Wellington, *Despatches*, II, 137–138.

55. Temperley, *The Foreign Policy of Canning*, pp. 114–118; Webster, *Britain and the Independence of Latin America*, II, 117. Polignac believed that France's

Although the Prince sensed shortly thereafter that he had been tricked, and tried to wriggle out of the bargain, the French received the memorandum with perfect equanimity. Villèle's government, although upon the point of becoming Ferdinand's mentor and guardian, had no intention of recovering Latin America for that wayward monarch. Villèle himself was rapidly regaining his former ascendancy over Louis XVIII; and from the first he had disapproved of the Spanish adventure. He remained far more interested in replacing English influence in Latin America with that of France than in becoming the sword and shield of Legitimacy. His problem was to avoid the dictates of the Eastern Powers —to break away from the restrictive doctrines of the rump Alliance—without bringing the wrath of its members down upon his head. A congress, at which Great Britain would assume the onus of refusing to cooperate in the reassertion of Ferdinand's authority over Latin America, seemed to Villèle the only feasible way of regaining for France her liberty of action. The Polignac Memorandum, with its ban upon the use of force, he regarded as a first step in the proper direction. That he believed Canning would attend such a congress, if only to disagree, gives support to the theory that in international affairs faith plays as important a part as logic.[56]

For the moment Canning was in no mood to disillusion Villèle; for this state of affairs was precisely the one that he had been laboring so long to create. By means of the Polignac Memorandum the danger of using force to settle the Latin American dispute had, to all intents and purposes, been eliminated. What was more, he had accomplished this feat without discouraging the Alliance from calling a congress. He had only to wait now until that selfsame Alliance, without Great Britain, had revealed its impotence. Once the revelation had occurred and Europe had reverted to that wholesome state of anarchy which he so prized, he could recognize the Latin American states with impunity and thereafter play the balance of power to his heart's content.

"entire abnegation in this grave question gave her the right and imposed upon her the obligation of opposing all enterprises on the part of other governments which would have as an object to obtain an advantage that she believed both her duty and her dignity required her to oppose." Polignac to Chateaubriand, October 10, 1823, William S. Robertson, *France and Latin-American Independence* (Baltimore, Johns Hopkins Press, 1939), pp. 270–271.

56. For the manner in which France received the Polignac Memorandum, see Harold Temperley, "French Designs on Spanish America in 1820–5," *Eng. Hist. Rev.*, XL (1925), 42.

With his chief objective well on the way toward realization, Canning could now adjust the lesser components of his policy. He had done nothing regarding British relations with Latin America since the beginning of the year; the shifting affairs of Europe and the negotiations with Rush had absorbed all his energies. But when on October 10 the news of the fall of Cadiz and the liberation of Ferdinand reached London, he responded immediately. Since the calling of a congress upon colonial affairs could be expected to follow closely upon the restoration of the Spanish monarch, he must have his own countermove in readiness. He exhumed the instructions drawn up in July, appointed commissioners to investigate the stability of the Mexican and Colombian regimes, and dispatched them upon their way.[57]

Only one other step remained to be taken. He must, it seemed, persuade Rush of the insignificance of the August and September conferences. The American was too well acquainted with British plans; he might encourage his own government to use that knowledge to its own private advantage. The fact that Rush knew too much was not the only difficulty either; he stood as a constant reminder of a moment's indiscretion. In October the course of their conversations must have seemed a piece of midsummer's madness to Canning. Clearly, for reasons of pride as well as of state, it had become necessary to remove the traces of that all too palpable error.

Unfortunately the days of assassinating foreign envoys had gone by; even having them recalled presented exasperating difficulties. But, although one was forced to abide with their presence, one could ignore completely such subjects as the Latin American states. Accordingly, for over a month, such was the tactic that Canning pursued in his relations with Rush. The American called at the Foreign Office on October 8, while the Polignac conferences were at their height. Canning "said nothing of Spanish American affairs, except barely to remark at parting, that he should send off consuls to the new states very soon, perhaps in the course of this month." [58] Here was an extraordinary change from their last interview when Canning had so hotly argued the merits of a joint declaration. But the treatment was as nothing compared with what followed. Rush called again on October 9 and found the

57. Canning to Hervey, October 10, 1823, Webster, *Britain and the Independence of Latin America*, I, 435–437.

58. Rush to Adams, October 10, 1823, Manning, *Diplomatic Correspondence*, III, 1500.

Foreign Secretary wrapped in a silence of glacial proportions. He "said not one single word relative to South America, although the occasion was altogether favorable for resuming the topic, had he been disposed to resume it. I therefore consider," Rush confided to Adams, "that all further discussion between us in relation to it is now at an end." [59]

But by the end of November Canning came to the conclusion that the wall of silence would no longer be necessary. Indeed, since the Polignac Memorandum was now a matter of common gossip, was this not the ideal moment to change tactics? To appear to confide in Rush? To emphasize, in the light of the memorandum, the shadowy and transient nature of their own conversations? To indicate their obsolescence, their informality, their title to oblivion?

Rush found himself at the Foreign Office once again on November 24. Canning promptly developed the new line by saying that the conference of September 26 at Gloucester Lodge, "having led him to conclude that nothing could be accomplished" between the United States and Great Britain, "he had deemed it indispensable, as no more time was to be lost, that Great Britain should herself, without any concert with the United States, come to an explanation with France." [60]

To indicate more emphatically to Rush that the door had been closed upon the whole unfortunate episode and that it would be positively rude to reopen it, Canning communicated to him an abbreviated copy of the Polignac Memorandum on December 13. The British had taken this step, Canning explained,

within a few weeks, after the last interchange of confidential letters between us. The result is before you. You will see that we are not unmindful of your claim to be heard: but I flatter myself that neither you nor we shall now have to lift our voice against any of the designs which were apprehended a few months ago.

I am sure you will feel, Sir [the Foreign Secretary concluded], and I trust it will be felt by your government that the confidence which I individually reposed in you is sacred; and that our intercourse in August not having led to any particular result, nor become matter of discussion between our respective Governments will be considered as having passed between two individuals relying upon each other's honour & discretion.[61]

59. Rush to Adams, October 10, 1823, *ibid.*, p. 1501.
60. Rush to Adams, November 26, 1823, *ibid.*, p. 1503.
61. Canning to Rush, December 13, 1823, *ibid.*, p. 1507.

Did Canning sense what was coming from the United States
and by such palliatives as these hope to forestall action? Perhaps,
but if this was the case his pleas for secrecy and quiescence were of
no avail. From the very first Rush had emphasized to Adams the
importance of the conferences and had added some acid comments upon the motivations of British policy.[62] Not unnaturally,
his communications aroused the utmost interest and concern in
the United States. The idea of proclaiming the Western Hemisphere to be a unit divorced from the politics of Europe had occupied the minds of American statesmen from the moment of the
republic's formation. The dramatic appearance of Russia upon
the northwest coast, the visions of expansion aroused by the
Transcontinental Treaty, the establishment of independent states
in Latin America, the menacing gestures emanating from Europe—these circumstances had already combined to suggest the
urgency of some such declaration. Rush's dispatches provided the
impetus to action.[63]

The first reports from London stirred up a great debate in
Washington. Should Canning's proposal be adopted or should
the United States continue in its aloofness from European en-
tanglements? Madison and Jefferson, summoned from their somno-
lent antiquity, advised cooperation; but Adams, shrewd, experienced, and overbearing, while favoring some sort of declaration
regarding Spanish America, preferred to see it made independently. Before a final decision could be reached Rush's accounts of
the impasse in the negotiations arrived.

The debate now resumed with greater energy, occupying Monroe's cabinet throughout November. Certain members of the administration expressed doubts as to the wisdom of taking any
action at all. But Adams, long so cautious, was at last convinced
that the moment was opportune for the United States to score a
resounding diplomatic triumph. Canning had finally exposed the
position of Great Britain in his conversations with Rush; she no
longer needed to be feared. As for the European Powers, Adams hardly thought that they would "ultimately invade South
America." Or, if they did, "they might make a temporary impression for three, four, or five years . . ." But he no more be-

62. Rush to Monroe, September 15, 1823, Hamilton, *The Writings of James Monroe*, VI, 376–377. See also Whitaker, *The United States and the Independence of
Latin America*, pp. 449–450.
63. Perkins, *The Monroe Doctrine, 1823–1826*, p. 69.

lieved "that the Holy Allies will restore the Spanish dominion upon the American continent than that the Chimborazo will sink beneath the ocean." [64]

In the end it was Adams who prevailed, and Henry Addington, the British chargé d'affaires in Washington, reported his manner as suddenly "open and cordial, and exempt from harshness or haughtiness. In truth, ever since the receipt of Mr. Rush's correspondence, he has been singularly cheerful and complaisant, and assumed a frankness and unreservedness in deportment and conversation altogether unusual to him." Addington did not quite grasp the feline quality of this new attitude. "Mr. Adams was evidently much pleased with the manner in which the proposition had been made," the chargé wrote blithely on December 1, "as well as the opening thus afforded for his country to play so prominent a part in the affairs of the world." [65]

How large that opening was, and the fashion in which it was to be filled, became evident a day later when the President, in his annual message to Congress, stated what has come to be known as the Monroe Doctrine. The substance of the President's declaration was quite simple. The Western Hemisphere could no longer be considered as available to colonization by any European Power; the United States proposed to hold aloof from European affairs; and conversely, Europe would be expected to adopt a similar attitude toward Latin America. The declaration, as phrased, included Great Britain in its strictures as much as it did the other members of the European Alliance.

Owing to a momentary indiscretion on the part of Canning and the acuity of Adams, the United States had found a way to garner for itself an enormous prestige as the guardian of liberty in North and South America. Whether American statesmen would implement the initial step in their daily diplomacy with the Latin American nations only subsequent years could tell. For the moment the apparent daring of the doctrine itself served to obscure the future.

Canning, of course, knew nothing of the declaration being made in Washington on December 2. For his peace of mind it was just as well. The business of the Foreign Office was settling into a more normal routine, and he could look into the future with cau-

64. *Ibid.*, p. 73.

65. Addington to Canning, November 20, December 1, 1823, Temperley, *The Foreign Policy of Canning*, p. 122.

tious optimism. He had regained—who could doubt it?—the initiative in foreign affairs; and as the days fled by only one incident occurred to mar the serenity. A regular official dispatch arrived from Addington recounting a conversation that he had had with Adams upon the proposals relayed by Rush. The contents of the dispatch could not have been in themselves particularly upsetting. The American government had been bound to learn the secret of the proposals. What seemed to concern Canning was that any record of them should appear in the Foreign Office files. Since no action would result from them, surely they were best forgotten. He had been overly nervous during the summer, perhaps even a trifle foolish. But why record his mistake?

At the behest of the Foreign Secretary, Lord Conyngham informed Addington that

the substance of your dispatch marked No. 18 is of so confidential a nature, that it should not have been the subject of an official Dispatch —but should have been communicated to Mr. Canning in a Private and Confidential letter.

It has therefore been withdrawn from the Official Correspondence of the Office, and is now returned to you in order that you may put it into the shape of a private letter.

Your No. 19 has been altered to No. 18—you will have the goodness to observe this in the numbering of your future dispatches.[66]

That was on December 8. On December 24, suddenly, appallingly, the routine was shattered. The Monroe Doctrine, arriving by special packet, fell into Canning's hands. Spread out in the bold type of the *National Intelligencer* were the shocking words:

. . . we should consider any attempt on their part to extend their system to any portions of this Hemisphere, as dangerous to our peace and safety . . . we could not view any interposition for the purpose of oppressing them . . . than as the manifestation of an unfriendly disposition towards the United States. . . . Europe is still unsettled. . . . Our policy . . . [is] not to interfere in the internal concerns of any of its powers . . .[67]

To Canning the words came as a harsh and unexpected blow. The United States had chosen the very moment when he was

66. Conyngham to Addington, December 8, 1823, Public Record Office, London, F.O. 5, Vol. 177 (Photostats in the Library of Congress).

67. Samuel Flagg Bemis, *A Diplomatic History of the United States* (New York, H. Holt, 1936), pp. 209–210.

gathering strength to defy the Alliance to challenge British influence in Latin America. If the Monroe Doctrine were allowed
to stand uncontroverted, the new states would surely look to North
America instead of Europe for leadership. Preferential trade
treaties might result. The whole Western Hemisphere might combine in a political league, with the United States at its head, to
create a new and disturbing element in the balance of power. Such
dangers as these must immediately be counteracted.

More dispatches from Addington were now arriving, elaborat-
ing upon the one that had been sequestered, but after a change of
numbers they were allowed to remain in the Foreign Office files.
Apparently there was no further need to conceal the nature of the
conversations with Rush. On the contrary, in view of the Monroe
Doctrine, Canning was now anxious to have these confirmations of
his influence. For he would spread it about that he himself had
inspired the presidential message; and having claimed credit for
it he would go even further. He would point to the Polignac
Memorandum, with its earlier date, and eventually assure for
Great Britain the title of exclusive benefactor to Latin America.

VIII

THE DILEMMA RESOLVED

IF Canning's political beliefs strike a jarring note; if, like
Palmerston, he loved to drive the coach of state close to the
edge and show how dexterously he could avoid falling over
the precipice, one must nevertheless admire the skill and resource-
fulness of his conduct. Certainly his first year in office would have
ruined a lesser man. Although he had carved out an impregnable
position for himself within the cabinet, his foreign policy had
not been an unmixed success. The French invasion of Spain could
be counted as an outright defeat for Great Britain, and the after-
math of the flirtation with Rush, if not a defeat, at least a most
embarrassing admission of weakness. Only in October, with the
Polignac Memorandum, had the wheel of fortune begun to favor
him; and even that secret triumph had been put in momentary
jeopardy by the Monroe Doctrine. Yet despite these contretemps
the worst was over, the obstacles ahead somehow loomed less
menacingly, and Canning, with his fierce energy and extraordinary
resilience, was not one to linger long by the wayside.

The attack which he opened on the Monroe Doctrine [1] remains as
a particularly dazzling example of his offensive diplomacy. It possessed variety, pace, and subtlety; it was executed with consummate
tactical skill. Taking the doctrine at its face value—that is, as
a message designed for domestic consumption—Canning forbore
from dignifying it with an official protest. Instead he challenged
only one of its principles and then devoted his energies to the task
of making the United States regret the emission of such a statement.

Rush went to the Foreign Office early in January, 1824, and
found himself the subject of an elaborate quizzing by the Foreign
Secretary. What was the meaning of the principle of noncoloniza-
tion, and against whom was it intended? The whole world? If so,

---

1. Although the President's speech was not referred to as the Monroe Doctrine
until January, 1853, I have given it that title here for purposes of convenience. For
the manner in which the doctrine got its name see Dexter Perkins, *The Monroe
Doctrine, 1826–1867* (Baltimore, Johns Hopkins Press, 1933), p. 233.

by what right? Rush lamely supposed that the paragraph in question must be directed against Russia's advance down the northwest coast of North America. In that event, replied Canning, there was no point in continuing the joint Anglo-American protests to the Tsar over his closing of the Behring Sea to foreign ships. Great Britain could hardly be expected to act in conjunction with the United States as long as it persisted in so objectionable a doctrine.

That was the first lash of the whip; other blows quickly followed. Negotiations to settle the fate of the Northwest Territory came to a halt; and Canning made at least one effort to stir up ill feeling between Russia and the United States.[2] As for the points raised by Adams as suitable for a treaty settlement, they soon became lost in a series of time-consuming and fruitless conferences. By the beginning of February Rush had come to the bitter conclusion that Great Britain would "avoid any further advance to a political cooperation with our system." [3] So much for the United States and its temerity in proclaiming the Monroe Doctrine.

In his dealings with Europe Canning chose to view the doctrine in a somewhat different light. To Sir William A'Court in Madrid he confided that a "frank communication was made to the American Minister, some months ago of the course which Great Britain intended to pursue, which was no doubt reported by that Minister to his Government before the opening of the Session of Congress." [4] Several days later, in an elaboration of these remarks, he expressed the opinion that Rush's "report to his Government of this *sounding* (which he probably represented as an overture) had a great share in producing the explicit declarations of the President." [5] To Sir Charles Bagot in St. Petersburg he told an equally circumspect tale.

I have very little doubt [he wrote], that the President was encouraged to make his declaration about the South American States by his knowledge of our sentiments. . . . Rush has avowed to me that he is convinced, his Government would *not* have spoken out, but for what passed

2. See Lieven to St. Petersburg, January 2, 1824, Perkins, *The Monroe Doctrine, 1823–1826*, p. 33.

3. Whitaker, *The United States and the Independence of Latin America*, pp. 528–530.

4. Canning to A'Court, December 29, 1823, Webster, *Britain and the Independence of Latin America*, II, 410.

5. Canning to A'Court, December 31, 1823, A. G. Stapleton, *George Canning and His Times*, p. 395.

between us; but that is a moral, not a political, an accidental, not a contrived much less a stipulated consequence of our intercourse.[6]

Abroad the impression quickly spread that Great Britain had inspired the Monroe Doctrine. Early in January, 1824, Chateaubriand remarked upon the similarity of purpose between the presidential message and the Polignac Memorandum and voiced the suspicion "that these doctrines were now set forth for the first time by the President in virtue of an understanding between the British and American Governments." [7] Canning in replying to this presumption denied that there had been any concert with the United States or that Great Britain had connived at the Monroe Doctrine. But the whole tenor of his note, admitting, as it did, the conversations with Rush, left the impression that Great Britain and the United States were not far apart in their respective points of view.[8] The entire campaign served to create an atmosphere of acute uncertainty upon the Continent. Canning did not stress the apparent coincidence of American and British policies to the point where Europe would feel obliged to draw back from a congress upon Latin American affairs. He merely left sufficient doubt in the minds of the Allies so that they approached the idea of a congress with extreme wariness—fully conscious of their dependence upon Great Britain. Psychologically the Concert was now ripe for disintegration.

With respect to Latin America itself, Canning subjected the Monroe Doctrine to an entirely different treatment. He counterattacked vigorously with the Polignac Memorandum. Toward the end of 1823 and early in 1824 he dispatched the memorandum to the British agents who were then investigating the stability of the Mexican, Colombian, and La Platan regimes. He also distributed it among his envoys at the courts of Europe. His general attitude toward the document, as he explained it to A'Court, was this: ". . . it must not be published; but short of that it cannot be too generally known. Its date is most important; both in reference to the state of things which then existed, and in reference to the American speech which it so long preceded." [9]

6. Bagot, *George Canning and His Friends*, II, 215–218.
7. Stuart to Canning, January 2, 1824, Webster, *Britain and the Independence of Latin America*, II, 131.
8. Canning to Stuart, January 9, 1824, *ibid.*, pp. 132–134.
9. Canning to A'Court, December 31, 1823, A. G. Stapleton, *George Canning and His Times*, p. 395.

By March, 1824, circumstances had so far changed that he was able to communicate the memorandum officially to the House of Commons. And although the Duke of Wellington protested such indiscriminate disclosure of diplomatic confidences, Lord Liverpool, in the House of Lords, went on to stress its precedence in time over the Monroe Doctrine. By the summer of 1824 even the Latin American press had got wind of what Canning had whispered into Polignac's ear; it could not have done so at a more opportune moment. For even as Canning's strictures became matters of common knowledge, Adams, in response to queries from his southern neighbors, found himself forced to place an extremely limited interpretation upon the Monroe Doctrine. The contrast in attitudes served to propel Great Britain to a position of the very first rank in the affections of the new states.[10]

Here was a highly satisfactory accomplishment. By a mixture of secrecy and well-timed publicity, veiled intimidation, and soft insinuation, Canning had turned an engine of anti-British sentiment into an instrument of his own diplomacy. During the first six months of 1824 one might almost have thought that the Monroe Doctrine was the premeditated result of his earlier activities. But he had still to accomplish his major objective—the destruction of the Alliance. Until the wreckage of that institution was visible for all to see he would not feel free to recognize the states of Latin America or deal the final blow to American influence in that area.

Fortunately, the Allies seemed determined to afford him every opportunity to effect his purpose. As early as October, 1823, they had invited Sir Charles Stuart to attend a conference upon Latin American affairs in Paris. Sir Charles had wisely refused the invitation and received in consequence a letter of approbation from his superior.[11] Canning himself had furnished a clue to his policy even earlier, in September.

Prince Metternich seems to be of opinion that all should be alike [he had written]; he is even for trying his hand upon us—to make our glory as like to that of the sun and moon of the Continent as possible: but he had better leave us quiet in our own sphere, or we shall make most unharmonious music.[12]

10. Temperley, *The Foreign Policy of Canning*, p. 164.
11. Canning to Stuart, October 28, 1823, *ibid.*, p. 134.
12. Canning to Sir Henry Wellesley, September 16, 1823, A. G. Stapleton, *George Canning and His Times*, p. 380.

His approval of Stuart's conduct brought the objectives of British policy into sharp relief. Indeed, was not the delineation a trifle too sharp? So it appeared, for in November, when the Allies persisted in their supplications, Canning adopted a more ambiguous role. He admitted that the presence of the United States at a congress was not wholly desirable; but he also declared that Great Britain's interests in the Spanish colonies "were of a nature so delicate, so diversified and different from those of other Powers that they could *not* be submitted to any general deliberation." Then he threw his audience into complete confusion by intimating that he might invite France to join with Great Britain in mediating the dispute.[13]

France, of course, was in no position to accept such an offer. Although she had relinquished her role as the military executor of Allied wishes by virtue of the Polignac Memorandum, she was still bound to act in this as in other matters in conjunction with the Concert. Moreover, as Ferdinand's benefactor and as a declared defender of the concept of Legitimacy she was deterred from acting toward the Latin American states in a friendly fashion, no matter what her commercial interests dictated. Her only salvation lay, so it seemed, in a congress with Great Britain in attendance—a congress which, if it did not frustrate English ambitions, would at least leave France free, in the ensuing deadlock, to satisfy her own.

As early as October a congress had become the great object of French policy. Now, in the face of Canning's ambiguous attitude, an effort was made to give the policy effect. Polignac, still under the influence of the Foreign Secretary's charm, advised that Great Britain might accept an invitation if Spain so requested.[14] Villèle confided to Stuart that "nothing would have been easier than to obtain a request in writing from the King of Spain for the departure of a joint French and Spanish expedition for Vera Cruz," but that respect for British susceptibilities had prevented him from taking such a step.[15] Chateaubriand informed Polignac, no doubt for Canning's benefit, that congresses had as painful memories for France as for England but that a less formal conference of Ambassadors might, in this case, serve as well.[16] Villèle poured

13. Temperley, *The Foreign Policy of Canning,* p. 121.

14. Polignac to Chateaubriand, October 31, 1823, *ibid.,* p. 134.

15. Stuart to Canning, November 3, 1823, Temperley, "French Designs on Spanish America in 1820–5," *Eng. Hist. Rev.,* p. 43.

16. Chateaubriand to Polignac, November 17, 1823, Temperley, *The Foreign Policy of Canning,* p. 134.

more oil upon the waters in the latter part of November. Conversing again with Stuart, he declared that France understood her interests to be the same as those of Great Britain upon many points, especially the colonial.[17]

The conspiracy of charm spread beyond French borders to Austria and Russia. Metternich became almost Circean and expressed the opinion that no Power should be prevented from proceeding "with respect to the Spanish colonies according to its own judgment and its real or imagined interests."[18] Count Lieven, the Russian ambassador in London, advocated invoking the mediation of Great Britain as the mandatory of the Allies. In St. Petersburg the Tsar himself shrugged his shoulders and remarked casually: "Everything is in confusion in America, let us leave this chaos for a while to reduce itself to order."[19]

Surely nothing more could be said to calm British suspicions of the Alliance system, and in December steps to activate that system followed the soothing words. France, in accordance with the Prince de Polignac's suggestion, exerted pressure upon Spain to issue an invitation to a congress. On December 1, 1823, Ferdinand obliged by dispatching a circular to the Allied Courts in which he requested their assembled advice upon the subject of Latin America. But this was not all that he did. With a perverse insight he avoided communicating his message to London, and at the same time he recommended the use of force as the most effective way of settling the entire question. Instead of being a gesture of conciliation, the circular, both in wording and in distribution, breathed defiance to Great Britain.[20]

The Allies reacted to this intransigeance with a mixture of confusion and irritation. The French quickly reminded Ferdinand of their obligation under the Polignac Memorandum not to use force or menace against the colonies. Even the mercurial Pozzo di Borgo struck a posture of disgust upon reading the invitation. Yet, despite the shower of protests and recriminations, Ferdinand continued upon his inscrutable way. Even as the circular went out to the Allies he issued a decree reasserting all his rights over the lost

17. Stuart to Canning, November 28, 1823, J. Holland Rose, A. P. Newton, E. A. Benians, eds., *The Cambridge History of the British Empire* (6 vols., Cambridge, Cambridge University Press, 1929–40), II, 251.

18. Metternich to Vincent, November 26, 1823, William S. Robertson, "Metternich's Attitude towards Revolutions in Latin America," *Hisp. Amer. Hist. Rev.,* XXI (1941), 545.

19. Perkins, *The Monroe Doctrine, 1823–1826,* p. 130.

20. Robertson, *France and Latin-American Independence,* p. 285.

dominions. The government gazette teemed with articles indicating a firm resolution to attempt their recovery, and by January, 1824, the stubborn monarch had succeeded in revoking all the concessions granted by his liberal predecessors. The atmosphere was scarcely conducive to the assembling of a congress on Latin American affairs.

The situation was therefore approaching that ripe state of confusion for which Canning had been waiting.[21] Throughout January he did his best to bring about complete pandemonium. On the eighth he stressed to Polignac the futility of holding a congress without the United States and confessed he knew that the United States would not attend. On the ninth he informed Lieven that the ineptitude of Sir Charles Stuart and the untrustworthiness of Pozzo di Borgo made such a meeting undesirable, at least from the standpoint of Great Britain.[22] On the twentieth Polignac received a second lecture. Conferences, Canning announced, "are useless or dangerous; useless if we are in agreement, dangerous if we are not . . ." Neumann, the Austrian chargé d'affaires in London, heard yet another story. Canning remained quite amenable to the free communication of ideas among the Allied Courts. That was a procedure which he favored as a matter of course. But he must immediately dispel the notion that Great Britain would attend a congress on Latin America.[23] The confusion reached a final, reeling climax when, on January 27, he informed Lieven that he repudiated the idea of a congress but might enter into conferences upon the colonial question. Sir Henry Wellesley, enjoying the rococo splendors of Vienna, confessed to complete bewilderment.

It is impossible [he told the Duke of Wellington] . . . to arrive at any correct notion of Mr. Canning's motives for refusing to assist at the conference upon the affairs of America, since he has assigned a different motive to me, to M. de Neumann, and to the government of France. According to my instructions I must maintain that Great

21. According to the London *Times* of November 25, 1823, a committee of two, representing the merchants of London, had called on Canning and Huskisson to learn the French attitude toward South America. They were told that France did not appear to have any designs on South America and that there was no immediate danger to British commerce in that region. See Lawson, *The Relation of British Policy*, p. 90. Professor Temperley does not mention this interview in his *Foreign Policy of Canning*.

22. Perkins, *The Monroe Doctrine, 1823–1826*, pp. 226–227.

23. Temperley, *The Foreign Policy of Canning*, p. 135.

Britain will not assist at a conference, grounding myself upon the Memorandum of the conference between Mr. Canning and M. de Polignac. The French government is led to believe, from the report of their Ambassador, not only that we decline the King of Spain's invitation, but that we are about to acknowledge the independence of the colonies; while M. de Neumann's reports justify a belief that, were the conferences to be held in London, Mr. Canning would not refuse to assist at them.[24]

Canning's equivocations proved especially painful to the French. The Allies had already begun a series of fruitless conferences on Latin American affairs in Paris, and Chateaubriand, without Great Britain, found himself being pressed to assume commitments with which the French interest had no specific concern. A note of desperation appeared in his communications to the British ambassador. The French government, he emphasized, was determined not to use force in order to re-establish Spanish ascendancy over the colonies. Secure in that knowledge, Great Britain would hardly wish to avoid a congress, particularly when an exchange of opinions there would involve no prearranged course of action.[25]

At one point Chateaubriand even suggested that the Monroe Doctrine was reason enough to predispose Great Britain toward cooperation with the other Allied Powers. When these pleas evoked no response he lost the last remnant of his poise. On January 26, 1824, denouncing the South American colonies as the breeding ground of militarism and anarchy, he demanded a congress, with Great Britain participating, in the name of Monarchy and Right.[26]

This wild cry gave the signal that the Alliance was on the verge of collapse. For the moment Canning refrained from answering Chateaubriand's indiscreet tirade and concentrated instead upon completing the destruction. He dashed off a dispatch to Sir William A'Court in Madrid on January 30, refusing flatly to attend a congress, "even, if it were perfectly clear, from the tenour of Mr. Ofalia's Instruction, that Great Britain is in fact included in the invitation to the Conference at Paris." [27] Three days later he assembled the Allied diplomats in London and informed them

24. Sir Henry Wellesley to the Duke of Wellington, February 10, 1824, Wellington, *Despatches*, II, 206.

25. Stuart to Canning, January 9, 1824, Webster, *Britain and the Independence of Latin America*, II, 135.

26. Temperley, *The Foreign Policy of Canning*, p. 135.

27. Canning to A'Court, January 30, 1824, Manning, *Diplomatic Correspondence*, III, 1517–1518,

of his decision. The fatal blow had finally fallen. The Eastern Powers, committed as they were to a settlement of the colonial question, found themselves, with France a reluctant fourth, impotent before the intransigeance of Great Britain.

Logic decreed that the Allies should now drop the entire subject. But logic had long since departed from the counsels of the Concert. Questions of prestige, and the wild hope that Great Britain might yet reconsider her stand, propelled the Continental Powers onward over the abyss. As Canning remarked, they still thought he was "throwing a little dust in the eyes of Parliament" and implored him to cease his "funning." [28]

Metternich condemned the folly of the Spanish government, admitted that with the Polignac Memorandum Canning had virtually isolated France from the Alliance, and expressed himself with great bitterness upon the refusal of Great Britain to confer upon the colonial question. The Prince, having rid himself of this spleen, went on to hint that Canning's rejection of a congress might well be interpreted to mean that England had surrendered her right to a voice in Continental affairs. [29]

Chateaubriand attempted to evoke the menace "of a project for extending the Federal System" from the United States to "all the states of America" and "thought it was an additional motive for the participation of the British government in the arrangements by which the Allied Powers hope to effect the pacification of those countries." He even offered to retract all the arguments contained in his letter of January 26—"if it were thought they were calculated to estrange the policy of France" from that of Great Britain. In a confiding burst to Stuart he said that Metternich had lost all interest in Spain's pretensions and would be satisfied to see the colonial question settled on a basis agreeable to the revolutionists—provided that in reaching such a settlement the usual forms and procedures of the Concert were followed. [30]

Other less garrulous efforts were made to cloak the proposed congress in a garb more suitable to British tastes. Ferdinand finally opened the colonial trade to nations friendly to Spain on February 9—and promptly ruined the gesture with restrictions which made the decree inoperative. As a result of further Allied

28. Temperley, *The Foreign Policy of Canning*, p. 136.

29. Sir Henry Wellesley to Canning, March 19, 1824, Webster, *Britain and the Independence of Latin America*, II, 27.

30. Stuart to Canning, April 15, 1824, *ibid.*, p. 150.

pressure the Spanish Foreign Minister, after tactlessly deploring
Canning's earlier refusal of a congress, renewed the invitation in
April.

To this, as to all the other, blandishments, Canning replied
with a haughty silence. He knew that what he had prematurely
anticipated a year earlier had at last occurred: the Alliance was
split into three distinct and separate parts. He learned through
Stuart that an Allied ambassadorial conference had extracted
from Chateaubriand a pledge not to recognize the new states. But
he also learned through Stuart that Chateaubriand, in retaliation, had reminded the conference of his equally binding pledge
under the Polignac Memorandum not to use force against them.[31]
As Canning remarked delightedly to Lord Granville:

The three Military Monarchies, with Russia at their head, would willingly *confer*, if they knew to what end to direct their Conference.
France wishes them to go on their own way, and to find a bye-way for
herself between them and us, but nearer to our way than theirs, and
with some slight inclination (if she knew how) to special French advantage.[32]

But he had "cut the knot of this twisted policy"; the Alliance
lay paralyzed. He could now recognize the Latin American states
free of its interference and, in the process, deal it a final, humiliating blow.

And yet there was a space of eight months between the collapse
of the Alliance and the recognition of the new states. What caused
the delay? Certainly not the country at large. The general enthusiasm for the new states, stimulated by the business community,
had reached a fever pitch; nothing could have been more popular than recognition; and under different circumstances Canning
would have willingly played to the gallery. But there still were
complications. The cabinet itself had come to no firm decision upon
policy. Lords Eldon, Westmoreland, and Bathurst, the Duke of
Wellington and the King all linked a distaste for Canning with the
fear that they were witnessing the final undoing of Castlereagh's
entire labor. To these men the Alliance, despite its manifold faults,
had become the symbol of European unity, and if recognition of
the new states represented a blow at that structure they would

31. Temperley, *The Foreign Policy of Canning*, pp. 136–137.
32. Canning to Granville, November 15, 1824, A. G. Stapleton, *George Canning
and His Times*, p. 405.

oppose the measure bitterly. Yet their opposition was not the determining factor in the delay. They hated Canning but they loved power more, and since Canning remained essential to their continuation in office they would, in the last analysis, sacrifice the Alliance and acquiesce in a policy of recognition rather than risk a dissolution of the government.

The delay resulted mainly from Canning's own stratagems. The Foreign Secretary was, and remained, a daring player; he designed his tactics to sweep the board. But for all his dash and boldness he retained a capacity to guard against the unforeseen. In this instance he had lured the Alliance into an untenable position; he had cleared the way for recognizing the new states. But he was substituting ridicule, logic, and precedent for violence, and there was need for circumspection in such a game. If he recognized the new states out of hand and without ample verbal justification he might find the precedent turned against him at a later date in some other part of the world. Or, if he ushered the new states into the family of nations before assuring himself of their pro-British orientation he might discover that he had reared a nest of serpents at his breast.

To decrease the danger of retaliation he twice offered Spain highly honorable conditions on which to settle her differences with the colonies. On January 30, 1824, when refusing Ferdinand's first invitation to a congress, he suggested an alternative arrangement by which the mother country would receive commercial advantages superior to those conceded to other nations.[33] When this offer was rejected he went even further. On April 2 he expressed a willingness to guarantee Cuba to Spain, "so soon as Spain shall on her side have adopted the suggestions of my other Despatch with respect to her Provinces on the Continent of Spanish America." [34] Surely this gesture indicated the last extremity of restraint on the part of Great Britain. But, to make the case more nearly perfect, Canning urged Mexico to originate some reasonable compromise in her dispute with the mother country so as to put Spain impossibly in the wrong. It was, as events proved, a superfluous step. In May Spain refused the guarantee of Cuba "which, if not clogged with such conditions, would have been most thankfully accepted . . ." [35]

33. Canning to A'Court, January 30, 1824, Webster, *Britain and the Independence of Latin America*, II, 415.
34. Canning to A'Court, April 2, 1824, *ibid.*, p. 424.
35. Temperley, *The Foreign Policy of Canning*, p. 139.

Canning required no further answer. The result of Spain's refusal, he announced in a public dispatch, was simply that Great Britain reserved the right to take whatever steps she might think proper, in regard to the Latin American states, without further reference to Madrid. In private he adopted a somewhat different tone.

We offered to guarantee Cuba [he wrote gaily to Bagot]:—which, for a power so shy of guarantees, was a great offer; and might, if accepted, have involved us in great difficulties. But it is refused. And there (as I have said) is an end.

A more prudent policy on the part of Spain, and one which I confess I apprehended, would have been to "bear us in hand" awhile:—to make it impossible for us to find an *apropos*, or to say as we now say, "there's an end." [36]

He was master of the terrain after that. He and his predecessor had offered Spain every reasonable opportunity to revise her position; her continued intransigeance in the face of long-exercised privileges certainly justified any step that Great Britain might take for their protection. Still, Canning was content to wait. There was no point in recognizing the new states unless he could be certain of their gratitude. Not only must his case be justifiable in terms of British interest and Spanish recalcitrance; it must also provide for Great Britain a new sphere of political influence. Recognition, in other words, must appear to Europe as a respectable and disinterested act, and at the same time bind Latin America firmly to England. Where the maneuvers with Spain had accomplished the first purpose, the reports of the commissions which he had dispatched to Latin America in the autumn of 1823 would allow him to judge the opportunity and time to accomplish the second.

The Mexican commission had reached its destination on December 31, 1823. Eighteen days later, after an investigation of the most superficial sort, undertaken at the very moment when a serious insurrection had flared up against the central authority, the commission sent off a report highly favorable to the existing regime.[37] Canning received their analysis late in April, 1824. He expressed a certain irritation over the speed with which his agents had worked

36. Canning to Bagot, May 29, 1824, Bagot, *George Canning and His Friends*, II, 240.

37. F. L. Paxson, *The Independence of the South American Republics; A Study in Recognition and Foreign Policy* (Philadelphia, Ferris and Leach, 1903), p. 219.

and complained that they had not studied the monarchical elements in the country with sufficient care. Nevertheless, he accepted their conclusions. The Colombian commissioners proved more conscientious. Not until October did their report reach England. Then it provided a flattering picture of General Bolívar, of his monarchical and pro-British predilections. Even more interesting were the dispatches from Buenos Aires. Woodbine Parish, who had been sent to the Plata, reported that half the public debt and most of the valuable property in Buenos Aires rested securely in English (or rather, Scottish) hands. Of the fifteen thousand foreigners in the city three thousand five hundred were British. Thirty-nine British commercial houses already were in business, with correspondents in Rio de Janeiro and Montevideo. They controlled almost the entire export and import trade.[38]

Canning, with the active support of Lord Liverpool, determined to act upon this latter case at once.[39] In July, 1824, over the opposition of Wellington, a cabinet minute went to the King, recommending that full powers be sent Parish to negotiate a commercial treaty—a treaty which inevitably "would amount to diplomatic recognition of the State with which it had been concluded." A month later Canning was able to empower Parish to take the all-important step.[40]

For a time the action remained a secret of the cabinet and the King. Piecemeal recognition was after all not quite dramatic enough to suit Canning's histrionic leanings or forceful enough to deal a last stunning blow to the Alliance. The disclosure was to come only when two more of the new states had been added to the list of eligibles and when circumstances had so arranged themselves as to make the act look like outright defiance of the Concert.

By November a suitable occasion had arisen. The Eastern Powers, together with France, were meeting in a series of conferences in Paris, solemnly discussing a problem over which they no longer exercised control. Russia and Austria through their ambassadors in London were busily engaged in a desperate intrigue to change the policy of the British government by ousting Canning from the

---

38 Parish to Canning, April 25, 1824, E. J. Pratt, "Anglo-American Commercial and Political Rivalry on the Plata, 1820–1830," *Hisp. Amer. Hist. Rev.*, II (1931), 305.

39. The Foreign Secretary was being bombarded with petitions from the most respectable businessmen in London, all of whom pleaded for recognition. Canning was not particularly impressed, however. "I do not think that the opinion of Messrs. Baring, or any other merchants, ought to guide our policy," he told the Duke of Wellington. See Wellington, *Despatches,* II, 294.

40. Temperley, *The Foreign Policy of Canning,* p. 144.

cabinet. Meanwhile France was being persuaded by her embittered associates not to relinquish the now burdensome occupation of Spain. Canning was well aware that the occupation came as an irksome duty to France.[41] He was equally conscious that the guardianship of Ferdinand prevented her from competing with Great Britain in the Latin American market. But he could not resist the argument, however superficial, that the occupation posed a threat to the balance of power—a threat for which Great Britain must have compensation.[42]

At Canning's instigation Lord Liverpool submitted a memorandum to the cabinet on November 30, favoring the recognition of Colombia and Mexico.

Let us remember . . . [he argued] that peace, however desirable, and however cherished by us, cannot last for ever. Sooner or later we shall probably have to contend with the combined maritime power of France and of the United States. The disposition of the New States is at present highly favourable to England. If we take advantage of that disposition, we may establish through our influence with them a fair counterpoise to that combined maritime power. Let us not, then, throw the present golden opportunity away, which, once lost, may never be recovered.[43]

When a majority of the cabinet, led by Wellington, remained unimpressed with this appeal Canning wrote directly to Paris and asked whether France would promise to evacuate Spain within a definite time. He received the looked-for response on December 9: both Damas, now Foreign Minister in Chateaubriand's place, and Villèle had evaded a direct reply to his question. As a result Canning was able to read a far more persuasive memorandum to the cabinet on December 14.

The great practical question . . . for us [he urged], seems to be how, in the event of an actual incorporation of the resources of Spain with those of France, such an accession to the power of France can best be

41. See Harold Temperley, "Canning and the Conferences of the Four Allied Governments in Paris, 1823–1826," *Amer. Hist. Rev.*, XXX (1924), 25.

42. As he explained himself to Granville, "If the French were reinforcing their army in Spain, we might have something to say; as they are withdrawing it, what would we more? Not surely help them with our suggestion, or encourage them with our applause, or preclude ourselves, by implication even, from summing up their Spanish Expedition in our own sense in Parliament, if occasion shall arise." Canning to Granville, November 11, 1824, E. J. Stapleton, *Some Official Correspondence*, I, 191.

43. Memorandum of November 30, 1824, Wellington, *Despatches*, II, 358.

counteracted. I have no hesitation in saying this must be by a separation of the resources of Spanish America from those of Spain; and it
is (at least in this point of view) a fortunate circumstance that this
state of things has already taken place; and that we are in a situation
to avail ourselves of it.[44]

The demand upon Damas and Villèle had served its purpose.
The Duke of Wellington, together with Lords Bathurst, Westmoreland, and Eldon, revolted for a moment, but when Canning
and Liverpool threatened to resign all opposition within the cabinet collapsed. A minute recommending the recognition of Colombia and Mexico was sent to the King on December 15; and Canning
went into transports of joy. To Lord Granville, who had replaced Sir Charles Stuart in Paris, he wrote: "The deed is done,
the nail is driven, Spanish America is free; and if we do not mis-
manage our affairs sadly, she is *English*." In his most expansive
mood he went on to explain:

. . . you will understand why I set you upon Damas and Villèle for
the answer about Spain. You see the use that it has been turned to in
the Minute. It was no less useful in discussion.

We—that is Liverpool and I—had made up our minds to be satisfied
with Mexico. But your dispatch enabled us to carry Colombia too.

Now that it has done its work, I do not want to persecute Villèle with
this question, nor get any ill humour into the discussion.[45]

The news of the British decision went off to Spain on December
31, 1824. After it had gone the Duke of Wellington worked himself into a fury, dashed off a bitter note of protest to the King,
and then, in conformity with cabinet custom, refrained from de-
livering his tirade. The government had hurried so, he grumbled
to Peel,

not from any cause appertaining to the case itself, but because we did
not choose to take the measures which we ought to have taken to draw
from France at first the explanation which the King of France has
since given in his speech to the Legislature, of the nature of the French
occupation of Spain.[46]

44. Harold Temperley, "The Later American Policy of George Canning," *Amer.
Hist. Rev.,* XI (1906), 781–782.
45. Canning to Granville, December 17, 1824, A. G. Stapleton, *George Canning
and His Times,* p. 412.
46. Wellington to Peel, January 2, 1825, Wellington, *Despatches,* II, 394.

George IV was equally furious. He asked his ministers for individual advice upon the measure, but when they refused, thereby setting an important precedent in English constitutional practice, he reluctantly gave his consent to recognition. Only a last childish gesture remained to solace his royal pride. When announcement of the decision was made in the King's speech to Parliament on February 7, 1825, he refused to read the message on the grounds that he suffered from the gout and had lost his false teeth. It fell to Lord Eldon, the bitterest opponent of the measure in the cabinet, to do so in his stead.[47]

The European chancelleries received the news with mingled grief and consternation. Villèle, sensing the deeper implications of the act, remarked to Lord Granville

that the Allies (and he did not conceal that he alluded more particularly to Russia) would consider this measure as one by which England placed itself upon a *different line* from the other great Powers of Europe, and that the Emperor of Russia, to whose moderation Europe was indebted for the preservation of the peace of Europe, seeing that the British Government had thought fit to pursue its own separate interests without concert and without regard to the opinions of other Courts, would no longer abstain from the prosecution of the natural objects of Russian ambition . . .[48]

Count Bernstorff, in Berlin, "could not but regret the adoption of this step . . ." while Metternich, who was growing ever more fearful of being left alone with the Tsar, belatedly deplored the widening breach between England and the Continental Powers.[49]

The Russian, Prussian, and Austrian ambassadors in London, in a forlorn effort at solidarity, presented verbal protests to Canning in the beginning of March. Their action proved to be a last fatal mistake. Canning turned their protests into official documents and proudly displayed them as confirmation of Allied impotence. He had publicly challenged the Concert; throughout 1824 it had sat in judgment upon Latin American affairs. He had ignored its advice and opinions; now he laughingly rejected its protests. In the sense of Castlereagh's original conception, the Concert no longer existed. Its members, bereft of prestige, would

47. Temperley, *The Foreign Policy of Canning*, pp. 151–152.

48. Granville to Canning, January 6, 1825, Webster, *Britain and the Independence of Latin America*, II, 162–163.

49. Clanwilliam to Canning, January 8, 1825, Granville to Canning, March 28, 1825, *ibid.*, pp. 286, 175.

henceforth pursue their separate interests with only spasmodic attempts at mutual consultation. Europe, according to Canning, was getting back to a wholesome state again.[50]

Latin America received the British decision to recognize its independence with universal satisfaction. Sucre's great victory at Ayacucho in December, 1824, had dislodged the Spaniards and their supporters from the Andean plateau. All that remained to the loyalists thereafter were small footholds in Chile, the fortress of Callao in Peru, and the bastion of San Juan de Ulua in Mexico. The natives, with British recognition, could now plan their future with a measure of security. Colombia, Buenos Aires, and Mexico quickly negotiated trade treaties with their benefactor, and, although the last was not finally ratified until 1827, the long-awaited commerce with Latin America could at once be placed upon a regular and predictable footing.

The effects of this diplomatic activity upon the English economy were not quite what the policy-makers had anticipated.

You cannot imagine how mad everyone here has gone over the companies in South America [Princess Lieven reported]. . . . Everybody, from the lady to the footman, is risking pin-money or wages in these enterprises. Huge fortunes have been made in a week. Shares in the gold-mines of Rial del Monte, bought at £70, were sold, a week later, for £1350. These sudden fortunes, and the passion for speculation, remind one of the Mississippi Bank in the time of the Regency.[51]

Mining companies, capitalized at over £14,000,000, sprang into existence to exploit the resources of the new states, and the banks and investing public absorbed loans of more than £20,000,-000.[52] A mania of speculation swept over the country, and in the final elaboration of the craze a group of investors organized the British Churning Company to export Scottish maids to tend Argentine cows.

The indiscriminate outpouring of money reaped its first harvest in 1826. The speculative bubble burst; warehouses bulged with unsalable goods; and scores of commercial houses crashed to ruin. The year 1827 saw a measure of order reintroduced into the sys-

50. Temperley, *The Foreign Policy of Canning*, p. 154.
51. Princess Lieven to Metternich, January 27, 1825, Quennell, *The Private Letters of Princess Lieven to Prince Metternich*, p. 343.
52. Rippy, *Rivalry of the United States and Great Britain over Latin America*, p. 108.

tem, but somehow the Latin American market did not fulfill the long-standing and golden anticipations. There were even those, like the Duke of Wellington, who felt that the protracted and involved struggle to capture it had wrought more harm than good.

IX

POLICY TESTED

THE impression of Canning which emerges from the diplomacy of Spanish American recognition is one of iconoclasm. For two years he drew upon the good will which Great Britain had accumulated among the new states while he maneuvered the Continental Powers into an untenable position. Then with great sound and fury he recognized Buenos Aires, Colombia, and Mexico, defied the Alliance, and rendered it the laughingstock of the Old World. From the relatively mild and impersonal wish that "for *Europe,* I shall be desirous *now* and *then* to read England," he had progressed to a point of venom where he was describing Metternich as "the greatest rogue and liar on the Continent, perhaps in the civilized world." [1]

But even Canning was not all iconoclast. "I was," he admitted, "I still am—an enthusiast for national independence; but I am not —I hope I never shall be—an enthusiast in favor of revolution." [2] Perhaps nowhere better than in his approach to Brazilian independence did he exhibit this respect for established forms. His desire to ridicule and annoy the Alliance was still evident. So too was his regard for the special British privileges in Brazil which Lord Strangford had wrung from Don John in 1810. But above and beyond these considerations Canning strove to establish in Rio de Janeiro both a center of British influence and a working model of the monarchical institutions which he so much admired.

His ultimate success in this object was due in no small part to the peculiar nature of the Brazilian movement toward independence. Don John as Prince Regent of Portugal had elevated his colony to the status of a kingdom in 1815. Upon the death of his mother he went a step further and assumed the title of King of Portugal, Brazil, and the Algarves. By a series of titular changes

1. A. G. Stapleton, *George Canning and His Times,* p. 364; Canning to Granville, March 11, 1825, *ibid.,* p. 427.
2. Temperley, *The Foreign Policy of Canning,* pp. 464–465.

Brazil graduated thus effortlessly from a position of dependency to one of theoretical equality with the mother country.

Three years sufficed to endow this new status with an air of permanence. In 1818 Castlereagh suggested that Don John should resume his duties in Lisbon; but the timid monarch preferred to linger on in Rio de Janeiro, away from the troublesome concerns of Europe. The revolution which swept over Portugal in 1820 so fixed him in this resolution that when the new Portuguese junta ordered him to return, he contemplated sending Pedro, the heir to the throne, in his stead. Events in Brazil shortly conspired to change his mind. A revolt which broke forth in Rio de Janeiro in April, 1821, rendered the colony an even less desirable residence than the mother country. Don John hastily appointed Pedro his regent in Brazil and fled to Lisbon, where he meekly swore fidelity to the constitution that awaited him. Brazil had become not only a kingdom; she also possessed her own sovereign.

What followed savors far more of outrageous travesty than of serious politics. The Portuguese Cortes, which had curtailed Don John's powers, now proceeded to exercise its own with extraordinary indiscretion. In a series of extreme and impractical decrees it attempted to reduce Brazil once again to the status of a colony. The reaction to this manifestation of constitutional liberalism was immediate. Satisfied that they had forever discarded their subordinate rank within the Portuguese empire, the Brazilians declared their independence on September 7, 1822, and on October 12 proclaimed Pedro their emperor. Nine days later to complete the act of defiance they declared war upon Portugal.[3]

Pedro's situation during this crisis had been one of extreme delicacy. Young and ungovernable, he nevertheless entertained a strong sense of loyalty to the House of Braganza. Although he had accepted the title of Emperor of Brazil without hesitation, he remained eager not only to preserve the authority of his family in both hemispheres but to secure his own right of succession to the Portuguese throne. Unfortunately such an attitude involved a dilemma. If he insisted upon liberty he would be disinherited in Lisbon; if he abjured independence he would be expelled from Rio de Janeiro. Any escape from such a dilemma obviously required the intervention of some outside force. The difficulty lay in obtaining such succor. If the circumstances had been spiritual Pedro might possibly have prayed for a miracle. Since they were

3. Webster, *Britain and the Independence of Latin America*, I, introd., 55–57.

political he turned to the more mundane influence of Great Britain.[4]

A Brazilian agent soon made his way to London with the object of securing recognition of Pedro's new title and the means to an honorable reconciliation with Portugal. He arrived at a propitious moment, for Canning, recently installed at the Foreign Office, saw in Pedro's predicament a way to inaugurate his own career with a striking diplomatic success.

Owing to the efforts of William Wilberforce and the "Saints," English public opinion had long been aroused to the necessity of abolishing the slave trade. Brazil, as matters fell out, represented the last great market for slaves. If, under the circumstances, he could force Pedro to accept abolition as a condition of recognition, Canning felt confident that he would win the gratitude of the country. He acted with customary vigor. In November, 1822, he proposed the measure to the cabinet; in February, 1823, he wrote to the British consul-general in Rio de Janeiro and offered to recognize Brazil if Pedro would abolish the slave trade. At the same time he instructed Lord Amherst, who was traveling to India by way of Brazil, to negotiate for a declaration against the "abominable traffic." [5]

Nothing came of these efforts. Pedro drew his main support from the great Brazilian landowners, who, in their turn, relied upon slave labor for the cultivation of their plantations. The young Emperor therefore found himself obliged to reject the conditions attached to British recognition.

Upon mature consideration Canning could hardly regret Pedro's decision. In his haste to score a personal triumph he had overlooked the real complexities of the situation. There were, he discovered after some further reflection, certain obstacles not to be overcome by the simple act of acknowledgment, for the importance of establishing British influence in an independent Brazil was equaled by the necessity of retaining it in Portugal. Brazil represented an excellent market for English manufactures; she also stood as the only potential monarchy in Latin America. But by a tradition verified in the Peninsular War, Portugal provided the gateway for Great Britain's military entry into Europe. Self-

---

4. *Ibid.,* introd., p. 60.

5. Cabinet Memorandum of November 15, 1822, *ibid.,* II, 398. Canning to Chamberlain, February 15, 1823, *ibid.,* I, 220–221. Canning to Amherst, February 18, 1823, Temperley, *The Foreign Policy of Canning,* p. 213.

interest required that the ancient guarantee of Portuguese integrity be preserved.

The reconciliation of these divergent aspects of British policy would have been extremely difficult under normal circumstances. What made it particularly trying in 1823 was the fact that a state of war existed between Portugal and Brazil. The war was of little consequence as long as Pedro remained unrecognized: the struggle could be considered as an internal one, outside the scope of the British guarantee. But with Pedro recognized and Brazil independent, matters would assume an entirely different aspect. The guarantee would at once become operative and Great Britain would be bound to support Portugal against the very state which she had acknowledged. Such a predicament could be got over only by renouncing the guarantee, by forcing Brazil to forego her independence, or by persuading Portugal to accept Pedro's new status. The first alternative was not to be considered except as a threat. In view of what was passing in Spanish America, the second was impracticable. Canning resorted to the third and tried to effect a reconciliation favorable to Pedro behind the screen of an impartial mediation.

As matters developed, Pedro was willing to wait upon Portuguese recognition; he even agreed secretly to suspend hostilities while attending that result.[6] But Portugal proved less amenable to persuasion. The reason for this intransigeance is to be found less in Don John's anger over the presumption of Pedro than in the diplomatic struggle between Great Britain and the Alliance.

Ever since Don John's return to Lisbon, the kaleidoscope of Portuguese politics had turned with bewildering rapidity. The liberals, with their inept reforms, had fallen from power. An absolutist party, led by the King's second son, held office for a moment and then followed the liberals into the wilderness. To the accompaniment of court intrigues, petty plots, and occasional violence, even the constitution disappeared from view. In theory Don John had now regained his royal prerogatives. In point of fact he had become a pawn in the struggle between Great Britain and the Alliance. Twice Hyde de Neuville, the French envoy, offered to intervene in Portuguese affairs. Twice Canning responded to the menace: in the one instance by the dispatch of a British

6. Chamberlain to Canning, July 14, 1824, Webster, *Britain and the Independence of Latin America*, I, 242.

squadron to the Tagus; in the other, by the offer of a detachment of Hanoverian troops (conveniently procurable without parliamentary consent).

Neither competitor quite gained his objective. Although Don John remained instinctively pro-British, he retained a deadly fear of the French troops in Spain. Eager to keep the British guarantee, he was equally anxious to retain the good will of the Alliance. In an effort to avoid the solicitude of his friends he appointed a ministry, absolutist and pro-French by inclination, yet in some measure subject to his own control. The result was political paralysis.

Canning's efforts to settle the Brazilian dispute suffered the inevitable consequences. Although the Portuguese cabinet recognized the necessity of obtaining British aid to bring Pedro to terms, they refused to consider a grant of independence as the proper method. Villa Real, the Portuguese minister in London, dutifully applied for mediation on September 23, 1823, but insisted somewhat less dutifully as he did so that Great Britain should neither recognize Brazil by herself nor condone Pedro's claim to the title of Emperor. Canning promptly rejected these conditions, whereupon Villa Real suggested that the Allies might be invited to mediate in his stead. Such talk only served to anger the Foreign Secretary. He announced in reply that "England would never recognize rights in the Allied Powers to intermingle in the affairs of the Colonies." Villa Real was wise enough to retreat a step; after further conferences he agreed to accept Great Britain and Austria as comediators in the case. Canning, for his part, promised to take no unilateral action for the time being.[7]

Austrian cooperation did not loom as a practical obstacle to Canning's plans. Metternich was far too pragmatic to concern himself with violations of Legitimist principle where there existed the possibility of preserving a monarchy. What was more, Pedro had married a Habsburg princess. Canning could therefore approach his task with moderate optimism and the assurance of some Austrian support. His own idea was to create a federative union in which each succeeding monarch would reside alternately in Rio de Janeiro and Lisbon. But when the conferences of mediation got under way in July, 1824, the area of disagreement proved far too wide to be bridged by this compromise. The Brazilian

7. Temperley, *The Foreign Policy of Canning*, pp. 213–214.

agents insisted upon outright and unfettered independence; Villa Real clung grimly to the principle of continued Portuguese sovereignty.[8]

Under the supervision of Canning and the Austrian chargé d'affaires five conferences took place, each of which resulted in deadlock. By the end of summer only two things had emerged from the discussions. The Alliance, acting through France, was encouraging the Portuguese to use obstructive tactics, while Pedro, in retaliation for Great Britain's failure to concede recognition, was maneuvering to cancel his obligations under the commercial treaty of 1810.

In a final effort to reach a settlement Canning brought forth his plan of federative union. When Austria refused to support it he pushed on boldly alone. In October he wrote directly to his minister in Lisbon, urged the benefits of federation, castigated the Alliance, and warned that he could not much longer withhold English recognition of Pedro. He got nothing for his pains. Don John responded to the threats and pleas with his customary evasions; the deadlock in the mediation conferences continued.[9]

In consequence, Canning passed to a more critical examination of the subject. If Villa Real continued to attend conferences he did so merely to throw the onus of their failure upon Brazil. The Portuguese cabinet, whose creature he was, had no desire to settle the dispute. They were merely circumventing the issue, gaining time to mount an attack upon Pedro. The scheme was as embarrassing as it was preposterous; but there it was. Under the circumstances what was England to do?

Can we suffer our squadron to remain in the Tagus [Canning asked Lord Liverpool], to protect (as it were) the fitting out of their expedition against Brazil?

Can we withdraw that squadron—at the risk of its being replaced by a French squadron—at all?

Can we do so, and leave the expedition to be fitted out under French and Russian protection, without marking our sense of the policy pursued by Portugal by a direct advance towards Brazil?

Can we, independently of these considerations, leave our relations with Brazil undefined much longer; the treaty being, by express

8. *Ibid.*, p. 217.
9. *Ibid.*, pp. 217–218.

stipulation, revisable at the requisition of either party, in February next?

To all these questions I am disposed to answer, No . . .[10]

The alternative was to force Don John to choose between Great Britain and the Allies. Only thus could Canning remove the ambiguity which had so far prevented the Brazilian negotiation from being brought to a satisfactory conclusion. The occasion called for vigorous diplomacy, and Canning responded nobly. Information had already reached him that the Portuguese were not only negotiating behind his back with the Allies but had actually sent two secret missions to Brazil in an effort to reach a direct settlement with Pedro. Using these instances of bad faith as the excuse, he proceeded on November 19, 1824, to suspend the mediatory conferences in London.[11] He also wrung from Villèle a written promise to recall Hyde de Neuville, the French envoy in Lisbon and the real leader of the anti-English faction, on account of certain indiscretions which that feckless soul had committed.[12] With the ground thus prepared, he turned directly upon Don John.

The King learned, in the beginning of 1825, that he must choose between Great Britain and the Alliance; there could be no further equivocation. The consequences of throwing in his lot with the Continental Powers involved the withdrawal of the British squadron from the Tagus and the outright recognition of Brazil. But if he chose England, he would receive her continued protection, together with aid in reaching a settlement with Pedro. Canning offered to send Sir Charles Stuart directly to Lisbon for the purpose of receiving Don John's consent to the recognition of Brazil. This done, Stuart would proceed to Rio de Janeiro and negotiate a treaty of separation wholly favorable to Portuguese interests.[13]

Such a solution provided little except balm for Portuguese pride, a way of accepting the inevitable with a semblance of good grace. Fortunately, Don John retained sufficient wisdom to realize that he could expect nothing more. Freed of the obnoxious presence of de Neuville and assured of British support in Europe, he

10. Canning to Liverpool, October 25, 1824, A. G. Stapleton, *George Canning and His Times,* p. 502.

11. At the same time he recalled the timid Sir Edward Thornton from Lisbon and replaced him with Sir William A'Court. See Temperley, *The Foreign Policy of Canning,* pp. 205, 218–219.

12. Canning to Liverpool, November 13, 1824, E. J. Stapleton, *Some Official Correspondence,* I, 195. See also Temperley, *The Foreign Policy of Canning,* p. 206.

13. E. J. Stapleton, *Some Official Correspondence,* I, 325.

summoned enough nerve to oust his ministers. Then he announced his readiness to receive Sir Charles Stuart.

Pray write to your Government [he told A'Court], that it is my earnest desire that Sir Charles Stuart should come out in a Line of Battle Ship at least. You do not know how much importance will be attached in the Brazils to such a circumstance. If he could be sent with a little squadron, so much the better, but a Line of Battle Ship is indispensable to the success of his Mission. Do not forget to write this to Mr. Canning, and that the sooner Sir Charles arrives at Lisbon the better.[14]

The tactics of the Alliance had gone for nought. Their pettiness and uncertainty had combined with Don John's instinctive predilection for Great Britain and her "Line of Battle Ship" to play into Canning's hands. He scored his triumph with the usual zest and venom. The Eastern Powers and France learned that his plan for recognizing Pedro would actually strengthen the very principle of monarchy which they were so busily advocating. What, in the name of Legitimacy, could they reply? Outmaneuvered, unwilling to risk a test of strength in Portugal, they gave their blessing to Stuart's odious mission.[15]

Canning presented Sir Charles with his instructions on March 14, 1825; two days later the envoy departed for Lisbon. After an interlude of procrastination Don John issued a *Carta Patente*, by which he transferred full sovereignty over Brazil to Pedro as King. Stuart underwent a metamorphosis, emerged as a Portuguese emissary, and proceeded to Rio de Janeiro. His path there had been smoothed in advance by Canning. On August 29, 1825, after a series of conferences and a minimum of bickering, he got his treaty. Pedro, after conceding that Don John should have the same title, became Emperor of Brazil. Pride and expediency had been served. The completed treaty reached Lisbon in November, and there final ratifications were exchanged. To Canning's great pleasure Brazil, in the very heart of South America, stood independent—and monarchical.[16]

The victory was sweet—doubly sweet in that the Alliance had again been defied—but, to Canning, no victory was complete until British interests had been served. Political altruism attracted

14. A'Court to Canning, January 15, 1825, Webster, *Britain and the Independence of Latin America*, II, 262.
15. Canning to Stuart, April 30, 1825, *ibid.*, I, 273.
16. Temperley, *The Foreign Policy of Canning*, pp. 220–222.

him only briefly; the clear ring of commerce exercised a more enduring spell. "Tell me," he asked the Portuguese minister in London, "if you believe that any Government here could throw away
the trade with Brazil in order to avoid the simple admission that
what is, is, viz. that Brazil is separated from Portugal." [17] Certainly he would not relinquish so rich a prize, despite his contention
to Lord Granville that

the treaties with Portugal (including even the odious and impolitic one
of 1810, which I, then Secretary of State, in vain remonstrated against
with the *then* Board of Trade, as grinding and vexatious to Portugal
and Brazil) are clogs upon us, in our new course of extended and liberal
commercial principles.[18]

On his mission to Brazil Stuart carried instructions to continue
the Treaty of 1810 "for two years from the day on which that
treaty becomes subject to revision, for the specific purpose of its
being deliberately revised and renewed. . . ." and to stipulate
that, in the revised and renewed treaty, "there shall be introduced
an Article for the immediate and effectual abolition by Brazil of
the Brazilian Slave Trade." [19]
Unfortunately Sir Charles could not resist the temptation to
depart from his instructions. Fresh from his triumph in the matter
of Brazilian independence, he plunged into a negotiation not to
extend the Treaty of 1810 but to revise all its detailed provisions.
His exertions met with almost instantaneous success. In the autumn
of 1825 Pedro agreed upon a new commercial treaty and promptly
published it in the newspapers of Rio de Janeiro.
The sequel to this episode was scarcely what Sir Charles had
anticipated. Instead of general acclamation and a peerage, he received a violent denunciation from Canning. Stuart had acted
in violation of his instructions. He had actually promised to discuss the absolute, the undiscussable, British right of search upon
the high seas in time of war. Even worse, he had included a most-
favored-nation stipulation in the treaty—a clause which in effect
nullified any special advantage that might accrue to Great Britain

17. Canning to Villa Real, January 16, 1825, *ibid.,* p. 219.
18. Canning to Granville, January 21, 1825, A. G. Stapleton, *George Canning and
His Times,* p. 509.
19. Canning to Stuart, May 12, 1825, Webster, *Britain and the Independence of
Latin America,* I, 279

under its terms.[20] If such a treaty were signed, Canning remarked angrily, "France will obtain just such another, and . . . then we shall have all the shame of grasping (in direct contradiction to our liberal professions) and at the same time be deprived of the advantage of our selfishness." [21]

Canning sent Stuart a special missive which must rank high among the masterpieces of publishable vituperation. Then he recalled the unfortunate envoy from Rio de Janeiro and consigned him to official oblivion. A new minister entered into negotiations with Pedro, and at last concluded more satisfactory arrangements on August 17, 1827, just eight days after Canning's death.

There was to be a curious sequel to all these diplomatic triumphs. So unpopular did the various treaties prove in Brazil that Pedro abolished his constitutional assembly and resorted to autocratic rule in order to enforce their terms. As a consequence, he alienated the influential native party of the great landowners; and from that moment Pedro's throne stood in jeopardy. Because of his insistence upon the commercial and slave trade treaties, Canning foredoomed to ruin the very monarchy which he had so painstakingly established.[22]

But the consequences of that decision were not discernible in 1825. Conscious of the importance of Latin America—indeed, overestimating its prospective influence—Canning was content to have established the European tradition of monarchy in Brazil. Monarchical institutions, together with British trade and British recognition, graciously bestowed upon the new states, would suffice, so he reasoned, to assure the cooperation of the entire continent in that elaborate game of balances which was the essence of his policy. Or at least so he argued as the question of Greek independence darkened the European horizon.

The recent events in the Western Hemisphere [he explained to his ambassador in Constantinople], have approximated, as it were, the different divisions of the world to each other, and have brought new Powers to bear on every question of political struggle or change, in whatever part of the globe it may arise. The Porte cannot doubt that

20. Canning to Granville, March 6, 1826, E. J. Stapleton, *Some Official Correspondence*, II, 16–17.
21. Canning to Liverpool, November 27, 1825, *ibid.*, I, 334.
22. Alan K. Manchester, "The Paradoxical Pedro, First Emperor of Brazil," *Hisp. Amer. Hist. Rev.*, XII (1932), 191.

all the inhabitants of both Americas to a man, are in their hearts favourers of the Greek cause, and might at no distant period become active co-operators in it. This is not the language of intimidation, it is that of truth.[23]

He might better have said that this was the language of exaggeration, for even as he wrote an old question arose to illustrate the fateful volatility of Latin American politics. In the revived dispute over the Banda Oriental not only did British influence prove fragile; Pedro's throne shook violently, Buenos Aires fell prey to anarchy, and the whole continent suffered paralysis.

Since the failure of the Allied mediation in 1819, Brazilian troops had occupied and Rio de Janeiro had ruled the Banda Oriental. The territory itself lay exhausted—its cattle-raising industry ruined, its population decimated, and its trade reduced to a fraction of its former lucrative proportions. Economically, the province no longer afforded any advantage to the occupying state; but its position on the Plata River endowed it with great strategic importance; for whoever controlled the Banda also controlled the mouth of the river.

The government of Buenos Aires had long been aware of this simple fact. In 1816 they had protested Don John's invasion and occupation of the Banda. In 1821 they had even refused to acknowledge the Brazilian conquest, although Don John offered to recognize Buenos Aires in return. But for nearly a decade they merely had maintained verbally their right to the Banda as legal successors to the Spanish viceroyalty of La Plata. Internal difficulties effectively prevented them from embarking upon a more vigorous course.[24]

In 1824 a new spirit became evident. The increasing stability and prosperity of the country enabled the government of Buenos Aires to press their claim in a more explicit fashion. They dispatched an agent to Rio de Janeiro and peremptorily demanded the return of the Banda. Pedro went through the motions of normal diplomacy. He conferred, argued, and made counterclaims. He then broke off the negotiations. Brazil refused to surrender the province, and the agent of Buenos Aires departed from Rio de Janeiro threatening war.[25]

23. Temperley, "The Later American Policy of George Canning," *Amer. Hist. Rev.*, p. 793.

24. Manchester, *British Preëminence in Brazil*, pp. 149–150.

25. *Ibid.*, p. 151.

News of the impending conflict sufficed to embarrass Canning upon several scores. War between Brazil and Buenos Aires would not only jeopardize the Brazilian monarchy; it would disrupt the British trade centering in the Plata basin. The struggle might even assume continental proportions, with eventual repercussions in Europe. A peaceful settlement of the dispute, arrived at under British auspices, seemed the only way of avoiding all these dangers. Yet mediation was, at best, a disagreeable and unrewarding task. If the mediator succeeded, he was likely to be reviled by one or both of the disputants. If he failed, British prestige was bound to sink to a low level, and British influence might well be replaced throughout Latin America by that of the United States. But not to act at all meant pursuing a course entirely alien to Canning's temperament.

Late in 1824, when the Foreign Secretary expressed a willingness to intervene, he did so in such a way as to reduce to a minimum the ill will of Buenos Aires and Brazil. He explained his attitude in this way:

It is not our intention to throw off lightly the question of any possible interference on our part to prevent hostilities between Brazil and Buenos Aires, but we wish to put that interference, if it takes place, on its right footing of a gratuitous act of friendship to both parties.[26]

As for his solution of the difficulty, it proved to be one for which neither he nor his government could be held entirely responsible. Just as the Allies had proposed in 1818, so now Canning suggested that Pedro surrender the Banda to Buenos Aires in return for a monetary compensation. The question of Montevideo was not in itself a new one, he told Woodbine Parish, nor new to Great Britain as a mediating Power.

It is one which Brazil and Buenos Ayres inherit from their respective Mother Countries. It is one which occupied three or four years of the deliberations of the Allies. The judgment which we concurred in giving, as between Spain and Portugal, it would be difficult for us to rescind, as between Buenos Ayres and Brazil. That judgment is upon record. The parties to the question are changed, but the substantial rights of the two sides of the question (by whomever represented) are not thereby altered.[27]

26. Canning to Parish, September 26, 1825, Webster, *Britain and the Independence of Latin America*, I, 128.
27. Canning to Parish, October 19, 1825, *ibid.*, p. 132.

So eager, indeed, did Canning grow to keep the dispute separate and distinct from those matters which concerned Great Britain directly that he ordered Sir Charles Stuart not to discuss it on his mission to Rio de Janeiro.[28] At one point he was even prepared to see the whole matter submitted to the assembled American states at Panama—a suggestion which he quickly retracted as soon as the larger implications of that assembly became apparent.

His efforts prevented a loss of British prestige; but they failed to engender a settlement. Both Brazil and Buenos Aires appeared to agree upon the desirability of British mediation, but Brazil eventually refused to surrender the province upon any terms. The fact that the inhabitants of the Banda had begun their own movement toward independence mattered little to the two contestants. The crisis deepened throughout the summer of 1825 and at last reached a climax in October, when the Congress of Buenos Aires incorporated the Banda into the United Provinces of Rio de la Plata. There ensued a final flurry of negotiations, and then on December 10 Brazil declared war upon her neighbor.

The conflict, which lasted from 1825 until 1828, followed what has since become a familiar pattern in South America. Despite frequent and bloody encounters neither side gained a decisive advantage. Buenos Aires scored the greater number of victories, but even as she did so her finances collapsed and a ruinous inflation gripped the country. Brazil fared no better. As defeat followed defeat, Pedro's popularity waned, expressions of dissatisfaction arose from his outlying provinces, and it soon became a question which offered the graver danger—the threat from abroad or the internal menace.[29]

The effects of the war upon British commerce in the Plata basin were extremely painful. When Brazil instituted a blockade of Buenos Aires, the British admiral on the South American station refused to recognize it; but upon legal advice Liverpool's administration countermanded his orders. British trade in the area dwindled rapidly in consequence, and in 1827 only two English vessels reached Buenos Aires. Canning, overwhelmed though he was with applications to interfere, nevertheless refrained from forcing upon Brazil a relinquishment of her maritime rights.

It is not for this country to stir unnecessary discussions upon abstract points of belligerent right [he maintained], so long as her own neutral

28. Manchester, *British Preëminence in Brazil,* p. 153.
29. *Ibid.,* p. 154.

rights are scrupulously respected, nor to endeavour to bring into disrepute an exercise of maritime power to which, as a belligerent, she has so often had, and must probably again, have recourse.[30]

Nevertheless it was becoming increasingly clear that he could not stand aloof from the conflict forever. British prestige in South America was falling at an alarming rate, as was British trade; and the danger was growing that Buenos Aires might act with Bolívar to turn the war into a crusade against the Brazilian monarchy. Canning therefore reverted to the instrument of mediation.

He still favored the cession of the Banda Oriental to Buenos Aires; he knew that Buenos Aires would pay Pedro a handsome sum to obtain the territory. Also, he felt, quite sincerely, that

unless by a general tacit agreement, the States of the New World be admitted to stand towards each other, in respect to geographical rights and limits, exactly as they stood when colonies, questions of the utmost perplexity will infallibly arise out of their rival and conflicting pretensions; and the whole continent of America, whether Spanish or Portuguese, will ultimately be laid open to the designs of any enterprising adventurers, who may think fit to carve out for themselves new dominions.[31]

To induce Brazil to renounce the Banda Canning was even prepared to guarantee freedom of navigation upon the Plata. But the likelihood of Pedro abandoning his original claim was, he must have realized, extremely small.

Was there not, then, a more feasible alternative: that of turning the Banda into an independent state? The irrepressible Sir Charles Stuart had originally broached this idea prior to the outbreak of the war, only to be coldly rebuffed. Canning's first reaction had been that such a solution would lay Great Britain open to the charge of self-seeking. It would be as though she had sought to create a buffer between Buenos Aires and Brazil, an island of British influence to be used in the control of their policies, a bridgehead into South America, or a colony in disguise.[32] But later, the knowledge of the separatist movement in the Banda, and Pedro's intransigeance, had the effect of placing Stuart's alternative in a more favorable light. The difficulty of the question, Canning

30. Canning to Parish, June 23, 1826, Webster, *Britain and the Independence of Latin America*, I, 149.
31. Canning to Ponsonby, March 18, 1826, Wellington, *Despatches*, III, 203.
32. Manchester, *British Preëminence in Brazil*, p. 154.

finally admitted, "lies in this, that the value of Monte Video to each party consists less perhaps in the positive benefit which they may expect to derive from it themselves, than in the detriment which they apprehend from its being in the possession of the opposite party." Still, he wished to preserve an air of impartiality, and since the cession of the Banda to Buenos Aires was a proposition of some sanctity, he pressed it as the preferable mode of settlement.[33]

Lord Ponsonby, a handsome, blustering gentleman, the former lover of the King's mistress, and therefore the minister-designate to distant Buenos Aires, received orders in March, 1826, to proceed to Rio de Janeiro and reduce Pedro to a reasonable frame of mind. The task proved impossible. Once in Brazil, Ponsonby found Pedro unwilling to consider either the surrender of the Banda to Buenos Aires or its erection into an independent state. The Emperor would concede no more than the establishment of Montevideo as a free port on the Plata. With this unsatisfactory concession in his pocket, Ponsonby proceeded to Buenos Aires. The war continued.[34]

Canning refused to be disheartened by this setback. Much as he wished to see the contest terminated, he refused to force a settlement upon the belligerents. His advice to Ponsonby was simple:

Nor perhaps can you better lay the foundation for a more efficient interference in His Majesty's name hereafter, when the events of the war may have sickened and exhausted both parties, than by declaring that you have fulfilled all your instructions on the subject of Mediation, and that your Government can only deeply lament that they have been unattended with any good effect.[35]

Before Canning's orders could take effect, Ponsonby had discovered the "undisputed fact that the Orientalists dislike being subject to Buenos Ayres *only less* than being subject to Brazil, and that Independency is their dearest wish." [36] He therefore pressed hard upon the government of Buenos Aires to assist in

33. Canning to Ponsonby, March 18, 1826, Wellington, *Despatches,* III, 202–205.
34. Manchester, *British Preëminence in Brazil,* pp. 182–184; Pratt, "Anglo-American Commercial and Political Rivalry on the Plata, 1820–1830," *Hisp. Amer. Hist. Rev.,* p. 325.
35. Canning to Ponsonby, November 27, 1826, Webster, *Britain and the Independence of Latin America,* I, 160.
36. Ponsonby to Canning, October 2, 1826, *ibid.,* p. 154.

turning the territory into an independent state. Late in 1826 the government agreed to accept the project as a basis for negotiation with Brazil; and in January, 1827, Canning graciously agreed "to engage to maintain the free navigation of the River Plate alike for Brazil, for Buenos Ayres, and for the newly constituted State of Monte Video." [37]

An agent from Buenos Aires proceeded to Rio de Janeiro in the spring of 1827 and, under the auspices of the British minister there, began to work out a peace settlement with Brazil. A preliminary treaty came to light on May 24. Great Britain was to guarantee the free navigation of the Plata; Buenos Aires would acknowledge the independence and integrity of the Brazilian empire; and, most astounding of all, she would renounce all claim to the Banda Oriental.[38]

The obvious fact that Brazil's military situation hardly justified such a triumph caused Gordon, the British minister, to be almost apologetic about his part in the negotiation. He had attempted, he told Canning, to act impartially between the contending parties. He nevertheless thought that peace was more important than boundaries; and he felt confident that Brazil would gain nothing from a continued sovereignty over the Banda.[39]

For once Canning showed no concern over a violation of instructions. Other more pressing matters were occupying his mind at this point. Lord Liverpool had been seized with an epileptic fit. A cabinet crisis had followed, during which Canning had waged a bitter struggle with the Duke of Wellington for the favor of the King. Late in April he had emerged victorious, his last ambition satisfied, as the first minister of England. He savored now the *engouements* of power, and all its clinging responsibilities. There was almost a note of mellowness in his dispatch of August 8, 1827, to Lord Ponsonby. The terms of the Brazilian treaty were quite satisfactory: after all, they served to end the war. As for the inhabitants of the Banda, if they still craved freedom, let them win it in peacetime.[40]

37. Canning to Gordon, January 3, 1827, *ibid.,* p. 317.

38. Joseph B. Lockey, *Pan-Americanism: Its Beginnings* (New York, Macmillan, 1926), pp. 463–464.

39. Gordon to Canning, June 8, 1827, E. J. Stapleton, *Some Official Correspondence,* II, 322.

40. Canning to Ponsonby, August 8, 1827, Pratt, "Anglo-American Commercial and Political Rivalry on the Plata," *Hisp. Amer. Hist. Rev.,* p. 326 n.

Lord Dudley, the new Foreign Secretary—handsome, kind, stuttering Lord Dudley—was somewhat more explicit:

It is true [he told Gordon], that the terms of the Preliminaries do not coincide with those which you were instructed to recommend to the adoption of the Belligerent Powers . . . ; nor indeed are they such as could have been proposed by a Government professing itself equally friendly to both the contending parties. . . . You have, however, judged rightly that the terms of the treaty are of less consequence than the putting an end to a contest mischievous to one country, destructive to the other, and hardly compatible with the free exercise of commerce with either.[41]

The citizens of Buenos Aires did not see the matter in quite the same light as Lord Dudley. They quickly rejected the treaty. They also dismissed their government who, in turn, blamed the British for the debacle. The war started up with renewed vigor, and the Brazilian fleet finally defeated a squadron from Buenos Aires. On land the leader of the Buenos Aires forces confessed to his superiors that he could not end the conflict. An effort to inveigle Bolívar into an attack upon Brazil failed; and once again internal anarchy threatened the republic.

In Rio de Janeiro and Buenos Aires Gordon and Ponsonby worked frantically on their own responsibility to halt the struggle. Pedro remained deaf to Gordon's pleas throughout the remainder of 1827; but Ponsonby by a more devious route succeeded in laying the foundations for a final settlement. Through an intermediary he established contact with Lavalleja, the new nationalist leader in the Banda Oriental. While advising Brazil and Buenos Aires to countenance the separatist movement, he urged Lavalleja to organize and strike out with a party of his own. By December, 1827, he could report that this last advice had borne fruit, and that the Orientalists were now strong enough to claim their independence. In the same month he persuaded Buenos Aires to declare herself openly in favor of that claim.[42] Only Brazilian resistance remained to be overcome, and in January, 1828, it too began to crumble. Faced with an enemy penetration into Brazilian territory and a plot to overthrow the government, Pedro's cabinet

41. Dudley to Gordon, August 28, 1827, Webster, *Britain and the Independence of Latin America*, I, 319.

42. Pratt, "Anglo-American Commercial and Political Rivalry on the Plata," *Hisp. Amer. Hist. Rev.*, p. 331.

suddenly gave heed to Gordon's pleas for an independent Banda. Early in February the belligerents agreed upon an armistice, and once again agents left Buenos Aires to conclude a preliminary peace.[43]

They departed at an opportune moment, for in London Lord Dudley had begun to lose patience with the whole affair. Ordinarily Dudley was a most phlegmatic man. During the previous six months, indeed, he had displayed an unusual self-restraint. In August, 1827, he had lost his friend and mentor: after a hundred days of power Canning had died. For some time thereafter Lord Dudley had endured the strange moods and frequent tears of Canning's successor, Lord Goderich. Now, still laboring assiduously in the sedate apartments of the Foreign Office, he suffered from the unalterable gruffness of another first minister, the Duke of Wellington. Certainly this was patience of the highest order.

But patience did not strike Lord Dudley as a virtue worth maintaining in the face of Latin American quarrels. Gordon had written that the conflict in the Plata basin was becoming one of Englishman against Englishman, that sailors were deserting their ships to join the fray, and that the social order in Brazil and Buenos Aires was bordering upon collapse.[44] Ponsonby had warned of the influence of the United States, "a nation whose readiness to interfere and depress the interests of Great Britain can hardly be questioned by any one well acquainted with the character of these people." [45] And in a memorandum written toward the end of 1827 a former British agent in Latin America had drawn a graphic picture of the havoc being wrought upon English trade in the area.[46] With the concurrence of the Duke of Wellington Lord Dudley prepared to take a stand, to break the Brazilian blockade of Buenos Aires and force some kind of peaceful settlement upon both belligerents.[47]

Fortunately for the British reputation in Latin America this new disposition became known only after the institution of the peace negotiations in Rio de Janeiro. Threats were superfluous.

43. Manchester, *British Preëminence in Brazil,* p. 156.

44. *Ibid.,* pp. 155–156.

45. Ponsonby to Canning, January 10, 1828, Pratt, "Anglo-American Commercial and Political Rivalry on the Plata," *Hisp. Amer. Hist. Rev.,* p. 327.

46. Rippy, *Rivalry of the United States and Great Britain over Latin America,* pp. 162–163.

47. Dudley to Wellington, March 1, 1828; Wellington to Dudley, March 2, 1828, Wellington, *Despatches,* IV, 288.

Even the presence of a mediator, in the person of Lord Ponsonby, proved unnecessary. Both Brazil and Buenos Aires had reconciled themselves to a separate existence for the Banda Oriental, and this sensible spirit soon manifested itself in a concrete fashion. On August 27, 1828, the two belligerents signed a preliminary convention which acknowledged the principle of independence for the province. On October 4 they exchanged ratifications of the final treaty. Two years later the new state of Uruguay emerged.

In Great Britain the preliminary settlement, where noticed, won general approbation. The primary purposes of British policy had been to promote a peace satisfactory to both belligerents and bring about the resumption of trade. With these ends gained even the Foreign Office passed over the particular terms of the treaty. It mattered very little what became of the Banda Oriental so long as hostilities had ceased.

The Duke of Wellington summed up the prevailing attitude in his usual abrupt fashion. "I think the republic of Buenos Ayres are mad if they do not agree to the preliminaries," he remarked, "and they are not true republicans if they have not possession of Monte Video as soon as Don Pedro will evacuate that place." [48]

Canning might have protested had he heard the Duke. But Canning, to the Duke's great relief, was no longer there to argue. Already the nervous preoccupations of the balancer were giving way to the less troublesome splendors of isolation.

48. Wellington to Aberdeen, October 25, 1828, *ibid.*, V, 171.

X

POLICY JUSTIFIED

THAT Great Britain would ever forsake voluntarily the role of balancer was inconceivable to Canning. His temperament abhorred the vacuum of isolation. Life, in his view, consisted of abstract strategems, with words as counters on a checkerboard of plots; true satisfaction resulted from intricate maneuvering. If placidity threatened the sea of affairs he would be the first to cast a stone. Moreover, his political heritage was that of the eighteenth century—formal, perhaps a trifle superficial, but nonetheless cosmopolitan. He regarded the world with a certain levity; there were overtones of insularity and cynicism in his methods; but the world was still a unit to which Great Britain must adhere.

So, too, must Latin America; that was a cardinal point of policy. Shortly after the recognition of the new states Canning explained himself quite clearly on that score to John Hookham Frere:

The thing is done [he wrote]. . . . The Yankees will shout in triumph; but it is they who lose most by our decision. The great danger of the time—a danger which the policy of the European system would have fostered, was a division of the World into European and American, Republican and Monarchical; a league of worn-out Governments, on the one hand, and of youthful and stirring Nations, with the United States at their head, on the other. *We* slip in between; and plant ourselves in Mexico. The United States have gotten the start of us in vain; and we link once more America to Europe. Six months more—and the mischief would have been done.[1]

No doubt Canning had reason to be proud of his achievement. He had struck a blow for freedom; he had outmaneuvered the Alliance; he had even kept his temper. And yet the link between Latin America and Europe—the fragile link of British recognition— did it justify the exultant letter to Frere? Surely not, if by recog-

1. Canning to Frere, January 8, 1825, Temperley, "The Later American Policy of George Canning," *Amer. Hist. Rev.*, p. 781.

nition alone Canning hoped to exercise an influence over the policies of each individual state in Latin America. The war between Brazil and Buenos Aires indicated how little progress he could expect in that direction. Essentially, the dispute over the Banda was to be resolved, not because Ponsonby and Gordon pleaded and advised but because the belligerents discovered that peace was mutually advantageous. Nor was the Banda to become free because these same emissaries favored its cause. A forceful desire on the part of the inhabitants of the territory rather than any outside intervention furnished the impetus to Uruguayan independence. In both instances British influence was to be the means to an end already determined, a convenient aid, but hardly in itself a determining factor.

If, on the other hand, Canning was working toward a less precise goal, was his boast to Frere perhaps not justified? He tended to regard Latin America less as a collection of states than as a unit, and he made no particular effort to establish a special position in any of its parts. Brazil, of course, was a long-established exception, but even Canning professed a certain reluctance to retain British privileges there. In one instance he refused to validate a treaty which would have granted Great Britain valuable concessions in Mexico.[2] On another occasion, when Bolívar pressed for an alliance, and what amounted to a protectorate, Canning fell into unaccountable delays and ambiguities.[3] During the years between 1822 and 1826 he preferred to rely upon the pervasiveness of British trade and the intangibles of prestige and example to win the general confidence of the Latin Americans.

Here, perhaps, was the essence of his policy, the clue to his success, and the source of his exultation. Where other Powers, less fortunately endowed, felt called upon to cavil and carp for particular privileges, he had but one request to make: equality of opportunity in the matter of trade. For the rest, he could afford an attitude of objectivity. He had no favors to ask; his was an air of reasonableness and of steady if somewhat supercilious concern for the welfare of Latin America. Supported as it was by the British fleet and a lavish stream of loans, how could such a policy fail to engender a reciprocal enthusiasm and trust?

So strongly did Canning come to feel upon the subject, so un-

2. Canning to Hervey, April 23, 1824, Webster, *Britain and the Independence of Latin America*, I, 451.
3. Lockey, *Pan-Americanism*, pp. 191–192.

remittingly did he strive to maintain the pose of the impartial and candid friend, that even in regard to monarchies for Latin America he refrained from putting himself forward. In a sense his restraint was surprising, for by party, by conviction, and by instinct, Canning was a royalist. Like Castlereagh he felt that monarchies in Latin America would provide stability and a European rather than a North American orientation. Indeed, where one already existed, as in Brazil, he was eager to see it survive. Where, on the other hand, it was a question of forcing the institution upon reluctant or undecided peoples, he passed the opportunity by.

He agreed "that the conservation of monarchy in *any* portion of South America will tend to break the shock of that inevitable divorce by which the New World is about to be divided from the Old." [4] And his policy toward Brazil was intended, in part, to lessen the shock. But, so far was

Great Britain from looking to any more intimate connection with any of the late Spanish Provinces than that of political and commercial intercourse, that His Majesty would not be induced by any consideration to enter into any engagement which might be considered as bringing them under *his* dominion.[5]

Undoubtedly this statement expressed Canning's true intent. There was, nonetheless, an obverse side to his policy. If he was unwilling to bring any of the new states under the dominion of Great Britain, he was equally unwilling to see them brought under the dominion of any other Power, particularly the United States.

I have no objection to monarchy in Mexico [he told A'Court]—quite otherwise. . . . But as to putting it forward, as a project or proposition of ours, that is out of the question. Monarchy in Mexico, and monarchy in Brazil would cure the evils of universal democracy, and prevent the drawing of the line which I most dread—America versus Europe.

The United States, naturally enough, aim at this division, and cherish the democracy which leads to it.[6]

To prevent such a division Canning's agents throughout Latin America waged a violent war of words upon the policy of the

4. Canning to Sir Henry Wellesley, August 13, 1824, Webster, *Britain and the Independence of Latin America*, II, 31.

5. Canning to Hervey, October 10, 1823, *ibid.*, I, 436.

6. Canning to Sir William A'Court, December 31, 1823, A. G. Stapleton, *George Canning and His Times*, pp. 394-395.

United States. They exchanged libels with their American counter-parts all the way from Mexico City to Buenos Aires. The air shook with charges and countercharges, and in Brazil the contest assumed an almost physical violence.[7] But these were mere skir-mishes, the cut and dash of light cavalry; the heavy artillery and the big battalions lay in London. Although Canning tolerated and even approved of his subordinates' activities he reserved the major battles for his own direction. In the engagements of Cuba and the Panama Congress the United States felt the full weight of his extensive armory.

Cuba not only remained one of the few real jewels in the Spanish imperial collection; because of strategic and economic considera-tions she had also become an object of interest to Great Britain and the United States. Each country suspected the other of having designs upon the island; neither was ready to subscribe to their execution. Canning suffered from the fear that the United States might annex Cuba in a sudden coup, and contemplated seizing Puerto Rico in retaliation.[8] Adams was equally susceptible. He imagined that Spain might cede Cuba to England in 1823; he raised the subject at a meeting of the cabinet; he even confided to Nelson, the American minister in Madrid, that he would prevent Canning from acquiring the island, by force if necessary.[9] But by the end of the year suspicions had softened somewhat. Both Powers professed to desire neither Cuba nor Puerto Rico. For the moment even Adams and Canning preferred to see the bone of contention remain in Spanish hands: Adams, because eventually the bone would be that much easier to take away; Canning, because a mon-archical outpost in the Western Hemisphere, even under Ferdi-nand's control, was less objectionable than a further diminution of European influence.

On the question of sovereignty, then, Great Britain and the United States were in temporary agreement. Where they differed and where Canning caused difficulties, was over the role that Cuba should play in ending the war between Spain and her former colo-nies.

That this enervating struggle should have lingered on after 1824 was due entirely to the folly of Spain. Driven from the

7. For the details of this and other contests see Rippy, *Rivalry of the United States and Great Britain over Latin America*.

8. Canning to Wellington, November, 1822, Perkins, *The Monroe Doctrine, 1823–1826*, p. 62.

9. Adams to Nelson, April 28, 1823, *ibid.*, p. 55.

mainland of Latin America, she nevertheless persisted in launching petty attacks upon the new states from her Cuban strongholds. The strategy was both pointless and costly. In retaliation Colombia and Mexico took to the sea. Their privateers swarmed into the Spanish Main, ventured into European waters, and snapped up prizes within sight of Gibraltar. Encouraged by these successes, the two countries turned next to an attack upon Cuba itself. In so doing they revived the diplomatic struggle between the United States and Great Britain.

To the United States, with Adams now raised to the presidency and Henry Clay at the State Department, the schemes of Mexico and Colombia came as a sudden and unpleasant surprise. Clay, the assertive advocate of Latin American independence, had long been possessed with the idea of ending the Spanish-American war. The danger to Cuba reinforced his determination; and in an elaborate campaign of dispatches he set out to reserve the island to the eventual mercies of the United States and win Spanish recognition of the new states. On the one hand Mexico and Colombia heard that he could not allow Cuba to be transferred to any other Power. On the other hand France and Russia learned that they should somehow assist the United States in bringing Ferdinand the Well-beloved to reason. Finally, in May, 1825, Clay took the boldest step of all. He offered to concert his policy with that of Great Britain not only to secure Spanish recognition of the new states but also to guarantee Cuba to Spain.[10]

Canning could arouse no enthusiasm for Clay's overture. A year earlier he himself had offered to guarantee Cuba to Ferdinand; but he had made his offer on the condition that Spain recognize the colonies beforehand. Now, with the colonies acknowledged by his own government, he saw no use in repeating the proposition. It was not that he wished to see the war continue; it was simply that taking the island under the protection of Great Britain and the United States did not strike him as the most effective way of ending the struggle. Quite the reverse. Not only would a guarantee encourage Spain to go on fighting, secure in the possession of Cuba; such an assurance would alienate Colombia and Mexico, who believed that they were entitled to attack the island. The most he would do was to revive the ancient offer of British mediation, if not to achieve any concrete results, at least to prove to the

10. Addington to Canning, May 2, 1825, Webster, *Britain and the Independence of Latin America*, II, 514–517.

Latin American states that he still had their interests at heart.[11]

In the light of this difference of opinion between Clay and Canning, one might have expected American and British policies to proceed along separate and distinct lines. If there was no ground for cooperation there hardly existed any basis for discord. The sum of their correspondence simply reveals a coincidence of determination—a common desire to embark upon the difficult but absorbing task of making Ferdinand see the light. In the delicate and involved affairs of state, however, it is rare indeed that policies do not become intermingled. The space for independent maneuvers is too narrow; motives intertwine, frictions set in. There occurs some jostling, a chain of minor reactions and irritations; and if men such as Canning are in the seats of power one finds oneself suddenly in the presence of a violent diplomatic contest. The case of Cuba proved to be no exception. Only here, owing to the introduction of a third element, the contest developed with startling rapidity.

The element in question consisted of an outburst of French activity in the Caribbean. Ever since Canning's refusal of a congress, France had been falling from embarrassment to embarrassment. Her occupation of Spain had proved unprofitable and unpopular. Her merchants were demanding that she establish regular relations with Latin America in defiance of Ferdinand. The Concert required that she abstain from recognition. And England, by virtue of the Polignac Memorandum, forbade the use of force or menace for the satisfaction of French demands. Caught among these conflicting currents, the ministers of France set out to gain by guile what they could not accomplish by more regular means. There was no concrete or far-flung plan—only a tentative probing, a series of efforts to assert French influence without stirring the ire of Great Britain or the Alliance. Two of these efforts attracted an unexpected degree of publicity during the summer of 1825. The first was the sudden and unexplained reinforcement of the French fleet in the Caribbean. The second consisted of the action by Governor Donzelot of Martinique in providing a naval escort for Spanish troops on their way to Cuba.

Clay, in whose satrapy the activity was occurring, immediately took alarm; but since he sought the assistance of France in bringing Ferdinand to terms, he couched his request for explanations

11. Canning to Zea de Bermudez, April 30, 1825, *ibid.*, p. 441.

in mild and friendly terms.[12] Canning was more peremptory. Suspecting that the French were up to no good in general and that Donzelot's action constituted a particular violation of the Polignac Memorandum, he demanded a clarification of intent from Paris. Damas was all apologies. He insisted that the Governor of Martinique had acted without instructions; but Villèle inadvertently let slip that Donzelot had actually been authorized to land troops in Cuba in order to preserve peace and order for Spain.[13] The possible consequences were intolerable. The initial desire to maintain peace and order might lead almost imperceptibly to a permanent occupation of the island by France. Canning immediately seized upon the careless admission and wrung from Villèle a complete disavowal of Donzelot's instructions.[14]

At this point all was still sweetness and light between Great Britain and the United States. Indeed, in castigating Villèle, Canning had not hesitated to remark upon the similarity of American and English views regarding the disposition of Cuba. Nor was he content to stop there. The outcome of his protests suggested a way not only of settling the Cuban question but of ending the war between Spain and Latin America. Instead of being the passive and cynical spectator, he now joined Clay in the quest for peace.

The first move came on August 1, 1825, when Canning wrote to Madrid. He refused once again to indulge in a guarantee of Cuba, but at the same time he disclaimed for Great Britain any desire to seize the island, and pointedly remarked that Ferdinand could best retain it by ending the foolish war.[15] On the same day the Foreign Secretary sounded France upon the possibility of signing a joint note which would express "our mutual and common determination, neither to aim at the occupation of the Spanish West India Islands ourselves, nor to permit such occupation of them by the United States of North America." [16]

He also broached the subject to Rufus King, the newly arrived minister from the United States. Essentially, what Canning proposed was that the United States should join with France and

12. Brown to Clay, July 15, 1825, Manning, *Diplomatic Correspondence*, II, 1412–1416.

13. Granville to Canning, June 6, 1825, Webster, *Britain and the Independence of Latin America*, II, 183.

14. Canning to Granville, July 12, 1825, *ibid.*, p. 185.

15. Canning to Lamb, August 1, 1825, *ibid.*, p. 449.

16. Canning to Granville, August 1, 1825, *ibid.*, p. 185.

Great Britain in a pledge not to occupy Cuba. Adherence to such an agreement, he explained, would put the Spanish mind at rest regarding the intentions of the three great maritime Powers, and might induce Ferdinand to make peace with the new states; for thereafter the only threat to Cuba could come from them.[17]

According to Canning's lights, King proved to be much less informed upon the subject than he had expected; he relied "with a simpleness which appeared quite childish on the good sense of the Continental Powers, for the advice which they would give to Spain and on the awakened good sense of Spain for listening to that advice when given." Or was it only simpleness? To Lord Liverpool Canning confided the suspicion that the United States was playing a deep and crooked game, in which case "the Yankees may be just the rogues that we have always hitherto taken them to be, but which I was willing to hope they might have resolved to be no longer." [18]

Nevertheless, he pursued King with vigor.

So long as peace with the new Powers is made a condition of the assurances of safety from the old [he explained], our exhortations will be heard with suspicion and repelled with resentment; whereas once soothed and softened by a solemn and unequivocal assurance as to the purity of our designs and as to the benevolence of our wishes . . . the Spanish Government may be induced to listen to advice in which it can no longer pretend to trace a lurking motive of self-interest, and to admit into a deliberation how Cuba can best be secured from invasion by Columbia or Mexico, Powers who have bound themselves by a common obligation neither to take, nor to permit the taking, of Cuba to either of themselves.[19]

He made no impression whatsoever. King, who lacked instructions, was too wary to pledge his government to a policy of abstention, particularly when Colombia and Mexico were not equally bound. On August 24 he rejected the overture.[20] Several days later, when France did likewise, the whole scheme fell to the ground.

17. Canning to King, July 28, 1825, Manning, *Diplomatic Correspondence,* III, 1553.

18. Canning to Liverpool, August 6, 1825, E. J. Stapleton, *Some Official Correspondence,* I, 283.

19. Canning to King, August 7, 1825, Manning, *Diplomatic Correspondence,* III, 1560.

20. King to Canning, August 24, 1825, Webster, *Britain and the Independence of Latin America,* II, 526.

Canning's reaction was one of undiplomatic pique. When King pressed him to support the American plan for ending the war he replied with a negative, and added a most ill-natured lecture.

Having been incessantly occupied for the last three years in endeavouring to persuade the Spanish Government to adopt those views with respect to the late Continental Colonies of Spain, which you concur with us in thinking the only sound and rational views, it is quite unnecessary to say that we heartily wish success to *any* new attempt to produce in the mind of H. C. Majesty that impression which we have attempted to produce in vain.[21]

Nor was Canning content simply to administer this rebuke. The affair with King was almost reminiscent of the conversations with Rush, with this difference: the roles were reversed; now it was the American position that contained the fatal defect. For while advocating with the one hand the cessation of hostilities between Spain and Latin America, the United States was attempting, with the other hand, to deprive the new states of their legal right to attack Cuba. Given the proper opportunity, Canning could expose American policy as motivated far more by self-interest than by sentiments of friendship toward Latin America. He sat back to await such an opportunity; for in that sensitive mind peace was secondary to retaliation.

Meanwhile in Washington Clay continued to be agitated over the presence of the French fleet in the Caribbean. The American minister in Paris had already received certain assurances from Damas, but these had lacked the customary Gallic precision. In October Clay decided to have Brown clear the matter up once and for all by stating explicitly the attitude of the United States toward Cuba.[22] Canning learned of this intention late in December and urged that Clay's communication be made to France "*in extenso*." "It is as pert a paper as a French Minister can desire to hear," he told Lord Granville, "and I flatter myself will lead Damas to regret that he did not close with my proposal of the three notes, or one tripartite one in the summer." [23]

Brown did as he was requested on January 2, 1826, much to Canning's enjoyment; but several days later, when King urged

21. Canning to King, September 15, 1825, *ibid.*, p. 530.
22. Vaughan to Canning, October 3, 1825, *ibid.*, p. 535.
23. Canning to Granville, December 26, 1825, A. G. Stapleton, *George Canning and His Times*, App., p. 609.

Great Britain to take a parallel step, the Foreign Secretary bluntly refused. With obvious relish he told King that Great Britain had already made a similar communication to France in July. To repeat such a move now would be to act, in appearance at least, at the beck and call of the United States.[24] This reply, and others in the same vein, constituted repayment in kind for King's refusal to subscribe to the Tripartite Agreement. If they served no particular purpose—if, in fact, they contrived to aggravate Anglo-American relations—Canning could congratulate himself upon having soothed his ego.

But a soothed ego was his only reward. Canning had given the United States a lesson in diplomatic procedure; he had not yet discredited that brazen country in the eyes of Latin America. For a moment, indeed, the quarry appeared altogether on the verge of escape. Clay, it is true, had been playing his part to perfection. On December 20, 1825, he had even gone to the lengths of requesting Colombia and Mexico to suspend their military projects against Cuba.[25] But Vaughan, the new British minister in Washington, had faltered and seemed about to spoil the chase. Not only had he encouraged Clay to take this step; he had actually given countenance to it.[26] Canning reflected all the outward signs of a frustrated sportsman. To Vaughan he wrote:

If it had been intended that you should treat . . . in a matter so delicate, as the proposed interference of neutral Powers to control the legitimate operations of belligerents against each other, you would not have been left without instructions . . .

The avowed pretension of the United States to put themselves at the head of the confederacy of all the Americas, and to sway that confederacy against Europe (Great Britain included), is *not* a pretension identified with our interests, or one that we can countenance or tolerate. It is, however, a pretension which there is no use in contesting, in the abstract; but we must not say anything that seems to admit the principle.[27]

That the United States actually nourished such a pretension was not a matter that Canning felt called upon to examine in any

24. James M. Callahan, *Cuba and International Relations* (Baltimore, Johns Hopkins Press, 1899), pp. 152–153.

25. William R. Manning, *Early Diplomatic Relations between the United States and Mexico* (Baltimore, Johns Hopkins Press, 1916), p. 142.

26. Vaughan to Canning, December 21, 1825, Webster, *Britain and the Independence of Latin America*, II, 536–537.

27. Canning to Vaughan, February 8, 1826, *ibid.*, p. 543.

detail. Reared in an environment laden with dislike of the United States, instinctively distrustful of its rising power, and thoroughly chagrined over the outcome of his conversations with Rush and King, he accepted the paper pronouncements of the Monroe Doctrine as sufficient evidence of evil and aggressive designs. The United States—who could doubt the evidence?—was moving to dominate the Western Hemisphere whence it would strive to upset the balance of world power. So Canning read his political lexicon; so the future would fall out, unless he met the threat. His fears regarding Vaughan turned out to be exaggerated; the frightened minister had refrained from putting his sentiments into writing. But the escape had been narrow, and the danger, in Canning's mind, remained great. Subtlety and caution were now the watchwords of his diplomacy.

As far as the United States was concerned caution, at least, was hardly necessary, for American statesmen were indulging in an orgy of indiscretions. Clay's note to Mexico and Colombia was already a matter of record. Alexander Everett, the breezy American minister in Madrid, made no effort to conceal his country's desire to see Cuba retained by Spain.[28] In March, 1826, even President Adams hinted at a similar determination in a special message to Congress. If Spain had ever thought of ending hostilities with Latin America these assurances quickly removed the inclination. Secure in the possession of Cuba, she lacked the incentive to act otherwise than as her sovereign's erratic conscience directed.

Not satisfied with his indiscretions in Madrid, Everett informed Clay, in a dispatch published for Congressional edification, that Great Britain was no longer interested in seeing the war ended.[29] This information, and all the utterances which had preceded it, was grist for Canning's mill; he ground the airy substance with slow and loving care.

As the mill ground, circumstances contrived to make a place for the product. Late in 1824 the idea of introducing a measure of unity to the Western Hemisphere occurred to General Bolívar. In 1826, as a result of his thought and effort, a congress convened for that purpose at Panama. The agenda of the congress was neither more nor less visionary than those of its eventual successors, nor were the results to have any greater significance. The assem-

28. Everett to Clay, February 13, 1826, Manning, *Diplomatic Correspondence*, III, 2103–2106.
29. Everett to Clay, October 20, 1825, *ibid.*, pp. 2069–2070.

bled delegates were asked to consider the conclusion of an inter-American confederation, the renewal of their alliance treaty against Spain, the disposition of Cuba and Puerto Rico, the implementation of the Monroe Doctrine, and the definition of neutral and belligerent maritime rights. As proposal followed proposal the task assumed staggering proportions.[30]

The Latin American states responded to Bolívar's agenda with varying degrees of enthusiasm. Out of the seven states recognized by Great Britain or the United States, four (Mexico, Central America, Colombia, and Peru) sent delegates to Panama. Buenos Aires flatly refused to attend. Brazil accepted an invitation, appointed a delegate, and then refrained from sending him. Chile nominated two plenipotentiaries over the protests of the American minister, who feared that Great Britain would dominate the assembly; but eventually a lack of money kept them away.[31]

Bolívar naturally expected to see the United States represented; but here fate, in the shape of Adams and Congress, decreed otherwise. When the subject arose the President vigorously advocated attendance. His pleas touched off a long and partisan debate in both Houses. Remarks offensive to the Latin Americans quickly found their way into print; their tenor made clear that an American delegation would be sent only to promote the national interest and that any deviation from a policy of strict neutrality, or any attempt to form entangling alliances, would be swiftly rejected. While the debate progressed the President nominated John Sergeant, a former member of Congress, and Richard C. Anderson, the minister to Colombia, as the American plenipotentiaries. The Senate confirmed the appointments only after a talented display of obstructive tactics. Anderson then died on his way to Panama while Sergeant, who dreaded the sea voyage, lingered on in the United States until after the Latin American delegates had adjourned their meetings.[32]

Canning's first reaction to Bolívar's vision was itself one of hesitancy. He confided his doubts to Lord Liverpool.

I have been reflecting a good while on the difficulty in which we are likely to be placed by the intended Congress of American States—

30. Lockey, *Pan-Americanism,* pp. 312, 325–326; Whitaker, *The United States and the Independence of Latin America,* pp. 572–573. For the evolution of these proposals see Harold A. Bierck, Jr., *Vida Publica de Don Pedro Gual* (Caracas, Ministerio de Educación Nacíonal, 1947), pp. 445–478.

31. Lockey, *Pan-Americanism,* p. 313.

32. Whitaker, *The United States and the Independence of Latin America,* pp. 578–580.

more especially if, as is not improbable, the U. S. of North America are invited to send a deputy to it.

Shall we send any Minister there, if invited or uninvited, or shall we take no notice of it?

Either is embarrassing: but I incline to think the last—though the easiest—the most dangerous course of conduct.

Yet if we send, to what specific purpose? [33]

Late in September, 1825, Ward, a British agent in Mexico, had furnished one startling if uninformed reason for sending a delegation. "The formation of a general American Federation from which all European Powers, but more particularly Great Britain, shall be excluded," was, he reported, one of the great objects of Joel R. Poinsett, the American minister in Mexico.[34] Richard Rush furnished Canning with yet another reason. The United States was eager to promulgate what it considered improvements in the maritime code, the former envoy confided, "by which we mean mitigating its severity in many respects, and this is an object that we hope to advance in this hemisphere by our Mission to Panama." [35] But it was the activity of Alexander Everett in Madrid that lent real purpose to the dispatch of an English mission. By the time Canning had received an official invitation to send an observer to Panama he had also become acquainted with the nature of Everett's communications to the Spanish government. He needed no further encouragement. In March, 1826, he selected Edward J. Dawkins as his agent and wrote for him an elaborate set of instructions.

Despite his original hesitations about a "specific purpose," Canning had found a great deal for his agent to do. Dawkins was to let it be known that Great Britain favored the adoption of her maritime laws as the general rule of conduct. "And you will take care to have it duly understood," Canning cautioned him, "that our determination to act upon these principles, as it has not been shaken by European confederacies, so it will not be altered by any Resolution of the States of the New World."

This admonition was only a beginning; Canning quickly warmed to his subject. Dawkins was to collect information "as to the views and policy of the American Governments, their feelings towards

33. Canning to Liverpool, June 6, 1825, E. J. Stapleton, *Some Official Correspondence,* I, 273–274.

34. Ward to Canning, September 30, 1825, Webster, *Britain and the Independence of Latin America,* I, 490.

35. Rush to Canning, November 2, 1825, *ibid.,* II, 535–536.

each other, and the degree of influence in their concerns which they may appear inclined to allow to the United States of North America." Dawkins was also to make clear the opposition of Great Britain to any project for putting the United States at the head of a hemispheric union. Upon this point Canning became almost tiresomely emphatic. He did not, he explained, object to an association made up solely of Latin American states; but the "association in such mutual engagements of any State not partaking of the Spanish character, would be viewed . . . with great jealousy as approaching to that species of League of the Americas as against Europe, which you are already apprized His Majesty could neither acknowledge nor approve."

Canning then reached the heart of the instructions. As illustrations of Great Britain's efforts to bring Ferdinand to terms with the new states, he handed Dawkins a whole sheaf of dispatches from Madrid. These would serve to discredit Everett's foolish and well-publicized assertions of the previous October. With them as his guide, Dawkins was ordered to observe "how earnestly it is desired by the United States, by France and by this country that Cuba should remain a Colony of Spain." He was also instructed to point out that the British government

are so far from denying the right of the New States of America to make a hostile attack upon Cuba . . . that we have uniformly refused to join with the United States in remonstrating with Mexico and Colombia against the supposed intention, or in intimating that we should feel displeasure at the execution of it. We should indeed regret it [Canning admitted], but we arrogate to ourselves no right to control the military operations of one belligerent against another.[36]

The chief purpose of the instructions was obvious: to contrast the attitude of Great Britain with that of the United States—to the marked detriment of the latter—and to make plain Canning's willingness to renew his mediation between Latin America and Spain. If such an offer, combined with the harsh and revealing light thrown upon American policy, did not defeat the pretensions of the United States surely Canning had misunderstood the complex arts of diplomacy. The quarry had come into view; the trap was set. Armed with these instructions Dawkins would know when to snap it shut.

36. Canning to Dawkins, *ibid.*, I, 403–409.

The British agent reached Panama on June 2, 1826. From the first he walked with a soft and unobtrusive tread. While awaiting the opening of the congress, he called upon the Colombian and Peruvian delegates. To the former he whispered that his mission was merely one of deference and consideration; but he talked business to the extent of exploring the possibilities of coming to an arrangement with Spain. To the latter he explained as best he could why Great Britain had so far failed to recognize Peru, and warned them tactfully "to avoid coming into conflict with the system of Europe, as well as to avoid arousing the prejudices of America." [37] He made an excellent impression. The Colombians found him charming, frank, and disinterested. His whole demeanor exuded friendliness and inspired a general confidence. It was an auspicious prelude to the labors that lay ahead.

The congress formally convened on June 22 and concluded its work a month later. One representative, a Peruvian, imputed to its deliberations an extraordinary significance.

An entire world is about to witness our labours [he announced]. . . . From the first sovereign, to the last inhabitant of the Southern hemisphere nobody is indifferent to our task. This will probably be the last attempt to ascertain whether Mankind can be happy. . . . Our names are about to be written either in immortal praise or in eternal opprobrium.[38]

He was mistaken, as events proved, upon all three counts. The labors of the delegates met with almost total indifference. Mankind continued in purgatory with a singular and zestful resilience. And the plenipotentiaries themselves? Their names stand etched on the brink of oblivion.

It was not that they shirked their responsibilities. They concluded four elaborate conventions, including one that provided for a species of inter-American union. But somehow the participating governments failed to act. Only Colombia, the sponsoring state, ratified the treaties, and then in the face of opposition from Bolívar himself. By 1827 the Liberator had turned against his inspiration and, "in a moment of disgust, likened it to the crazy

37. Lockey, *Pan-Americanism*, pp. 372–373. See also Bierck, *Vida Publica de Don Pedro Gual*, pp. 491–492.

38. Temperley, "The Later American Policy of George Canning," *Amer. Hist. Rev.*, p. 786.

Greek who of old sat on a rock in the midst of the sea and tried to direct the ships that sailed about him." [39]

But Dawkins could not have been happier. Throughout the course of the congress he tripped quietly among the delegates, dispensing advice with an impartial and invariable solicitude. As an unofficial observer he was of course barred from attending the sessions of the conference, but this disqualification mattered very little as far as his own mission was concerned. In the absence of a rival delegation from the United States he could exert his influence as and when he chose. Without competition, his duties seemed almost too facile, for a majority of the subjects which he raised met with responses highly favorable to the British point of view. One wonders, indeed, whether his presence in that cruel and enervating climate was not after all superfluous. Could it be that, despite the apprehensions of his master, he had wasted his talents in the slaying of shadows?

Upon two points only did Dawkins meet with stubborn opposition. He stoutly maintained that a reconciliation with Spain was possible, provided that the new states would make a handsome contribution to Ferdinand's depleted treasury; but the delegates flatly refused to consider such a proposition.[40] In the matter of maritime rights a wide divergence of opinion prevented him from winning acceptance of the British point of view. But since in both instances the attitude of the United States received no more consideration than his own, there was little room for real disappointment.[41]

In regard to Cuba the result was different. Here the trap set by Canning snapped shut with businesslike effect. Dawkins found the Colombians already cognizant of the dangers surrounding an attack upon the island. But on June 26 he came upon Pedro Gual, their principal delegate, avidly and angrily reading Everett's published dispatch from Madrid. This was the moment for which Canning had so carefully prepared. When Gual questioned the motives of the British government in not helping to end the war, Dawkins flatly denied Everett's impudent assertions and several days later furnished the evidence to disprove them. The quarry had been hunted down at last. Gual contritely withdrew his accusations

---

39. Lockey, *Pan-Americanism*, p. 316.

40. *Ibid.*, pp. 373–374.

41. Rippy, *Rivalry of the United States and Great Britain over Latin America*, p. 245.

and, in penance, actually proposed that the congress employ English good offices to effect a settlement with Spain. His suggestion came to nought, but thereafter such was the moral pre-eminence of Great Britain that the United States fell into a dark and chilling shade.[42]

So great did Dawkins' influence become after this incident that when, on July 15, he learned of the signature of a general confederative treaty and expressed some concern as to its contents, Gual allowed him to read and comment freely upon the whole text. When Dawkins inquired whether the United States might become a signatory, Gual replied: "Certainly, if they will declare war against Spain." Since there was little possibility of this last occurrence Dawkins complacently allowed the matter to drop.[43]

On the same day the congress adjourned. The fund of common agreement which existed among the new states—and it was an uncommonly small fund—had been fully exploited. Yellow fever was threatening the delegates; strong tensions had arisen between the Colombians and the Mexicans. There was much mutual felicitation, a tentative decision to reconvene at Tacubaya in Mexico, and then the delegates went home. Dawkins received an invitation to Tacubaya, but he lacked the necessary authority and returned to England instead. Mr. Sergeant, the tardy representative of the United States, appeared in Mexico shortly thereafter, presumably to participate in the new assembly. But in this expectation, alas, he was doomed to disappointment. Despite the earnest professions of good will which had emanated from all sides, the Congress of Tacubaya failed to convene.[44]

Dawkins presented Canning with a lengthy account of his accomplishments in October, 1826. It was a singularly modest report; but then, why should it not have been? The contest envisaged by Canning had proved quite one-sided, and Dawkins had won by default. "The general influence of the United States," he confessed, "is not, in my opinion, to be feared. It certainly exists in Colombia, but it has been very much weakened even there by their protests against an attack on Cuba, and by the indiscretions they have committed at Madrid." It would be resisted by powerful pro-British factions in Mexico and Peru—of that much he felt quite

42. Dawkins to Canning, July 7, 1826, Webster, *Britain and the Independence of Latin America*, I, 413–420.
43. Temperley, *The Foreign Policy of Canning*, p. 180.
44. Lockey, *Pan-Americanism*, pp. 345–346.

sure. As for the republican principles of the new states, they had appeared far less sinister under the microscope at Panama than London had originally conceived. Dawkins did not think that they would contribute materially to a further division between Latin America and Europe.[45]

What more could Canning ask? The European Concert was dead. As he told his cousin: "You have no reason to dread being shackled in your march by the Holy Alliance. They no longer march *en corps*. I have resolved them into individuality and having done so, I employ the *disjecta membra* each in its respective place without scruple or hesitation.[46]

The fate of Latin America as an independent weight in the balance of world power likewise seemed assured. Under Canning's guidance British prestige on that distant continent had risen to an eminence unequaled by that of any other Power. In a moment of assured complacency he could rebuke Lord Ponsonby for supposing that Great Britain would advise the retention of the Brazilian constitution. England, he explained, had a predisposition toward monarchical institutions; but her general policy was one of nonintervention, and she would therefore no more mix in the internal affairs of Latin America than in those of Russia.[47]

There was another measure of his self-confidence. Secure in the sources of his power he could even resort to jokes. To Sir Charles Bagot, now ambassador at the Hague, he sent off a coded dispatch, marked "separate, secret, and confidential," which read:

Sir,

> In matters of commerce the fault of the Dutch
> Is offering too little and asking too much.
> The French are with equal advantage content,
> So we clap on Dutch bottoms just 20 per cent.
> (Chorus)—20 per cent, 20 per cent.
> (Chorus of English Custom House Officers and French Douaniers):
> (English) We clap on Dutch bottoms just 20 per cent.
> (French) Vous frapperez Falck avec 20 per cent.

I have no other commands from His Majesty to Your Excellency To-day.[48]

45. Dawkins to Canning, October 15, 1826, Webster, *Britain and the Independence of Latin America*, I, 422–424.

46. Temperley, *Life of Canning*, p. 218.

47. Temperley, *The Foreign Policy of Canning*, p. 184.

48. Canning to Bagot, January 31, 1826, Bagot, *George Canning and His Friends*, II, 321.

But was there not a flaw in the serenity that enveloped him in 1826? Unchecked, he approached the summit of a long and uneven career. One might truthfully say that he stood at the very center of the balance of power, moving the equilibrium as he chose, in an easy, proprietary manner. And yet an air of curious uncertainty seemed to cling to his actions still. Could it be that in his own lifetime he sought the accolade of posterity?

The spring of 1826 found storm clouds gathering about Portugal; Don John's throne was in danger once more. A small army of deserters, favoring the absolutist pretensions of his second son, was threatening the decrepit King from secret bases on Spanish territory. In this affair Canning certainly perceived the necessity of fulfilling the British guarantee to Portugal. In the drama of events did he not also sense the glimmerings of immortality?

In September he embarked upon a journey to Paris to concert his policy with that of France. Villèle, despite his sins and omissions of the previous summer, proved helpful with regard to Portugal and positively loquacious in respect of another question. His government had actually intended to evacuate the French garrisons in Spain. But what, he asked Canning, "are we to do? can we withdraw our army at this moment—at the risk of seeing a corps of royalist volunteers make an armed irruption into Portugal the next day? Would to God! we had never gone into Spain!" [49]

Canning drank in the conversation and warned Villèle that ultimately he must give some kind of answer to the constant questions in Parliament regarding the French occupation of Spain. In October he left Paris armed with a letter which gave explicit assurances of France's determination shortly to evacuate her troops.

For over a month thereafter Canning busied himself with the Portuguese crisis. Daily the menace from the deserters in Spain became more pressing; by winter the necessity of dispatching troops to the aid of Portugal could no longer be avoided. On December 12, having made his preparations, Canning entered the House of Commons to announce the decision. Somberly attired in a long black frockcoat, his face a ghastly white, already dying yet somehow vividly alive, he left a memorable impression as he declared: "We go to plant the Standard of England on the well-

49. Canning to George IV, October 1, 1826, A. Aspinall, ed., *The Letters of King George IV, 1812–1830* (3 vols., Cambridge, Cambridge University Press, 1938), III, 166.

known heights of Lisbon. Where that Standard is planted, foreign dominion shall not come!" His audience was suitably impressed.[50]

Then, from nowhere, came the old, taunting question. What did he propose to do regarding the French occupation of Spain? There were the assurances of Villèle, and a pledge from the King of France himself, to be revealed; or, if that was not politic, there was the same haughty silence that had served so well in the past. But suddenly neither would do. Instead Canning launched into an elaborate and carefully rehearsed reply. "It would be disingenuous indeed not to admit that the entry of the French Army into Spain was, in a certain sense, a disparagement—and affront to the pride—a blow to the feelings of England," he announced as he began a new peroration. "Was there nothing then to be done? . . . What, if the possession of Spain might be rendered harmless in rival hands—harmless as regarded us—and valueless to the possessors? Might not compensation for disparagement be obtained, and the policy of our ancestors be vindicated by means better adapted to the present time?" Witnesses noted that the voice crept up to a higher note and that the haggard face became more mobile. "If France occupied Spain, was it necessary in order to avoid the consequences of that occupation, that we should blockade Cadiz?" Here the voice rose to a shrill and piercing crescendo:

No. I looked another way. I sought materials of compensation in another hemisphere. Contemplating Spain, such as our ancestors had known her, I resolved that if France had Spain, it should not be Spain *"with the Indies." I called the New World into existence to redress the balance of the Old.*[51]

Exhausted from the effort, Canning sank back on the Treasury Bench. A moment of profound silence followed, broken only by the sound of faint mocking laughter from a corner of the chamber; and then a wild burst of cheering and applause sped through the House. In that delirious instant Canning could be sure that the recording angel had noted his name.

Later the speech aroused criticism; but then certain negative reactions were to be anticipated as a matter of course. There was Cobbett, referring contemptuously to Canning as "Aeolus," and

50. Temperley, *The Foreign Policy of Canning,* p. 380.
51. *Ibid.,* pp. 380–381.

Mr. Creevey, remarking scornfully upon "his late lies at the expense of his colleagues and Castlereagh, in setting up for the sole deliverer of the new world." [52] When the excitement had died down even Canning himself seemed almost contrite. In a private letter he explained his motives thus to Lord Granville:

You will see that the occasion, which I so often predicted to Villèle, arose, and that I was obliged to justify in the best manner that I could (that is to say, in the very manner in which I told him I would, and must do so, if compelled), our tame acquiescence in the continuance of the French army in Spain.

But, as far as he himself was concerned, he went on, in a more defiant mood,

I cannot regret the extremity to which I was driven; for, if I know anything of the House of Commons . . . or if I may trust to what reaches me in report of feelings out-of-doors, the declaration of the obvious but unsuspected truth, that "I called the New World into existence to redress the balance of the Old," has been more grateful to English ears and to English feelings ten thousand times, than would have been the most satisfactory announcement of the French Government to withdraw its army from Spain. [53]

Must the curious inquirer assume from this equivocal statement that Canning's most spectacular phrases consisted of bombast? The evidence is not entirely clear. Mrs. Canning, herself a political student of some acumen, maintained, in regard to the policy of recognition, that the French invasion

certainly hastened, but it did not produce that measure—for the year before Mr. C. had declared to Spain that such an event must soon take place. The "profit" to us therefore might have been obtained at any time without reference to France but, in hastening it and executing it at the moment it was due, it was a blow to the pride of France through Spain and made the conquest which she had obtained not only incapable of being made profitable—but in fact a burthen—of which she was anxious to be rid. [54]

52. Maxwell, *The Creevey Papers*, p. 461.
53. Canning to Granville, December 14, 1826, A. G. Stapleton, *George Canning and His Times*, pp. 546–547.
54. Mrs. Canning to A. G. Stapleton, n.d.; Harold Temperley, "Joan Canning on Her Husband's Policy and Ideas," *Eng. Hist. Rev.*, XLV (1930), 413.

Mrs. Canning might further have remarked that, quite independently of the circumstances of French action, the policy of recognition had become almost inevitable by reason of Lord Castlereagh's ceaseless and unsparing efforts during the decade of his power. But that is perhaps more than could be expected of an adoring wife. What, after all, was there to say of that enigmatic aristocrat, that icy and impenetrable figure, who had dared to temper the stern realities of the balance of power with odd notions upon international cooperation?

Yet despite the conflicting evidence is it not possible that if Canning failed to utter an exact truth he expressed truthfully enough, in that ringing sentence, the essence of his political catechism? Could it not be that in the wreckage of the Grand Alliance and in the independence of Latin America—in the balance of forces established in and among three continents—he himself, like Castlereagh, saw a vision—a vision of Great Britain, ever alert, dispensing a just peace from the center of a universal equilibrium? Or was it after all that disturbing laughter, so light and so ironic, which had caught the essence of his role?

BIBLIOGRAPHICAL NOTE

BRITISH diplomacy between 1804 and 1828 remains the subject of detailed historical analysis. The period dealing with the Napoleonic Wars, the Congress of Vienna, and the Quadruple Alliance attracts scholars not only for its intrinsic interest but also for its relevance to the problems following upon the first and second world wars. Nor is this interest confined to the details of British diplomacy in Europe. Students have made an equally intensive examination of British policy in its relation to the independence of Latin America. The most important dispatches, state papers, and speeches concerning it have been published. The diaries, correspondence, and memoirs of almost all of its principal architects are now available; and there exists a number of monographs and articles dealing with its various aspects. Yet, as well known as British policy toward Latin America has become, there is no single work which attempts consistently to trace and evaluate its development throughout these crucial years. What Arthur P. Whitaker has done for *The United States and the Independence of Latin America, 1800–1830* (Baltimore, Johns Hopkins Press, 1941), and William S. Robertson for *France and Latin-American Independence* (Baltimore, Johns Hopkins Press, 1939), remains to be executed for Great Britain. Professor Charles K. Webster made such an attempt in the introduction to his documentary collection, *Britain and the Independence of Latin America, 1812–1830* (2 vols., London, the Ibero-American Institute of Great Britain, Oxford University Press, 1938), but it is a summary one and omits the formative years. J. Fred Rippy covered almost all of the vital period in *Rivalry of the United States and Great Britain over Latin America, 1808–1830* (Baltimore, Johns Hopkins Press, 1929), but he placed primary emphasis on the clashes between English and American agents in the several areas of Latin America rather than on the development of either country's policy. *The Cambridge History of British Foreign Policy, 1783–1919* (3 vols., Cambridge, Cambridge University Press, 1922–23), and *The Cambridge History of the British Empire* (6 vols., Cambridge, Cambridge University Press, 1929–40), are even less helpful than the monographs. Latin America receives only passing attention, although some effort is made to relate Great Britain's policy there to her European diplomacy.

The critique which follows is designed to acquaint the student with works which will provide a general appreciation of British policy toward Latin America between 1804 and 1828. In this connection several cautionary remarks are in order. Aside from the documentary collections and personal records, there is much that is partisan in the literature on the period. One school, predominantly American, stresses throughout the selfishness, rapacity, and reactionary conduct of English statesmen. Another school, primarily British, is so intent upon defending the record of those statesmen that it fails to evaluate their policies in terms of basic English interests. Lastly, the continuation of the ancient feud between Tory and Whig inclines historians to judge their subjects less upon skill than upon party allegiance.

Bibliographical Aids

FOR students who wish to explore fully the ramifications of this subject, the following general bibliographies are recommended:

Samuel Flagg Bemis and Grace Gardner Griffin, *A Guide to the Diplomatic History of the United States, 1775–1921* (Washington, U.S. Govt. Printing Office, 1935).

Grace Gardner Griffin, *Writings on American History, 1906–*   (New York, New Haven, and Washington, 1908–   ).

Handbook of Latin American Studies (Cambridge, Harvard University Press, 1936–   ), edited by Lewis Hanke until 1940, and thereafter by Miron Burgin.

Writings on British History (3 vols., London, A. Cape, 1937–40), compiled by Alexander Taylor Milne for the Royal Historical Society.

Bibliographies of especial value to the subject of British policy and the independence of Latin America may be found in:

Charles K. Webster, *The Foreign Policy of Castlereagh, 1812–1815* (London, G. Bell, 1931).

———, *The Foreign Policy of Castlereagh, 1815–1822* (London, G. Bell, 1925).

Harold Temperley, *The Foreign Policy of Canning, 1822–1827* (London, G. Bell, 1925).

Dexter Perkins, *The Monroe Doctrine, 1823–1826* (Cambridge, Harvard University Press, 1927).

Documentary Collections

THERE is an embarrassment of riches in this group. *British and Foreign State Papers* and *American State Papers, Foreign Relations* contain the important public documents for the period; they do not reveal the inner motives for the great decisions of state. Two other collections, *Britain and the Independence of Latin America, 1812–1830,* ed. Charles K. Webster (2 vols., London, the Ibero-American Institute of Great Britain, Oxford University Press, 1938), and *Diplomatic Correspondence of the United States Concerning the Independence of the Latin-American Nations,* ed. William R. Manning (3 vols., New York, Carnegie Endowment for International Peace, Oxford University Press, 1925), are more helpful in this respect. Of the two, Professor Webster's work possesses the greater value, not only because the documents are British in origin but also because their selection shows a finer discrimination. Manning's collection is the larger, and certain portions of it, dealing with the Rush-Canning conversations and the Anglo-American rivalry over Cuba, are indispensable. But some of the documents have been unduly edited, others have been omitted, and the Panama Congress has been entirely ignored.

Of a different order but of equal value are the *Correspondence, Despatches, and Other Papers of Viscount Castlereagh, Second Marquess of Londonderry,* ed. Charles W. Vane, Marquess of Londonderry (12 vols., London, H. Colburn, 1848–53), and the *Supplementary Despatches, Correspondence, and Memoranda* (15 vols., London, John Murray, 1858–72), and *Despatches, Correspondence, and Memoranda* (8 vols., London, John Murray, 1867–80), of the Duke of Wellington, edited by his son. Many of Castlereagh's papers were lost in a shipwreck; still more remain unpublished. Nevertheless, the available collection provides a satisfactory guide to his objectives and diplomacy as Foreign Secretary from 1812 until 1822. The scope of the Wellington papers is breath-taking. The Duke either witnessed or participated in the formation of British policy from 1806 until his death in 1852. He was particularly concerned at all times with Latin American affairs. In the twenty-three volumes of correspondence, which include letters to and from all the great personages of the era, there is an accumulation of information, often indiscriminately arranged, which still remains to be exhausted.

There are, in addition, several useful special collections. *Select Despatches . . . Relating to the Formation of the Third Coalition against France, 1804–1805,* ed. John Holland Rose (London, Royal Historical Society, 1904), go far to explain why Pitt never embarked seriously upon a policy of expansion in Latin America. *Manuscripts of J. B. Fortescue, preserved at Dropmore* (10 vols., London, H.M. Stationery Office, 1892–1927), edited by the Historical Manuscripts Commission, record in detail the difficulties and indecisions of the Ministry of All the Talents. *British Diplomacy, 1813–1815* (London, G. Bell, 1921), ed. Charles K. Webster, is valuable for the light that it throws upon Castlereagh's peace policy. Finally, *British Consular Reports on the Trade and Politics of Latin America, 1824–1826,* ed. R. A. Humphreys (London, Royal Historical Society, 1940), serves as a useful guide to British commercial objectives in Latin America.

Speeches, Correspondence, Diaries, Memoirs

THE speeches, correspondence, diaries, and memoirs for the period are uneven in both distribution and quality. *Parliamentary Debates* and *The Annual Register* reflect the general opinion of the day, but since foreign policy, even under Canning, was not considered as an appropriate matter for public discussion, the picture is a formal one. For the rest, the editing having been done primarily by the Victorians, the student will find an excess of reticence, eulogy, and partisanship. On Pitt's last ministry there is virtually nothing between his unpublished private papers and the general works which are mentioned elsewhere. The Earl of Malmesbury's *Diaries and Correspondence* (4 vols., London, R. Bentley, 1844), furnish some insight upon European strategy but contain no mention of Latin America.

Lord Grenville's administration fares somewhat better. Aside from the *Dropmore Papers,* there are the Duke of Buckingham's *Memoirs of the Court and Cabinets of George III* (4 vols., London, Hurst and Blackett, 1853–55), *The Journal and Correspondence of Lord Auckland* (4 vols., London, R. Bentley, 1861–62), *The Diary of the Right Hon. William Windham, 1784–1810* (London, Longmans, Green, 1866), unduly edited by Mrs. Henry Baring, and *The Windham Papers* (2 vols., London, Herbert Jenkins, 1913), which do not appear to have been edited at all. Of these, Windham's diary is the most relevant to Latin American affairs.

Although the Marquess Wellesley was Foreign Secretary from 1810 until 1812, neither his colleagues nor his contemporaries judged him as particularly suitable for remembrance. Three meager collections exist in *The Despatches and Correspondence of Marquess Wellesley, K.G. During His Lordship's Mission to Spain . . . ,* ed. Montgomery Martin (London, John Murray, 1838); *Memoirs and Correspondence of the Marquess Wellesley,* ed. R. R. Pearce (3 vols., London, R. Pearce, 1846); and *The Wellesley Papers* (2 vols., London, Herbert Jenkins, 1914). They are hardly more relevant than the Duke of Buckingham's angry *Memoirs of the Court of England during the Regency, 1811–1820* (2 vols., London, Hurst and Blackett, 1856).

Castlereagh's papers are dealt with elsewhere. Of Canning there remain some luminous traces. A. G. Stapleton's *George Canning and His Times* (London, J. W. Parker, 1859), although marred by the eulogy of a private secretary, is redeemed to a certain extent by the revealing personal correspondence which it contains. E. J. Stapleton has rendered a more useful service with *Some Official Correspondence of George Canning* (2 vols., London, Longmans, Green, 1887), particularly in furnishing some explanation of the speech of December 12, 1826. *George Canning and His Friends,* ed. Captain Josceline Bagot (2 vols., London, John Murray, 1900), conveys much of Canning's wit as well as his correspondence. The letters to Bagot, written after the appearance of the Monroe Doctrine, deserve more attention than Professor Temperley allotted to them. These works, together with *The Speeches of the Right Honourable George Canning,* ed. R. Therry (6 vols., London, J. Ridgway, 1836), provide some of the intimacy, warmth, and mischievousness of the man that a more self-conscious collection would lack.

Certain American collections are indispensable to an understanding of British policy in Latin America. First and foremost among these are the

Memoirs of John Quincy Adams, ed. Charles Francis Adams (12 vols., Philadelphia, J. B. Lippincott, 1874–77) ; and the *Writings of John Quincy Adams,* ed. Worthington C. Ford (7 vols., New York, Macmillan, 1913–17), which cease abruptly in 1823. Both of these works are too well known to require comment. Richard Rush's *A Residence at the Court of London* (3 vols., London, R. Bentley, 1833, 1845), suffers from having been written to improve Anglo-American relations and reflects less accurately his opinions and experiences than do his official dispatches. Nevertheless, it is valuable for its discussion of the conversations with Canning. Less important, but necessary to an understanding of the Monroe Doctrine, the Panama Congress, and the Cuban controversy, are *The Writings of James Monroe,* ed. Stanislaus M. Hamilton (7 vols., New York, G. P. Putnam's, 1898–1903) ; the *Works of Henry Clay,* ed. C. Colton (10 vols., New York, G. P. Putnam's, 1904), rich in speeches but meager in official or even personal letters ; and the voluminous *Life and Correspondence of Rufus King,* ed. C. R. King (6 vols., New York, G. P. Putnam's, 1894–1900).

Special Works

THE quantity of special works dealing with the period is such that only those most immediately relevant to British policy in Latin America are listed. Among them is one so broad in scope that it deserves pre-eminent notice. It is Albert Sorel's *L'Europe et la révolution française* (8 vols., Paris, E. Plon, Nourrit, 1904). For an understanding of the period as a whole Sorel's history stands by itself.

For the years between 1804 and 1810, when British policy alternated between revolution and conquest, the most useful study is a biography. William S. Robertson has not been notably successful in evoking a life in *The Life of Miranda* (2 vols., Chapel Hill, University of North Carolina Press, 1929) ; but as a chronicler of events and a student of painstaking accuracy, he has left, with the aid of Miranda's private papers, a remarkable account of the General's relations with four English administrations. In the variety of those relations may be found the essence of British policy during its formative years. The military consequences of that policy, in both Europe and America, are discussed with strong Tory bias by John W. Fortescue, *A History of the British Army* (13 vols., London, Macmillan, 1902–30), Vols. IV–VI. In addition, two contemporary records, *Minutes of a Court Martial . . . of Capt. Sir Home Popham* (London, 1807), and *The Proceedings of a General Court Martial . . . for the Trial of Lieut. Gen. Whitelocke* (2 vols., London, Longman, Hurst, Rees, and Orme, 1808), provide information about the attempt against Buenos Aires, not to be found elsewhere. In the diplomatic sphere Pierre Coquelle's *Napoleon and England, 1803–1813* (London, G. Bell, 1914), and André Fugier's superb multiarchival study, *Napoléon et l'Espagne, 1799–1808* (Paris, F. Alcan, 1930), suffice to explain in some measure the inconsistency of British policy in Latin America. The economics of the war, which had so much to do with England's original interest in the Spanish colonies, may be gleaned from Audrey Cunningham, *British Credit in the Last Napoleonic War* (Cambridge, Cambridge University Press, 1910), and Eli F. Heckscher, *The Continental System, an Economic Interpretation* (Oxford, Clarendon Press, 1922).

For the years between 1810 and 1812, the period of attempted mediation, the most satisfactory general account, based upon English and Spanish sources, is Wenceslao Ramirez de Villa-Urrutia, *Relaciones entre España é Inglaterra durante la guerra de la Independencia* (3 vols., Madrid, F. Beltran, 1912). With the aid of Foreign Office dispatches John Rydjord discusses "British Mediation between Spain and Her Colonies: 1811–1813," *The Hispanic American Historical Review*, Vol. XXI (1941), as does C. W. Crawley, in "French and English Influences in the Cortes of Cadiz, 1810–1814," *The Cambridge Historical Journal*, Vol. VI (1939). In both instances conclusions are sacrificed to an inordinate display of detail.

The most concise account of the circumstances surrounding the Congress of Vienna proceeds from W. Alison Phillips, *The Confederation of Europe* (London, Longmans, Green, 1914). Harold Nicolson's recent work, *The Congress of Vienna* (New York, Harcourt, Brace, 1946), follows it closely in both material and judgments and is distinguished chiefly for its charm. Neither man pretends to the scope, the authority, or the scholarship of Charles K. Webster. In *The Foreign Policy of Castlereagh, 1812–1815* (London, G. Bell, 1931), a work based upon Continental as well as English archives, Professor Webster combines these qualities with uniformly satisfactory results. Nowhere is Castlereagh's peace policy more lucidly described. In two articles entitled "Castlereagh and the Spanish Colonies," *The English Historical Review*, Vol. XXVII (1912), and Vol. XXX (1915), Professor Webster analyzes Castlereagh's Latin American policy in elaborate detail. Essentially the same material is embodied in his multi-archival study, *The Foreign Policy of Castlereagh, 1815–1822* (London, G. Bell, 1925), which is devoted primarily to a study of the European Concert.

Critics have taken Professor Webster to task on two scores: for being too partisan toward Castlereagh and for glossing over the less edifying aspects of the Foreign Secretary's policy in Latin America. Whatever the merit of these criticisms, they overlook two larger faults. Partisanship has led Professor Webster to concentrate on the minutiae; there is an excess of detail, with the result that the Concert of Europe emerges as a living organism rather than a convenient instrument for operating and softening the effects of the balance of power. By the same token, Professor Webster, in describing Castlereagh's Latin American policy, fails to relate and subordinate it to the quest for peace in Europe.

What Professor Webster is to Castlereagh, Harold Temperley is to Canning. His *Foreign Policy of Canning, 1822–1827* (London, G. Bell, 1925) represents the fruits of two decades of labor among the archives of Great Britain and Europe. Canning's Latin American policy is examined in great detail, and if I have differed from Professor Temperley in many respects, the differences have been ones of interpretation rather than of fact. Professor Temperley sees Canning as the proponent of liberalism, the defender of national self-determination, and the enemy of reaction. I see him as the father of Palmerston's noisy excesses and a grandparent of "splendid isolation." Professor Temperley describes his Latin American policy in the form of episodes, without real continuity or motivation. I understand that policy first as the means by which to smash the European Concert and then as an attempt to create a balance of world power.

That Professor Temperley's own ideas were not entirely settled may be judged from two later articles, "The Instructions to Donzelot, Governor of Martinique, 17 December, 1823," *The English Historical Review,* Vol. XLI (1926), and "Joan Canning on Her Husband's Policy and Ideas," *The English Historical Review,* Vol. XLV (1930). In the first essay Professor Temperley relents a trifle from his original contention that Canning actually feared the French in Latin America. In the second, he presents sufficient evidence to make the Foreign Secretary's sincerity in his speech of December 12, 1826, a matter of some doubt.

Professor Temperley's changed attitude may have resulted partly from the classic exposition by Dexter Perkins, *The Monroe Doctrine, 1823–1826* (Cambridge, Harvard University Press, 1927), a study based upon the American and European archives. If Professor Perkins does not entirely explain Canning's diplomacy during the spring and summer of 1823, neither does he ascribe it to mere hazard and emotional reflex, as is so often the case. The change in Professor Temperley may also have been due to the biting portrait of Canning which Élie Halévy contributes in *A History of the English People, 1815–1830* (London, T. F. Unwin, 1926), a work as striking for its comments on foreign affairs as for its representation of the domestic scene.

In addition to Professor Temperley's "The Later American Policy of George Canning," *The American Historical Review,* Vol. XI (1906), and "French Designs on Spanish America in 1820–5," *The English Historical Review,* Vol. XL (1925), there are several American monographs which contribute materially to an understanding of the direction of British policy, once the Latin American states had been recognized. William R. Manning offers a careful study of the Cuban controversy, based on the American and Mexican archives, in *Early Diplomatic Relations between the United States and Mexico* (Baltimore, Johns Hopkins Press, 1916). Joseph B. Lockey's *Pan-Americanism; Its Beginnings* (New York, Macmillan, 1926), is similarly useful for the Panama Congress; while Harold A. Bierck, Jr. explores that subject in even greater detail in *Vida Publica de Don Pedro Gual* (Caracas, Ministerío de Educación Nacíonal, 1947).

British policy toward Brazil is hardly mentioned by Professor Webster and is dealt with by Professor Temperley only as it affects Anglo-Portuguese relations. Alan K. Manchester provides a more comprehensive, if involved, account, based upon Foreign Office dispatches, in *British Preëminence in Brazil: Its Rise and Decline* (Chapel Hill, University of North Carolina Press, 1933). Enrique Ruiz-Guiñazú, in a carefully contrived study of *Lord Strangford y la Revolucion de Mayo* (Buenos Aires, Bernabé y cía, 1937), does much to clarify Dr. Manchester's more obscure passages. E. J. Pratt makes an equally welcome contribution regarding the Banda Oriental dispute with his "Anglo-American Commercial and Political Rivalry on the Plata, 1820–1830," *The Hispanic American Historical Review*, Vol. XI (1931).

Biographies

THE great personages who ornamented British politics in the period between 1804 and 1828 possess an extraordinary interest for the biographer. In one way or another almost all of them come into conflict with their surroundings. From their original environment they derived the aristocratic worldliness of the eighteenth century. They were not only supreme individualists; they took for granted their right to rule. Yet at maturity, at the very moment when their convictions had become settled, they found the familiar world of the eighteenth century disintegrating about them. Romanticism was rapidly replacing the more restrained classic postures; the middle classes were demanding a share of their power; even their individuality was being called into account by a more conventional morality. How they adapted themselves to these circumstances, and the effect which their internal conflicts had upon the government of England, presents a recurring challenge to the biographer. It has not often been happily met.

Pitt has received adequate treatment at the hands of J. Holland Rose. His two volumes, *William Pitt and National Revival* (London, G. Bell, 1911), and *William Pitt and the Great War* (London, G. Bell, 1911), combine profound scholarship with a measure of psychological insight. George M. Trevelyan has created a sympathetic portrait of *Lord Grey of the Reform Bill* (London, Longmans, Green, 1920). And Philip Guedalla marshals the best elements of contemporary biographical method in *Wellington* (New York, Harper, 1931).

On the other side of the ledger Lord Liverpool lies embalmed in *The Life and Administration of Robert Banks, Second Earl of Liverpool* (3 vols., London, Macmillan, 1868), by C. D. Yonge; Castlereagh suffers from the uncontrolled piety of Sir Archibald Alison in *Lives of Lord Castlereagh and Sir Charles Stewart* (3 vols., Edinburgh, W. Blackwood, 1861); while Canning parades woodenly through Augustus G. Stapleton's *Political Life of the Right Honourable George Canning* (3 vols., London, Longman, Rees, Orme, Brown, and Green, 1831). Lords Grenville and Wellesley are more fortunate: they have no biographers at all.

For brief sketches the student may fall back upon the *Dictionary of National Biography* (22 vols., London, Smith, Elder, 1908–   ), but despite their general excellence these are inadequate substitutes for the full-length portraits that one is entitled to expect, at least of Castlereagh and Canning. Secondary political studies such as H. M. Hyde, *Rise of Castlereagh* (London, Macmillan, 1933), Harold Temperley, *Life of Canning* (London, J. Finch, 1905), and Dorothy Marshall, *Rise of George Canning* (London, Longmans, Green, 1938), need to be supplemented by works of a more intimate design. It no longer suffices to record events; the biographer must strive to evoke a spirit and re-create a life.

INDEX

A'COURT, SIR WILLIAM, 145, 165, 166, 171, 188 n., 189, 203

Adams, John Quincy: and British policy in Latin America, 165, 167, 204, 205, 211, 212; mistrust of British, 80, 107, 108; and Monroe Doctrine, 151, 152, 159–162; policy toward Latin America, 113, 114, 118, 122; views on Latin America, 123, 127. *See also* United States

Addington, Henry U., 161–163

Aix-la-Chapelle, Congress of, 95–98, 117, 118, 120, 121, 133, 138. *See also* Grand Alliance

Alexander I (Tsar of Russia), 135, 146, 165, 179; attitude toward Latin America, 112, 119, 120, 133, 169; character, 83, 84; European ambitions, 98–99, 101; peace plans, 78–80, 87, 88, 124; postwar security projects, 83–85, 89; relations with Grand Alliance, 91–92, 95–97, 99–102, 129, 141, 142; wartime policy, 3, 13, 30, 31, 34, 65. *See also* Holy Alliance, Russia

Alexander VI, pope, 5, 57

All the Talents, Ministry of, 18, 22, 25, 32, 35, 37, 38

American Revolution, the, 8, 9

Amherst, Lord, 184

Amiens, Peace of, 2, 15

Anderson, Richard C., 212

Antwerp, 79

Apodaca, Admiral, 46, 63

Artigas, José, 59, 60, 115, 116

Asiento, 6, 7

Auchmuty, Sir Samuel, 26, 28, 32

Auckland, Lord, 26, 29

Austerlitz, battle of, 16

Austria: and Latin America, 169, 186, 187; and Neapolitan revolt, 99–101, 141; and postwar settlement, 81, 85, 87–89; relations with Great Britain, 91, 128, 176; resistance to Napoleon, 46; and restoration of Ferdinand VII, 145, 146, 148; and Third Coalition, 1–3, 16. *See also* Metternich

BAGOT, SIR CHARLES, 91, 113, 114, 118, 149, 165, 175, 218

Baird, General, 23

Balance of power, 4, 163; ideas of Canning, 138, 139, 177, 191, 200, 201, 219; ideas of Castlereagh, 81–83, 86, 89–91, 104, 222

Banda Oriental (Uruguay), 57; British interest in, 115–117, 133, 193–198; independence of, 199–203; Portuguese designs on, 57–59; war in, 59–62, 115, 192–198. *See also* John VI, Pedro I, Strangford

Bankhead, Dr., 134

Barbados, 20

Bardaxí, Don Eusebio de, 66, 67

Baring, Alexander, 176 n.

Basel, 85

Bathurst, Lord, 97, 138, 173, 178

Behring Sea, 165

Belgrano, Manuel, 62

Bentham, Jeremy, 52

Beresford, Col. John, 23–25, 28, 31, 49

Bernstorff, Count, 179

Bolívar, Simon, 51, 52, 176, 202; influence in Latin America, 62, 121, 128, 195, 198; mission to England, 50–53, 61, 63; and Panama Congress, 211, 212, 215, 216

Bonaparte, Napoleon, 1, 2, 54, 61, 77, 78, 93, 130; defeat of, 74, 80, 85, 86, 88; military strategy, 8, 12, 16, 30, 31, 34, 37, 40, 43, 46, 65, 69; negotiations with Great Britain, 19, 25, 26, 28, 47

Brazil, 212; and Banda Oriental, 59, 60, 115, 116, 192–200; British policy toward, 57–60, 182–189, 193–200, 203, 204, 218; British treaties with, 55, 56, 61, 190, 191, 202; independence of, 37, 54, 55, 182–189. *See also* John VI, Pedro I

Brougham, Henry, 137

Brown, James, 209

Buckingham, Marquess of, 29

Buenos Aires (Argentina), 136 n., 212; and Banda Oriental, 59–60, 115, 116,